NUMBER NINE

Peter T. Flawn Series in Natural Resources

A THIRSTY LAND

The Making
of an American
Water Crisis

Seamus McGraw

UNIVERSITY OF TEXAS PRESS ◆◆ AUSTIN

The Peter T. Flawn Series in Natural Resource Management and Conservation is supported by a grant from the National Endowment for the Humanities and by gifts from various individual donors.

Requests for permission to reproduce material
from this work should be sent to:
 Permissions
 University of Texas Press
 P.O. Box 7819
 Austin, TX 78713-7819
 utpress.utexas.edu/rp-form

The paper used in this book meets the minimum requirements of
ANSI/NISO Z39.48-1992 (R1997) (Permanence of Paper). ∞

Library of Congress Cataloging-in-Publication Data

Names: McGraw, Seamus, author.
Title: A thirsty land : the making of an American water crisis /
 Seamus McGraw.
Description: First edition. | Austin : University of Texas Press, 2018. |
 Includes bibliographical references and index.
Identifiers: LCCN 2018002642
 ISBN 978-1-4773-1031-1 (cloth : alk. paper)
 ISBN 978-1-4773-1680-1 (library e-book)
 ISBN 978-1-4773-1681-8 (nonlibrary e-book)
Subjects: LCSH: Water resources development—Texas. | Water resources
 development—Government policy—Texas. | Water resources
 development—Environmental aspects—Texas. | Water-supply—
 Social aspects—Texas. | Water-supply—Political aspects—Texas. |
 Water-supply—Texas—Management.
Classification: LCC HD1694.T4 M34 2018 | DDC 333.91009764—dc23
LC record available at https://lccn.loc.gov/2018002642

doi:10.7560/310311

CONTENTS

A THIRSTY LAND

PROLOGUE

IT IS A HARSH LAND, this bone-dry twenty-one-thousand-square-mile expanse of cacti and rocks and rattlesnakes that sprawls out as far as the eye can see in all directions from the confluence of the Rio Grande and the Pecos in Texas. It is a land that yields little, and even now, for what little it gives—a little water, a little food, a little fuel—it demands much in return.

It is a land that demands sacrifice.

A desert landscape violently interrupted by rugged canyons, it is stunning in its stark beauty. It is what every child in the East or the North or the Deep South imagines when they close their eyes and conjure up an image of the American Southwest, though for most, if they ever see it all, it simply will be a Wild West backdrop for a cross-country car trip along Interstate 10.

That is a pity. Because you only have to venture a comparatively few miles from that highway—that single strand of a weblike monument to our modern American belief that we can engineer our way through any problem and enjoy the benefits of those advances in splendid isolation—to find a very different monument to a very different way of looking at the world and our place in it.

Hidden in a rock shelter, a few hundred feet above the Pecos, there is a mysterious mural. It is one of scores in the region painted sometime between two thousand and four thousand years ago by a vanished people, linked to the Yaquis and other Native American cultures. But in many respects, this silent cacophony of seemingly unrelated images—of strange characters, and prancing deer, and odd snake-like lines whirling around a headless figure with a red line across its neck—is perhaps the most puzzling.

Long known as the "White Shaman," it doesn't depict a shaman at all, says Carolyn Boyd, an artist turned archeologist who has been trying to crack the code of the murals for more than twenty years. "Actually, that figure is a prototypical moon goddess."

And if you were to visit that rock shelter on the winter solstice, you would see that the act of creation that those ancient painters set in motion thousands of years ago continues to this day. As the sun rises on December 21, it illuminates one portion of the mural after another, until at last it stops, going no farther than that bright red line across her neck, effectively decapitating her.

It is, Boyd contends, a sacrifice, the goddess giving her life to bring about a new beginning for her people, and it continues to play out, year after year, centuries after her people have gone.

Concealed within these images there is a story of creation, how, in their mythology described dismissively by some as "primitive," they believed that the world was once a formless, watery void somewhere in the east, and how, led by a divine deer, people bearing torches were led to the sunlight, emerging from a sacred mountain, and how that act repeated itself each year, as the moon emerges from a water world, ascends, forms a union that brings forth the sun, and then declines, before the whole cycle begins again. It is a story of balance.

But Boyd has teased more out of the mythology as well. The very act of painting those images, she said, was an effort not to memorialize a distant past but to make it real and present. The act of re-creation was actually an act of creation.

And sacrifice. In a complex ritual, those ancient people brought the materials to make the pigments used in the painting, minerals wrenched with great toil from the ground, vegetable matter hard to come by in a merciless desert, and animal fat, precious beyond words to a people living always on the edge of starvation.

Even the minute mechanics of the act of painting itself was a ritual act of continuing creation. Science has given us the tools to suss out how it was done. First the black paint was applied, a communion with that ancient watery world. Then the red—you can see it in the flaming antlers of the mystical deer that leads them out of the darkness—then yellow, then white, which represented the fullness of the cycle, from water to land to light and to a balance between fire and water, between sunlight and rain.

They did not believe that they were simply the inheritors of creation. They believed that they were actors in it, that with each stroke, each dab of paint, they were summoning and completing creation itself.

It would, of course, be fanciful, poetic, and maybe even a little patronizing to imagine that somehow these ancients living hand to mouth at the far edge of an unforgiving desert, lacking all but the most rudimentary tools, fully comprehended the complex forces that defined their existence. There is no reason to imagine that they had the clarity of vision to see into their future any more clearly or courageously than we can face our own. It would be presumptuous to believe that they could have somehow pierced the veil and peered back into the beginning of time.

We will leave it to mystics and philosophers to ponder whether there was something etched in their DNA that led them to fashion a creation myth that in many respects reflects the geological record. We are a modern people. We trust in facts and science. Or so we tell ourselves.

And yet, modern science tells us that indeed, eons before any human being ever set foot in Texas, this parched corner of the world was in fact born in water. As recently as sixty-five million years ago, as a sea that once stretched all the way from the Gulf of Mexico to the Arctic retreated eastward, this very rock shelter where these ancients acted out the moment of their mythical creation in order to sustain that creation likely still was hidden beneath the waters at the western edge of the Gulf.

That sea helped form the land that this lost people knew, and the one that we—an increasingly urban people insulated from a direct connection to the land—still inhabit today. It left behind towers of sandstone that the relentless winds of Texas sculpted into monuments. It left behind limestone deposits aboveground and, more critically, below it, subterranean deposits that in some cases would be carved by the slow, relentless trickle of water into underground channels like the Edwards Aquifer that—taxed though it is—still provides water to millions of people in much of Central Texas. It left behind salt deposits in other parts of Texas, mostly to the west, and it is the ghost of that ancient sea which even today taints significant water sources, like the Upper Brazos River Basin, and less significant ones, like the Hueco Aquifer, which serves at least a couple of hundred residents of the colorful desert ghost town of Terlingua.

And just as these ancients imagined, in a confluence of water and fire some forty million years ago, violent volcanic activity, triggered perhaps by larger tectonic forces that created the Rocky Mountains, hoisted sea bottoms toward the sky. And from those mountains, in the fullness of time, rivers flowed and water percolated through the alluvial deposits to form what would become the Ogallala Aquifer, a source of life and livelihood for farmers and ranchers and city folks from Texas to Nebraska, now in danger of going dry within our lifetime.

Elsewhere in Texas, there are other ghosts of that ancient sea—lignite, and more critically oil and gas deposits, formed by the decaying remains of the life that once teemed there. The ancients who celebrated the interconnectedness of water and fire could hardly have imagined that we, the people who ultimately supplanted them, would someday draw our fire from what was once a creature of the water. But we do. And with the advent of hydraulic fracturing to force even more fire from the dead sea, we use vast amounts of water to do it. It is perhaps ironic that the ghost of those ghosts, the carbon, the methane, that we release as we burn those fuels is now considered by most scientists who study such things to be a significant cause of the shifts in our climate, shifts that are making our storms more savage, our droughts more punishing. Or maybe we just see it as ironic because we are modern people. Sophisticated. Those poor primitives might not have recognized the irony. They might have simply seen it as evidence that everything is interconnected.

It wasn't until five thousand years ago, some ten thousand years, scientists tell us, after the earliest known humans in Texas—and perhaps on the continent—left shards of their stone tools at a settlement along Buttermilk Creek near Georgetown,[1] and perhaps as little as one thousand years before these rock painters in the Pecos held their rituals, that the coastline of Texas achieved the form it has today.

Even still, it is changing. Powerful forces, some beyond our ability to control, some beyond our willingness to, and some we can and will control, continue to alter the landscape, to—in water and in fire—describe our destiny.

It is October 2015, and a column of smoke and ash swirls up into the sky on a hilltop near Hidden Pines in Bastrop County. At the side of a farm road, a half-dozen sooty red fire trucks idle, their diesel engines droning, their emergency lights pulsing. A dull yellow bulldozer slumbers a few yards away. Nearby, a small platoon of firefighters has waded into the blackened brush, deploying a hose that will spray a few thousand gallons of water pumped out from under this place, from an aquifer that serves a growing, thirsty community where water is precious enough that whole cities will compete for it.

They don't talk much. An occasional order barked from a distance by a supervisor in a white helmet will do to move them a few feet to the left or to the right. They don't need to talk much. These firefighters are experts. They know what they are doing. Many are veterans of the last big conflagration that hit this area, the 2011 drought-fueled blaze that ripped through this area, killing two people and destroying more than sixteen hundred homes in what was at the time the single most destructive wildfire in Texas history.[2] Later, there will be time to talk about whether enough fire trucks and helicopters and bulldozers had been deployed to prevent the 2015 blaze from burning more than forty-five hundred acres or destroying sixty-four homes.[3]

Maybe there will be time to talk about how the cycles of killer floods and devastating fires, drought and torrential rains that have plagued Texas since the days of the cave painters may have contributed to this. There might even be time to wonder whether in our headlong rush to become the most urbanized state in the union we have blurred the boundary between the urban and the wild, making ourselves even more vulnerable to those cycles, perhaps even exacerbating those cycles while at the same time we overtax the very resources—like water—that could help us mitigate those risks. That is a point that would be driven home mercilessly to millions in East Texas when, in the later summer of 2017, Hurricane Harvey slammed into the densely populated cities and struggling agricultural communities along the Gulf Coast with a kind of fury that would once have seemed almost unimaginable, leaving shattered lives, at least eighty-two corpses,[4] and by some estimates almost $200 billion worth of destruction in its wake.[5]

But at this moment, that is not uppermost on the minds of the firefighters as they move in unison, almost as if it is a ritual, drowning one of perhaps a hundred hot spots still smoldering from the most recent brushfire and then moving on to the next. Nobody there that day gives much thought to where the water to douse the embers comes from. Or how it got to the hose. Nobody gives much thought to the power that it takes to pump that water, how the fossil fuel that powers the pumper truck was itself formed from an ancient sea, and how in all likelihood it was forced out of the earth in a torrent of a million gallons or more of water. Nobody gives much thought to how all of these things are interrelated.

This is a crisis, and there is no time to dwell on such things. For now, we will leave that to scientists and engineers. We are a modern, civilized, and technologically advanced people, with our red fire trucks, our black hoses, our white helmets, and our yellow bulldozers. We are nothing like those who lived here thousands of years before us. We are the masters of our world. And we have a fire to put out.

This is a book about water. And Texas. But it is more than that.

If Texas is unique—and it is—that is not because the challenges it faces are necessarily peculiar to Texas. What makes Texas unique is the fact that virtually all the maddeningly complicated issues in an increasingly complex and unstable world can be found there, from its parched deserts and its overburdened rivers to the high plains in danger of running out of groundwater to its storm-prone coastal lowlands.

Those challenges seem clearer in Texas, perhaps, because it is a place of extremes, a place where it is often hard to ignore the whims of nature. The lessons that can be learned from that age-old battle to bend nature to our will, and to submit when she refuses, go way beyond Texas as well. Texans have always struggled to rise to that challenge, sometimes succeeding, often failing, but usually doing it first while the rest of the nation takes notes.

Yes, this is a book about how the immutable laws of geology and hydrology and the limits they place upon us increasingly chafe against the laws of human nature; and, yes, the peculiarities of politics and culture in Texas play an important role in this story.

But human nature doesn't stop at the Texas state line.

And so this book is about much more than water and much more than Texas. It is about dwindling resources and the battle over them in a world that is growing by leaps and bounds. But mostly, this is a book about us. It is a book that asks whether we have it in us, as those ancients along the Pecos did, to seek out an understanding of how crucial a role water plays in our lives—regardless of where we live, how much we demand of it, and perhaps more importantly, how much it demands of us.

Once upon a time, a lost people in a forgotten rock shelter daubed paint on a wall.

Black. Red. Yellow. White. Pigments made of stores of the stuff of life, sacrificed at great cost by a people who could barely afford to make that sacrifice, transfigured and animated by water, the most precious of all the desert's resources, and applied in a ritual of faith and in the supreme belief that creation is an ongoing act—that, like everything else in that harsh, unforgiving corner of the world, we each have a hand in that creation.

CHAPTER 1

PIPE DREAMS: THE 1968 STATE WATER PLAN

IT HAD BEEN A LONG, hot, and dry summer in much of Texas, but it was not hot enough on that August day in 1969 to keep Texans from flocking to the polls by the hundreds of thousands.

After all, these were Texans. Hardy people. They were used to the heat. They were used to the dry. Most of them had somehow managed to survive one or more of the punishing droughts that assailed Texas from time to time, and anyone old enough to vote that day was old enough to remember the worst of the most recent ones, the drought of the 1950s that visited ruin on all but a few lucky corners of the state. More than a few of them were old enough to remember the droughts of the 1930s that had chased farmers all across the middle of America, from the Dakotas to the Texas Panhandle, from their lands, one step ahead of roiling clouds of choking dust that blocked out the sun.

In fact, for many of them, it was their painful personal memories of those unforgiving days not so long ago, when the bleached and rainless skies turned against them, that drove them to the polls that day. That, and the belief that the Texas they now lived in was different than the one they had known back then.

On the ballot that day was a measure that, according to its supporters, among them the most powerful people in the state, would summon all the might, the ingenuity, the technological mastery of

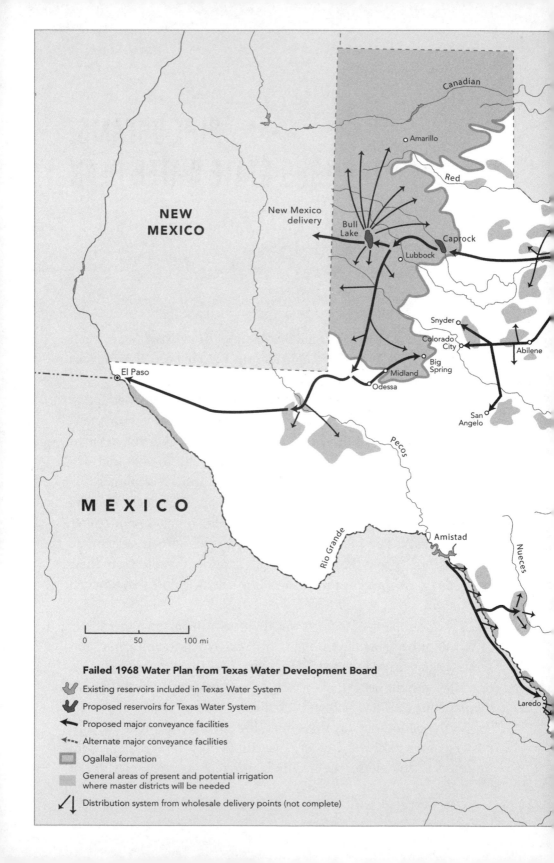

Canadian

○ Amarillo

Red

**NEW
MEXICO**

New Mexico
delivery

Bull
Lake

Caprock

Lubbock ○

Snyder ○

Colorado
City ○

Abilene

El Paso ○

Midland ○

Big
Spring

Odessa ○

San
Angelo ○

MEXICO

Pecos

Rio Grande

Amistad

Nueces

0   50   100 mi

Laredo ○

Failed 1968 Water Plan from Texas Water Development Board

Existing reservoirs included in Texas Water System

Proposed reservoirs for Texas Water System

Proposed major conveyance facilities

Alternate major conveyance facilities

Ogallala formation

General areas of present and potential irrigation
where master districts will be needed

Distribution system from wholesale delivery points (not complete)

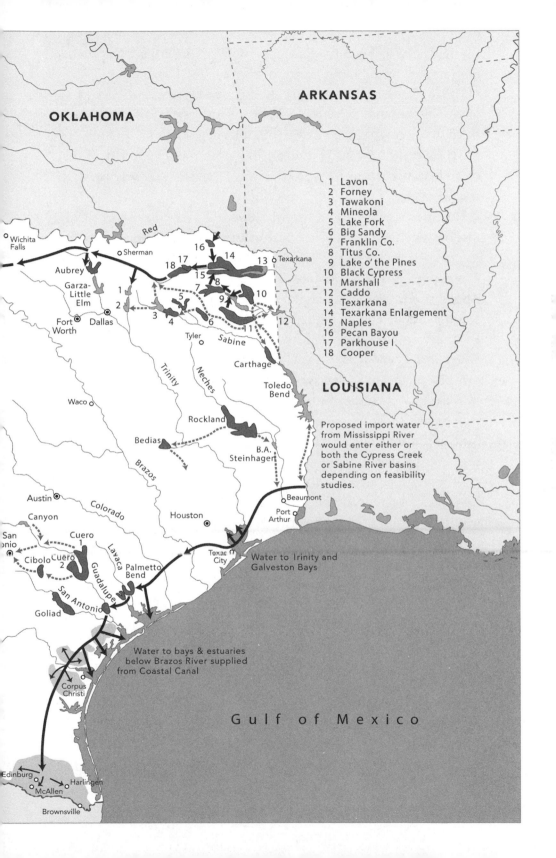

OKLAHOMA

ARKANSAS

1 Lavon
2 Forney
3 Tawakoni
4 Mineola
5 Lake Fork
6 Big Sandy
7 Franklin Co.
8 Titus Co.
9 Lake o' the Pines
10 Black Cypress
11 Marshall
12 Caddo
13 Texarkana
14 Texarkana Enlargement
15 Naples
16 Pecan Bayou
17 Parkhouse I
18 Cooper

Wichita
Falls

Red

Sherman

Aubrey

Garza-
Little
Elm

Fort
Worth

Dallas

Tyler

Sabine

Carthage

LOUISIANA

Texarkana

Waco

Trinity

Neches

Toledo
Bend

Rockland

Bedias

Brazos

B.A.
Steinhagen

Proposed import water
from Mississippi River
would enter either or
both the Cypress Creek
or Sabine River basins
depending on feasibility
studies.

Austin

Colorado

Houston

Beaumont

Canyon

Port
Arthur

San
onio

Cuero
1

Lavaca

Texas City

Water to Trinity and
Galveston Bays

Cibolo

Cuero
2

Guadalupe

Palmetto
Bend

San Antonio

Goliad

Water to bays & estuaries
below Brazos River supplied
from Coastal Canal

Corpus
Christi

Gulf of Mexico

Edinburg

Harlingen

McAllen

Brownsville

the new Texas to guarantee that an event like those crushing droughts of years past would never harm them again.

It was less a ballot measure than it was a profession of faith, a pledge of allegiance to new Texas, proud and certain of its ability to bend the forces of nature to the will of its people.

There was little reason to doubt the power and authority of that creed that August day in 1969. The world that summer was awash in testaments to it.

Just two weeks earlier, the whole world viewed the most awe-inspiring technological accomplishment in human history up to that moment. A rocket to the moon and back, with three men aboard, had slipped the "surly bonds of Earth," and from the instant that Apollo 11 cleared the launchpad at Cape Kennedy to the moment the capsule splashed down in the Pacific, Houston was calling the shots.

That stood to reason, at least in the minds of Texans. Back then, Houston was the face Texas wanted to show to the world. Brash, prosperous, inventive, it was a city that retained that ineffable essence of Texas, that peculiar southern grace with a western swagger—only now it was swaggering along the edge of what John F. Kennedy called the New Frontier, one that stretched as far up as the moon and maybe someday, beyond.

The very fact that Houston, of all the places in America that could have been selected, had been chosen as the site of Mission Control was itself a way of flexing Texas's prestige. Furthermore, it had been chosen in no small part because of a bit of political wrangling by a local congressman, Albert Thompson, who managed to first horse trade with John F. Kennedy and then got the space center named after Kennedy's successor, a president of the United States who himself seemed to embody the ethos and the contradictions of Texas.

To put it another way, Houston and all of Texas in the summer of 1969 wanted the world to see Texas as a place where big people did big things, technologically and economically, even if, from time to time, it had to rely on the largesse of big government programs like the National Aeronautics and Space Administration to do it.

And Houston was getting bigger by the day.

Between 1960 and 1980, the population of Houston expanded

by half a million people, from about 938,000 to almost 1.6 million, and nearly half of those new faces had turned up on the census by the time Apollo 11 lifted off.[1] Similar growth was taking place in other Texas cities. Dallas, which at the time of its deepest infamy, on November 22, 1963, was little more than a glorified cow town of just under 700,000, had by 1969 grown by nearly a third. San Antonio was keeping pace. And all of this was happening at a time when, overall, the state's population was growing at a significantly less volatile rate of just over ten percent.

Though Texas had, for reasons we will explore shortly, already begun to see a migration of a significant portion of its rural population to its cities and towns, the growth in cities was driven by immigrants. Overall, Texas in 1969 was still largely rural. There were small pockets of population separated by vast expanses of agricultural property as well as wild and empty land. But her cities, just like a moon-bound rocket struggling to lift itself from the earth and then gathering speed, were on the ascent, an ascent that continues unchecked to this day.

Immigrants have shaped the history of Texas since King Philip V of Spain first enlisted fifty-five families from the Canary Islands to populate a remote, desolate, and inhospitable settlement he was trying to establish in San Antonio three centuries ago.[2] These latter-day, mid-twentieth-century immigrants, however, mostly were not the often-vilified Mexicans sneaking across some international boundary. Instead they were, like those who followed Stephen Austin into Texas 130 years earlier, coming from the east and the north. They were by and large more affluent and more mobile thanks to both their wealth and advances in technology as well as nationwide improvements to infrastructure, like the burgeoning interstate highway system. They were part of a nationwide migration to the Sun Belt that took place in the decades after World War II.

These were newcomers with big dreams and big expectations, and they were placing gigantic demands on the resources of a state that had always yielded the most precious of those resources reluctantly.

Water.

In the late 1960s, oil may have flowed copiously in Texas. But that oil wouldn't have flowed without water. It takes water to drill oil or gas wells; it takes water to flush out the dregs when those wells start to fade. The cities and towns that are built on the wealth of that oil need water too, a lot of it. It takes water to convert that crude resource into gasoline to fuel the newcomers' cars and energy to light and heat and air-condition their homes. The people flooding into Texas, then as now, needed to be fed and clothed, and the food and the fiber to do that often came from farms and ranches in Texas, and they needed water too. In fact, in another peculiarly Texan twist, the legislature and the courts effectively had guaranteed those farmers and ranchers that much of that water was theirs to do with as they liked and without question.

But from the time that Coronado stumbled onto the parched Llano Estacado in 1541, with a thirsty band of soldiers and priests in search of gold, strangers have always been lured to Texas in search of riches, only to learn once they got there that water was every bit as precious and often just as rare. The problem was not then, and is not now, that Texas didn't have enough water. The problem in Texas always had been that it didn't have enough water in the places where it was most likely to be needed, and often it had far too much water in the places where it wasn't.

Texas always has been a place of extremes when it comes to water. East of the hundredth meridian, which basically bisects the state, annual rainfall that engorges rivers and replenishes aquifers increases with each mile until you reach the Sabine River, where annual rainfall is more than sixty inches a year, making it one of the top thirty rain-soaked places in the country. The highest single-day total rainfall ever recorded anywhere in the United States occurred at Alvin, Texas, in 1979 during Tropical Storm Claudette, when three and one-half feet of rain fell. Head west, however, and rainfall drops off precipitously until you hit El Paso, where if you poured every drop of the average 8.81 inches that falls there each year into the average high school football field, you would end up with a puddle that comes up not much higher than the top of your cowboy boots.

It would be challenging enough to manage growth and development, to sustain aquifers and allocate the water that flows in the state's fifteen major rivers and thirty-seven hundred named streams to the growing cities and suburbs and the far-flung farms and ranches, if the built-in inequity in precipitation was all with which you had to contend.

But Texas has always been wickedly capricious in terms of water as well. That is partly because it is, both climatologically and culturally, a kind of battleground, where the hot, water-laden air from the Gulf of Mexico sweeps north and west until it collides, usually from October to June, with cool air heading south. Sometimes those contending forces trigger wild thunderstorms, tossing off tornados in their wake. In May of 1953, one of those marched through Waco, killing 114 people.

Other times, hurricanes rush in from the Gulf, causing unfathomable destruction. On August 20, 1886, what would now be classified as a Category 4 hurricane roared ashore with 150-mile-per-hour winds and a fifteen-foot storm surge that overwhelmed the unsuspecting and ill-prepared town of Indianola on Matagorda Bay. Reports from the time describe a hellscape, as all that remained of drowned buildings on several blocks burned to the waterline.[3] Forty-six people were killed. It was not the first hurricane to have hit Indianola. Eleven years earlier, another hurricane had claimed almost ten times as many lives there. Nor would it be the last. That would come five weeks later, in 1886, when yet another storm surged ashore, drowning what was left of the town. The remains of Indianola, once a rival to Galveston in terms of influence and prestige, were abandoned beneath the waters of the bay, where they remain to this day.

Fourteen years later, Galveston itself would be in the crosshairs of a disastrous Category 4 hurricane—to this day the most destructive storm in US history—that leveled three thousand homes and killed up to twelve thousand people. Though the city, much reduced, survived, it lost forever its role as Texas's preeminent port, ceding it to Houston.

Those vicious storms, the prolonged soaking rains that turn arroyos into killer cauldrons of roiling water, can drop two or more feet of golf-ball-sized hailstones. Often, the storms come at the end of equally vicious droughts. The storms that drowned Indianola came at the end of a drought. The hailstorm that buried parts of the High Plains under four feet of hail in 2012 followed a nearly ten-year drought.

Moses Austin, the man who opened Texas to Anglo settlement, never got to live there because he died of pneumonia, reportedly after getting caught in a driving Texas rainstorm while trudging back home to Missouri from Mexico, where he had pleaded his case. The next year, his son Stephen's first colony nearly died out because of a drought.

It is a peculiarity of Texas, which sits astride the same latitude as the Sahara Desert, that in any year, according to a study conducted in 1987 by George Bomar and Robert Riggio for the Texas Water Commission, it is more likely that a significant drought will occur somewhere than it is that the average amount of rain will fall.

Peer far enough back in history and you will find evidence in tree rings and the like that Texas has always been subject to epic droughts. In 2011, one year into a three-year drought that cost Texas $7.62 billion in crop losses and livestock deaths, the National Weather Service dryly noted that the state was in the grips of the driest—and second-hottest—year on record. And there probably will be, scientists say, even worse droughts to come as the planet, in the throes of an unprecedented warming period, endures increasingly volatile weather patterns that will make wet places wetter, and dry places, like much of Texas, profoundly, dangerously drier.

Yet to this day, the devastating drought that gripped virtually all of Texas from roughly 1950 to 1957 remains the drought against which all others are measured.

They call it the drought of record. But it was more like a reckoning. Beginning in 1950, the drought spread across a ten-state area of the West and the Southwest. Much of the afflicted area received less than one-third of its average annual rainfall. Some places received significantly less. And no place was harder hit than Texas. Rivers ran dry. Springs, including Comal Springs, the largest in Texas, ceased to flow. In some western reaches of the state all but the most tenacious vegetation withered and died, and in the drought's wake the parched earth cracked and split and heaved until it looked like leprous scabs.

It was relentless. Year after year it went on until you would have been hard-pressed to find a Texan who wasn't touched by it. It was longer and deeper than the drought their parents had experienced a generation earlier, longer and deeper even than the one their grand-parents had survived a generation before that. As the late Elmer Kelton put it in *The Time It Never Rained*, his epic 1973 novel about the drought of record:

> Farmers watched their cotton make an early bloom in its stunted top, produce a few half-hearted bolls and then wither.
>
> Men grumbled, but you learned to live with the dry spells if you stayed in West Texas; there were more dry spells than wet ones. No one expected another drought like that of '33. And the really big dries like 1918 came once in a lifetime.
>
> Why worry? they said. It would rain this fall. It always had.
>
> But it didn't. And many a boy would become a man before the land was green again.

By the time the drought of record came to an end, all but 10 of Texas's 254 counties had been declared federal disaster areas. At its height, one percent of all Texans—more than 100,000 in a state of 9.8 million people—were unable to wholly feed themselves and found themselves dependent on some sort of government food assistance. Despite federal programs to deliver feed to farmers and ranchers, nearly 100,000 farms and ranches failed. The number of active ranches dropped from 345,000 to 247,000. The drought itself, as well as the valiant but vain efforts by the ranchers and farmers Kelton described battling the drought the only way they knew how— by sticking it out and doing what they had always done, only doing it harder—had left the land so wounded, so parched, that when the winds blew from the north, they sent up great choking clouds of dust that rivaled the Dust Bowl days a generation earlier.

And just as the Dust Bowl had sparked a mass exodus, the dry times of the 1950s drove farmers and ranchers by the thousands from their land. A lot of those farmers and ranchers moved to town. Many never went back. By the time the drought was over, rural areas of the state, which had boasted one-third of the state's population, now accounted for about one-quarter.

The cities they fled to didn't escape the consequences of the drought either. Dallas, for example, came within weeks of running out of water from its traditional sources and had to begin wholesale pumping from the salty Red River, with the salt eating away at pipes and equipment.

In another time and in another place, a drought like the drought of record that crippled Texas might have sparked a profound questioning, a period of self-reflection perhaps, and a discussion about whether the growth Texas was experiencing was sustainable and, if so, for how long. It might have led some to debate that notion of balance, just like those lost Native Americans who re-created creation in the rock shelters along the Pecos, and to ask whether maybe those earlier inhabitants might have been on to something.

But this was Texas on the cusp of the modern age, a proud and growing state that prided itself on the fact that it was pointing the way toward that last great frontier, a place where people were conditioned to believe that you didn't submit to nature, no matter how brutal she could be. It was a Texas that believed that with grit, inventiveness, and the gifts of technology and science, and—as was the case with the interstate highway system and the Johnson Space Center—government largesse if need be, you could bring the most awesome, the most fearsome forces of nature to heel.

It is said nowadays that when it comes to prodding the legislature even to begin to slice through the Gordian knot that is water policy in Texas, you have to have two things. The first is a punishing drought, the kind of devastating event that focuses the mind like the sight of the noose. The second involves marshaling the enlightened self-interest of hundreds of lawmakers, many of them fiscally conservative and all of them devoted principally to the parochial, often conflicted interests of districts all across the diverse bag of bobcats that is the state of Texas, and focusing those lawmakers on a single purpose.

That rarely happens. But it did in the wake of the drought of record.

By the end of the drought, leading voices, among them some of the state's most prominent engineers, began molding public opinion in favor of a staggeringly ambitious response to the drought and to the destruction by the floods that followed it. In newspapers, on the radio, and on the still-untested medium of television, they made the case for bold action, and they did it convincingly enough to begin to turn reluctant lawmakers.

Few of those advocates were more influential than Marvin Nichols, the Fort Worth engineer and senior partner in what today is among the most powerful engineering firms in the state, Freese and Nichols.

Nichols himself was a man with a high profile. Before an unfortunate—and embarrassing—turn of political events a few years earlier, the self-avowed states' rights Democrat had been on track to be President Eisenhower's choice to head the US Bureau of Reclamation, the agency principally responsible for the construction of most of the major dams in the American West.

Ike quietly dropped the nomination when it came to light that there had been allegations of corruption (none of them touching Nichols himself) at an American-owned nickel mine in Cuba while Nichols was at the helm.[4]

If the scandal, such as it was, tarnished Nichols's reputation elsewhere, there is no evidence that it hurt him much in Texas. In part because of the efforts of Nichols and his fellow engineers, in mid-1957 the legislature approved a $200 million bond issue that lawmakers argued would spark three times that much investment in water conservation and long-term projects across the state. Voters approved the measure by a substantial margin that November. A six-member panel—dubbed the Texas Water Development Board (TWDB)—was named that December, and Governor Price Daniel appointed Marvin Nichols its first chairman, a post he held until 1962.

Between 1957 and 1966, that board took on significantly more responsibility than simply administering loans. It also took on the task of assessing the state's water needs, not just at the moment but looking forward to 1980, in effect establishing what would become the every-five-year process of developing the Texas State Water Plan, which continues to this day.

There was a sense of urgency to the challenges that Texas faced, and it wasn't just because of the lingering effects of the drought or the rapidly increasing demand for water caused by development. Texas always has been unique among western states in that under the terms of its admission into the Union one and one-quarter century earlier, it had ceded none of its land to the federal government. Thus, the kind of projects undertaken elsewhere in the nation, such as dams like the Hoover and Grand Cooley, had never been done on anything like that scale in Texas.

By the 1960s, however, there was growing concern among states' rights Texans that things were beginning to change. As early as 1953, the Bureau of Reclamation had begun circulating plans to rechannel the waters of some rivers, and by 1964, the rumblings from Washington had become loud enough and Governor John Connally had become alarmed enough to demand that Texas come up with a comprehensive plan to address its water deficit before the US Army Corps of Engineers and the Bureau of Reclamation did.

As Connally's statement to policy makers said at the time,[5]

I am increasingly concerned about drought conditions in Texas and progress of our efforts to develop adequate sources of water for all our State.

The Bureau of Reclamation and the Corps of Engineers have proposed broad water development projects for Texas far beyond the plans of the Texas Water Commission report, "A Plan for Meeting the 1980 Water Requirements of Texas."

In my opinion, these plans fall short of satisfying the water needs for all of Texas.

Furthermore, the Congress is presently considering a Federal water pollution control bill which will supplant state authority in this field. I have long been concerned that the State exercise its responsibility in all areas of water conservation and development.

The threat of federal action spurred Texans to take action. And that action was, in many respects, classic Texan—big, brash, ambitious beyond anything else proposed anywhere else in the country or the world.

As originally proposed, the 1968 State Water Plan was Pharaoh-like. It called for transporting water from the rain-soaked eastern section of the state hundreds of miles in a concrete-lined canal, southward to the Rio Grande Valley. It took some political arm-twisting to get that much through the legislature.

As ambitious as that was, though, it was not ambitious enough for Nichols. The way he saw it, the plan all but ignored West Texas. It was, as he told a reporter at the time, "a plan for only half the state,"[6] and he urged the state to go back to the drawing board.

What emerged was far more elaborate, far more costly. At an estimated cost to Texas of $3.5 billion, more than ten times the cost of the Apollo 11 moon shot, a third more than the cost of the entire Apollo program, in fact (the federal government was to have picked up an additional $5.5 billion of the overall $9 billion cost of the water plan), the state proposed nothing short of replumbing almost all of Texas.

The revised 1968 water plan envisioned the construction of not one, but two, major canal networks. By far the most daunting was the northern canal, which effectively would pump millions of acre-feet of Mississippi River water uphill from nearly sea level to four thousand feet above it, across the northern half of Texas to Lubbock, where some would be diverted to New Mexico, some to the Trans Pecos and El Paso, and the rest used to water the Panhandle and replenish the Ogallala Aquifer, which even then was well on its way toward being overpumped.

All in all, thirteen million acre-feet of water would have been diverted to Texas. The seven million kilowatts of electricity necessary to pump that water where it needed to go would have required, according to some estimates, that Texas expand its power-generating capacity by one-third.[7]

Turning this plan into action, however, would require a constitutional amendment to authorize the TWDB to issue $3.5 billion in bonds to cover Texas's portion of the tab.

It was a sign of those heady, ambitious, we-can-do-anything times in Texas, and maybe a testament to the influence of men like Nichols, that the plan had won the support of many in the Texas state legislature, despite the staggering cost, a sum that dwarfed the $200 million appropriated just a few short years earlier. It also had widespread support in places like Amarillo and El Paso. The *El Paso Herald* on its front page touted it as a "bold and imaginative plan for meeting the water needs of Texas for the next 50 years."[8]

But there were also opponents. There were more than a few voters in places like Houston who expressed a sense of reluctance about watering West Texas and the Rio Grande Valley. And the nascent environmental movement was also beginning to take hold in Texas, and groups like the Sierra Club made their opposition to the 1968 water plan abundantly clear. One of those early foot soldiers in the war against the plan was Carol Patterson, a Yankee from the lush, elm-shaded suburb of Montclair, New Jersey. She and her husband, Kirk, had just returned to his native Austin when the campaign against the state plan began and soon found themselves drawn into the struggle against it. "We didn't come itching for a fight," she recalled. But Kirk Patterson had just graduated from Harvard Law— he had done his third-year paper on the impacts of nuclear power on water resources—and was casting about for something to do when they stumbled into the local Sierra Club office. "They were in the midst of fighting the . . . plan," Carol said, and after Kirk did some quick calculations, they signed on to the effort to block it. The way they saw it, the environmental costs—the land lost to reservoirs, the disruption of natural areas, the immense energy demands of moving all that water—far outweighed the benefits. There was also, she conceded, a Saul Alinsky–esque distaste given that the bulk of the money spent would wind up in the pockets of well-heeled and politically connected engineering and construction firms like Freese and Nichols and Brown and Root (now KBR). And the lawyers who would draft the contracts. And the financial firms that would skim their cut off the top of the bonds that would be issued.

It was, Carol said, an early foray against an axis of powerful interests. "It was the engineering firms that would build it, but it was also the bond firms that would subsidize it. And it was the lawyers. That was the group that was gung ho to build any project for any reason. They had a lot of swat in the legislature."

The way the Pattersons saw it, the plan was the kind of thing that resonated with powerful interests in Texas: a big, dramatic, home-grown poke in the eye of federal agencies that would dream of challenging it if it became law. In their view, if the plan was going to be defeated, voters in cities like Houston would have to turn out against it. But that, Carol said, wouldn't be enough.

As it turned out, she said, it wasn't just environmental eggheads and me-first city dwellers who viewed the plan with a measure of suspicion. There were quite a few rural, fiscally conservative Texans, particularly in rain-soaked East Texas, who had grave doubts about the plan Marvin Nichols so enthusiastically had promoted.

You could find them in places like the tiny Piney Woods city of Gilmer in East Texas's Upshur County, where they were especially hostile to the notion that they would have to foot the bill for the Panhandle's water. As the *Gilmer Mirror* put it in a blistering editorial a few weeks before the vote, the proposal would saddle all Texans, city dwellers as well as residents of the soggy east, with the staggering cost of the proposal—up to $100 per acre-foot for the water when all was said and done—and few of the benefits. Instead, those benefits would flow to farmers in the west. The solution, the paper's editorial writers concluded, was not to water the west but to build new reservoirs in the east and make sure that future development took root there. "We believe the lowest cost way to solve any 50-year water distribution problem in Texas is to gradually put new families, new plants, new growth and new cities where the water is. This will not cost billions of dollars nor obligate taxpayers over the whole state.

And it makes economic sense to let industry and people come to where the water is, rather than to spend billions elsewhere . . . and then use it chiefly for irrigation."[9]

Those reservations were not entirely unreasonable given the monumental scope of the plan. In addition to pumping water from the Mississippi, the plan called for the construction of sixty-two major reservoirs, to provide four million acre-feet of water, that would have drowned some forty-five hundred square miles of bottomland, most of it in East Texas, especially in the Sulphur River Basin, which would have essentially been dammed from Dallas to the Louisiana state line.

Large swaths of valuable old-growth timber, a rarity in Texas, would have been swept away, locals said. Farms and homesteads, some of them dating before the birth of the Republic, would have been purchased or condemned and then consigned to the bottom of some reservoir, which would then be named after some famous Texan with little or no connection to the region. Cemeteries containing the headstones of those ancestors who first trekked into the place would be lost.

A culture as old as Texas's and yet always, throughout her history, overlooked and undervalued by the powers that be in Austin and elsewhere would be pried up by the roots.

It wasn't that such concerns carried no weight among the boosters of the 1968 water plan. Nor was it that they necessarily dismissed them, or even that they were necessarily dismissive of those who harbored them. It was just that the way they saw it, there was little time for such sentimentality in the new Texas.

The state, in the midst of a spiraling population boom, was facing a serious challenge to its 1960s-era image of itself as a forward-leaning citadel of progress, economically, technologically, and even culturally. Serious men, like Marvin Nichols, had a serious plan to rise to that challenge. And they were confident that the people of Texas would see things their way.

And so, on August 5, 1968, two weeks after Houston successfully guided the first humans to the moon and back, the boosters of the plan were optimistic as 625,312 Texans went to the polls to decide the fate of the most ambitious water proposal ever developed in Texas.

What they apparently failed to recognize, however, is the one fact that every leader in Texas since Sam Houston has learned: if there is one thing that is more predictably unpredictable than the wild cycles of rain and drought in Texas, it is Texans themselves.

The measure failed by 6,277 votes, just over one percent of all the votes cast. It failed by a respectable margin in Upshur County, the *Gilmer Mirror* reported on August 7. The vote there was 858 against to 651 in favor. Even in parched Pecos County, where the measure passed by an almost three-to-one margin, there were still 197 stiff-necked Texans who voted against it.[10]

But by far, just as the Pattersons had hoped, the loudest no came from the voters of Harris County and from Houston in particular. There, United Press International reported at the time, the measure was trounced by a stunning five-to-one margin, with 67,719 voting against the measure and 13,431 supporting it.

We will leave it to historians and political scientists to debate whether the narrow defeat of the funding mechanism for the state water plan that day was a rejection of big government spending or whether something else was a play, the beginning of a shift in power, perhaps, away from the historical rural power base that had long called the shots in Texas and toward the growing cities. But it might be worth noting that on that same day, voters in Texas by a two-to-one margin generously agreed to raise the maximum amount they would be willing to spend on aid to families with dependent children—welfare—from $60 million a year to $80 million.

Stunned by the razor's-edge defeat, state officials gritted their teeth and gamely pledged to try again. Like a jilted lover, Howard Boswell, then the executive director of the TWDB, told United Press International that the next time the skies dried up, a lot of those voters would come crawling back. "Our water problems haven't disappeared, and if we have a recurrence of drouth, we will have still more people interested in the plan," he said.[11]

The vaunted vision of men like Nichols of a virtual moon shot that would reengineer the entire state of Texas, to soak its deserts and refill its thirsty aquifers with the waters of the Mississippi, reached its high-water mark on the morning of August 5, 1969. By the time the polls closed and the votes were counted, that vision had become a pipe dream.

CHAPTER 2

WHEN MINE IS YOURS AND YOURS IS OURS

"WHEN IT COMES TO WATER IN TEXAS, it's yours, mine, and ours," a noted attorney who has spent decades navigating the state's water laws once said.

On the surface, that understated acknowledgement—that water is not a single resource but the lifeblood of a confounding and complex system on which hundreds if not thousands of competing interests depend—sounds almost egalitarian, enough so that it might be considered suspect or downright socialist in some parts of the state.

But that is not what the lawyer meant. And just to make that abundantly clear, he added that the way it works in Texas is, "if I'm pumping it, it's mine. If you're pumping it, it's ours. And if it's polluted, well then, it's yours."

That deeply ingrained and conflicted sensibility—that water is often at once a personal possession and one that also must be viewed as a public resource—has always been part of the ethos of the American West in general. Nowhere has that been more true than in Texas. It was that duality that Marvin Nichols and the other advocates of the sweeping 1968 water plan were trying to harness and channel with their grand scheme. And, despite their narrow defeat, to some degree they keep trying, every five years with each new iteration of the state water plan.

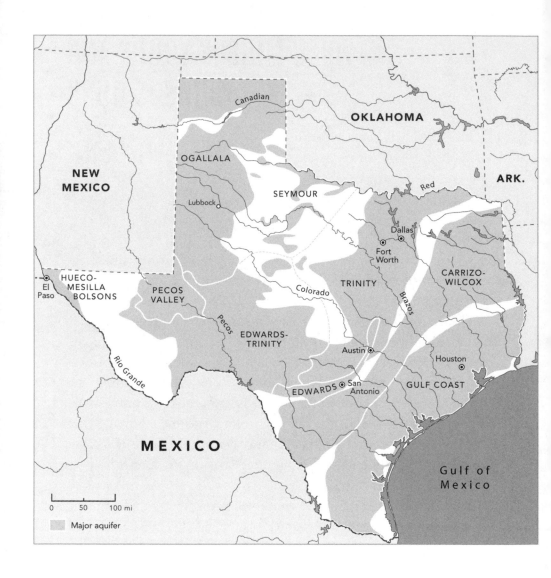

NEW
MEXICO

OKLAHOMA

ARK.

Canadian

OGALLALA

SEYMOUR

Lubbock

Red

Dallas

Fort
Worth

TRINITY

CARRIZO-
WILCOX

HUECO-
MESILLA
BOLSONS

El
Paso

PECOS
VALLEY

Pecos

Colorado

Brazos

EDWARDS-
TRINITY

Austin

Houston

Rio Grande

EDWARDS

San
Antonio

GULF COAST

MEXICO

Gulf of
Mexico

0   50   100 mi

Major aquifer

There has been some progress toward that goal. Over the past few decades, with the establishment of nearly 100 regional groundwater districts, the state has made strides in at least creating a mechanism to monitor and set some limits on the unfettered right to pump as much water from underground aquifers as a landowner might choose. And progress has been made in determining who has the right to draw water from the state's five thousand miles of rivers and thirty-seven hundred named streams and when they can draw it.

But as we will see later in this volume, that progress been inconsistent and often self-defeating. More than one water expert in the state has likened it to a giant game of Whack-A-Mole, where you address one problem, say subsidence over an aquifer that serves the wet green counties of the eastern part of the state, only to set in motion a chain of unexpected consequences that somehow or other turns into a fight over whether weekenders have an inalienable right to waterski on man-made lakes north of Austin, and that somehow or other morphs into a battle over whether it is a wise decision to raise rice in the desert outside Fort Stockton. Water experts will tell you that it is a bottom-up and parochial system, one that often pits region against region, sometimes neighbor against neighbor. But for now, and perhaps for the foreseeable future, it is the best we have got.

Further complicating those efforts, of course, is a distinctly Texas-style wrinkle. Though they are linked in countless ways, one often replenishing the other, in Texas, surface water and groundwater are viewed as utterly separate and legally disconnected. As in most states, not just in the arid West but across the country, surface water is considered public property, and in Texas, rights to it are granted by the state on what amounts to a first-come, first-served basis. "First in time, first in right" is the way it is essentially distilled. Along most of Texas's rivers and streams, those who have the oldest rights get priority when times get tough and the rivers run low, and those who came later have to reduce their consumption first.

Underground water, however, is viewed entirely differently. It is first and foremost a property right. Under a system abandoned in the rest of the West as long as a century ago because it was found to be unworkable in the arid West—though it still remains in place in a handful of states in the usually more water-rich East—the view in Texas is that a landowner in Texas controls everything above and below his or her lands from the skies to the center of the earth. And that includes the water, which, with very few exceptions, the landowner can pump to his or her heart's content.

That makes Texas unique among western states. As State Representative Lyle Larson, the San Antonio Republican who chairs the Natural Resources Committee, puts it, "We're the only state that has abdicated a global view of water."

This system also puts Texas at odds, as we will see later, with some of its neighbors, particularly those that share the overdrawn Ogallala Aquifer. New Mexico and Colorado, for example, use a "first in time" prior appropriation system similar to the one applied to surface water in Texas to limit the amount of water that can be drawn from an aquifer. Oklahoma, taking its cue from a system that developed in California over a century ago, has taken a more universalist view. Recognizing the indisputable fact that groundwater often feeds and is fed by surface water supplies, those states have adopted what is known as a correlative rights doctrine in which ownership of a piece of land entitles you to a percentage of the water in the underlying aquifer, but you don't have an absolute right to groundwater or an unlimited right to pump it. Nebraska, which also sits above the Ogallala, uses a similar system but also demands that whatever water you do pump must be put to a beneficial use, though as we will see later, there is no real definition of that use and it can be a remarkably elastic term.

It is not that Texas doesn't have the right to regulate groundwater more aggressively. More than a century ago, in 1917, the voters explicitly gave the legislature that right when, after two deep droughts, in 1910 and again in 1917, they approved an amendment to the state constitution that stated in no uncertain terms that "the preservation and conservation of . . . natural resources of the State are each and all hereby declared public rights and duties; and the Legislature shall pass all such laws as may be appropriate thereto."[1]

Yet, for whatever reason, be it that Texans are by nature and history a stiff-necked, individualistic bunch or that the courts have been unwilling to legislate from the bench or, as more than one critic has put it, that the Texas legislature has seemed reluctant to legislate from Austin, the rule of capture remains the dominant feature of Texas water law.

As Texas Supreme Court Justice Nathan Hecht put it in his concurrence to a 1999 case in which the rule of capture was upheld (albeit reluctantly), "Not much groundwater regulation is going on."[2]

If you imagine that such a bifurcated system in which groundwater rights and surface water rights are treated as entirely discrete entities is a recipe for conflict, you are right.

It has been said, "Whiskey's for drinking, water's for fighting over." It is perhaps telling that the precise origin of that phrase, widely and perhaps incorrectly attributed to Mark Twain, is, like many other aspects of water issues in Texas, shrouded in mystery.

It is as clear as a Hill Country spring that Twain, or whoever it was who first coined that phrase, wasn't talking specifically about Texas when he uttered those words. He was talking about the American West in general, but it is also crystal clear that those words distill a certain ethos that was carried into the state, and to the West in general, by those pilgrims and pioneers who first stumbled into the lands formerly held by Spain and then Mexico.

Though it was no doubt intended as a wry rebuke, in effect it became an exhortation, to meet the challenge accepted by those who came first and by all those who came after them to grab everything they could, from a bottle of red-eye to vast expanses of rangeland or farmland and everything that lay beneath it, and to grab it with both hands.

It has been repeated so often it has become almost a creed. And in the first third of the nineteenth century, in the sometimes arid, sometimes flooded hinterlands of Texas, it was a revolutionary creed. To understand just how revolutionary it was, and to grasp how deeply it is still imbedded in us today, it is essential to go back to the beginning, to the first real Spanish settlement worth the name.

The San Antonio of the early twenty-first century, a driving modern metropolis of 1.4 million people, the second-most populous city in Texas, the seventh-most populous city in the United States, is a far cry from the desiccated, all but ghost town of roughly eight hundred people that American settlers first saw when they began spreading west toward San Antonio from Stephen Austin's first colony in the east in the mid-1820s. Crippled by cycles of drought followed by floods, followed by more droughts, ravaged by war and a brutal and bloody revolution, the place had been practically de-peopled. But those few who stayed behind, either out of hardiness or simply because they had no place else to go, remained tethered to the land, in part by the network of canals, or *acequias*, that had been meticulously built over one hundred years earlier by missionaries and their Native American laborers.

But that resident population was also tied to the land, and to some degree sustained on it, by a concept in both law and culture—*derecho*, a Spanish word for which there is no direct English equivalent. It is most directly translated as "straight," or "on the up-and-up," but what it really connotes is a kind of justice, of fair play, and the ancient court records are full of cases in which what was seen as right or just trumped what might have been written in the law.

As applied to the issue of water, at least in San Antonio in the colonial and Mexican era, the law effectively ordained that all the water that flowed upon the surface, from the moment it gurgled out of the various springs into the San Antonio River, or from there into the *acequias*—the hand-hewn canals—belonged to the King of Spain, and later to his various civil successors. It declared that water was in effect a public trust, to be administered for the public good, and shared by the landholding members of the public. It was, as far as it went, a reasonably enlightened policy—it even demanded a level of conservation requiring that all unused water be returned to the system—and it was workable enough that it continues to this day to remain a critical component of water law in Texas, at least as it relates to surface waters.

The principle, carried with the earliest Spanish settlers from their own rain-starved lands in Iberia and based upon lessons they had learned there during harsh droughts dating all the way back to the days of Augustus Caesar, was workable enough to sustain the kind of subsistence farming communities the Crown needed to keep its settlers and Native Americans well fed and watered enough to fend off the occasional foray into the region by French adventurers and by those Native American cultures that did not wholly sign on to the idea of delivering vast swaths of their ancestral land to Christ and Spain. In effect, it ordained that every person had a right to the water they needed for domestic use and to water their livestock and that everything above that was shared. In San Antonio, people would take turns diverting water to the *acequias* and from there to their fields. And for the most part, they waited their turns patiently.

There were, of course, drawbacks, related not to the amount of water but to the quality of it. Cholera, a waterborne disease, had appeared twice, in 1849 and again in 1866, killing as many as seven hundred people in what was then a city of twelve thousand.[3] The carnage was appalling. In an April 1849 dispatch, the *Texas Democrat* reported that "there had been as many as 35 deaths in the space of twenty-four hours."

Abbé Emmanuel-Henri Domenech, a French missionary who happened to be in town when the outbreak of 1849 occurred, described the city this way in a letter home. "San Antonio, which a few days before was so gay, so crowded with people . . . was now silent as the grave. The streets were deserted, and the church bells no longer tolled the ordinary. Had they done so, the tolling would have been continuous night and day. The parish priest could find no time even to say mass."[4]

The outbreaks were, to a great extent, the product of the city's dependence on the river and the *acequias*, which by then—perhaps by dint of the fact that the population had quadrupled in the years after Texas joined the Union,[5] placing a burden on them that they were never designed to bear—had deteriorated to the point at which many of them were little more than stagnant cesspools. There was at first little civic will to invest in the kind of infrastructure improvements that would be required to meet the growing demand, until eventually, over time, the condition of the *acequias* and the overall issue of water as a matter of both quality and quantity became a subject of scandal.

Adding to the indignation was the sense that the old concept of *derecho*, though it had in the past bound the people by their own sense of justice and responsibility to each other as much as it bound them to the Crown and successive governments, had faded. The concept also smacked of the kind of subordination of the individual to the larger good that was anathema to some newcomers,

There is an incident documented by Charles R. Porter Jr. in his seminal book, *Spanish Water, Anglo Water*, that casts the decline of that community bond in stark relief. In 1840, a physician who lived along one of the *acequias* decided to supplement his meager income by providing human skeletons for research and had begun boiling down human remains, saving the bones and tossing the soapy, potentially contaminated slop directly into the *acequias*.

It was the kind of story that even then provoked outrage and revulsion among the populace, but truth be told, it didn't spark much in the way of action, certainly not on the part of the city fathers.

And yet, as a principle, the Spanish concept behind surface water rights even managed to survive initial contact with the Anglos who melded it with the English common law concept of riparian rights, the notion that those who lived along the edge of flowing waters had a natural right to use that flow and that those who were first in time at the water's edge had rights that could not be siphoned off by those who came later, even if they settled upstream. Over time, the riparian rights established in English common law evolved to include the concept of prior appropriation, which essentially institutionalized the "first in time, first in right" concept, though it did permit anyone with riverfront property to siphon off two hundred acre-feet of water a year for domestic and livestock use.

It is far from a flawless system. Over time there were competing claims for water rights, and at last, in an effort to settle them all, the legislature adopted the 1967 Water Adjudication Act, under which the state, in an effort essentially to quantify its surface water supplies, undertook a decades-long study to determine who had rights to what free-flowing water and discovered to its chagrin that, at least when it came to dry times, many of the state's waterways had been overappropriated. In other words, there were more people who had rights to water in some regions than there was water, and if everybody drew everything they could, there would not be enough to go around, meaning that those with older claims to the water would take precedence. As we will see later, that is precisely what happened during the drought in 2012, when rice farmers in East Texas found themselves cut off from their traditional water allocation from the Colorado River.

Further complicating matters was evolving Texas law, which didn't make it easy to ship water from one river basin to the next in hard times. If you had priority rights to, say, a few hundred thousand acre-feet on the Guadalupe River and wanted to sell it to San Antonio, you could do so, but you would lose your senior water rights, making the land a less attractive investment for a prospective buyer looking for a steady and reliable water supply for those dry times, said Carlos Rubenstein, former chairman of the TWDB who also served as watermaster for the Rio Grande for nine years, overseeing all allocations from the river below the Amistad Reservoir.

And yet, for a very long time, the basic concept of surface water rights has survived and allowed Texas to thrive. It was a good enough idea to keep San Antonio afloat and to allow for the settlement of San Marcos and even more arid places, like Uvalde. But in a region like South Central Texas, which gets roughly half the annual rainfall of Houston, and where the rain either falls in buckets or not at all, sometimes not for years, reliance on fickle nature and on even more fickle human nature was not enough. It was certainly not enough, as the prevailing sentiment of nineteenth-century America would demand, to make the desert bloom.

To do that, to turn dry land into farms, to make ranges blossom, to turn towns into glistening American cities (and later suburbs), those Manifest Destiny–era settlers would have to find and exploit another source of water, and they would almost certainly have to concoct another formula for parceling it out, one that rewarded individual grit and gumption and that held property rights as something almost sacred.

They didn't have to look far to find the resource. The water, at least, was right beneath their feet. Sometimes, anyway.

As far as those earliest Anglo settlers were concerned, groundwater was an entirely separate beast. It was not subject to the law of *derecho*. Because it was groundwater it was subject to a different kind of law. *The rule of capture* is the way it is described in the bloodless language of jurisprudence. What it essentially means is that whatever lies beneath a person's land belongs to him, subject to no sovereign but him, and he can do whatever he wants with it, even if what he wants to do is draw out every drop of water from the ground, right out from beneath the feet of his neighbor if it need be. There is a less bloodless way of describing it: "Whoever has the largest pump wins."

As a legal doctrine in Texas, the rule of capture erupted like a geyser in 1904, a year after California effectively abolished it, in what was then the little railroad town of Denison, Texas, about seventy-five miles north of Dallas. And much like Houston in the 1960s, Denison owed a lot to the burgeoning technology of the day, railroads. In fact, Denison owed its very existence to the railroads. It was laid out in 1872 by a speculator, who in a bid to win the esteem of the railroad named the town after the vice president of the rail line. His tribute paid off. By the turn of the century Denison had about ten thousand residents who apparently thought very highly of the railroad and the role it played in Denison's genesis and its continued prosperity. Well, most of them did anyway.

W. A. East appears to have been the exception. Most of the details of East's life have been lost to history, but this much is known: by the early 1900s East had acquired three small lots and had drilled small, shallow water wells in them for his domestic use, wells that were, he thought, "inexhaustible."[6]

As it turns out, East's expectations for the continuing bounty of water may have been overly optimistic. In August of 1901, drillers, hired by the railroad to find water to slake the thirst of the steam-belching locomotives that huffed into town like clockwork, sunk a deep well on a property adjacent to East's property and, with the help of a steam-powered pump, sucked twenty-five gallons a day from right underneath East's land as well as that of some his neighbors.

Within a few months, East's wells went south.

He sued. And lost. And appealed. And won. And then the railroad appealed to the Texas Supreme Court and in so doing set the stage for water battles in Texas for the next hundred years.

The unique and defining character of Texas groundwater law begins with that landmark case, *W. A. East v. Houston and Texas Central Railway Company*. The Texas Supreme Court, drawing its inspiration from English common law and its particulars from the way it had evolved in Texas to cover oil and gas law, ruled that the railroad had every right to drill a water well and siphon out every drop it could, even though it completely sucked dry the pitiful little water well a neighboring landowner used for household purposes.

It is, perhaps, no surprise that a court in Texas at the turn of the twentieth century ruled in favor of a railroad over a small-time landowner. Courts, in Texas and elsewhere, reflect the prevailing political winds of their times.

The upshot was that the court effectively declared that groundwater from the state's nine major and twenty-one minor aquifers was "mysterious and occult," so much so that it was beyond the scope of the court to regulate it and that individual property rights were sacrosanct. Still, in a throwaway line hidden deep in the decision, the court also seemed to muse that it might not be entirely impossible for the state, at some point in a more enlightened future, to adopt regulations that would, if not level the playing field for all users, at least calm the waters a bit under that field. It would take the better part of the next century, and the threat of federal court action, for the state even to begin to circumscribe the rule of capture.

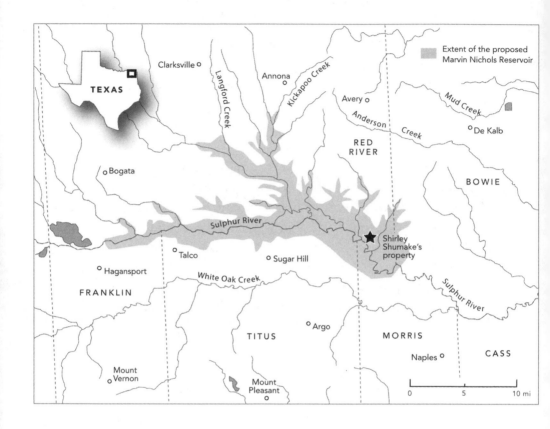

TEXAS

Clarksville ○

Annona ○

Kickapoo Creek

Langford Creek

Avery ○

Anderson   Creek

Mud Creek

De Kalb ○

Extent of the proposed
Marvin Nichols Reservoir

RED
RIVER

BOWIE

Bogata ○

Sulphur River

★ Shirley
Shumake's
property

Talco ○

Sugar Hill ○

Hagansport ○

White Oak Creek

Sulphur River

FRANKLIN

TITUS

Argo ○

MORRIS

Naples ○

CASS

Mount
Vernon ○

Mount
Pleasant ○

0   5   10 mi

CHAPTER 3

"THAT'S THE KIND OF THINKING THAT WILL GET YOUR LAND TOOK FROM YOU"

Maybe it was the way the summer sun glided through the lush leaves of the white oaks, the pecans, the hickories, and the ash on the far bank. Or maybe it was the way it splintered into a thousand glistening sunbeams that danced that late afternoon on the surface of the slow-moving Sulphur River that marked the border of her family's land.

Or maybe it was the sound of the boys who, having already fed all the hot dog buns she had brought to the ravenous catfish and given up fishing for the afternoon, laughed as they cannonballed into the water and dunked each other in the tawny flow.

She wanted the river to flow, just like that, forever, she thought.

But as Shirley Shumake leaned back against a massive old white oak, sixteen feet around, that had been there before her great-grandmother's family trudged into this part of Texas more than 160 years earlier, somewhere, deep down, she had a feeling that one day, maybe soon, all of this would be gone.

The rumors had been circulating for a while by that afternoon in the late summer of 2000. The cities of Dallas and Fort Worth, now morphed into a single "metroplex" that was growing like salt cedar on a river bank, and their water purveyors, including the Tarrant Regional Water District, had long been casting a covetous eye on this all-but-forgotten corner of Texas.

Of course, that is the way things had always been in these hardwood bottomlands an hour or so west of Texarkana.

When the rest of Texas needed timber to frame its houses, this is where they came, in the process spawning a $15.8-billion-a-year industry that directly employed hundreds in the region and indirectly employed three thousand. When they needed forage for their cattle or feed for their horses, they came here. And when they needed soldiers for their wars, from the Texas revolution of 1836 through Vietnam and Operation Desert Storm, they came here. Pretty much every man Shirley knew had been in the service, her brother Max included.

Now they were coming for the water. The rumor was that Fort Worth, the North Texas Municipal Water Authority, the Tarrant Regional Water District, and to a lesser extent, the City of Dallas had developed plans with the powerful and politically well-connected engineering firm of Freese and Nichols to develop a staggeringly ambitious reservoir project along this very stretch of the Sulphur River. It wouldn't be the first dam on the Sulphur River. A decade earlier, Shumake had watched as her neighbors a few miles to the west were driven from their lands to make way for the nineteen-thousand-acre Jim Chapman Lake. A few decades before that, what would become the twenty-thousand-acre Wright Patman Dam was built.

But this was a different proposal altogether. As originally planned, the new reservoir eyed for this stretch of the Sulphur River would drown seventy-two thousand acres of land under two hundred feet of water, and that wasn't even counting the tens of thousands—perhaps as much as 150,000—acres of land that would have to be surrendered by either purchase or condemnation to make up for all the timberland that would be lost to the flood. That is because the federal government requires that when a dam is built, the damage must be mitigated, and lands of similar quality must be set aside. And because there was only so much comparable land in Texas, and most of it was within a few miles of Shirley Shumake's eight-hundred-acre ranch, even landowners miles removed from the proposed reservoir site could lose control of their land in the process of providing the growing metroplex with affordable water.

It would, advocates said, be the last of the truly grand-scale reservoirs ever to be built in Texas, the last vestige of that grandiose 1968 water plan that would have reengineered Texas. In fact, it was to be named after one of the godfathers of that failed plan. Right after the voters had rejected that proposal, the sons of that godfather, and the old man's partners at Freese and Nichols, had lobbied the legislature to change the name of the lake that might someday be built.

It was now called the Marvin Nichols Reservoir.

It was to be a stunning project: a $2.1 billion investment in somebody else's future that would threaten Shirley Shumake's past and that of her neighbors, taking their homes, their history, the land they were raised on, and the land in which their ancestors were buried. And though she didn't fully realize it at the time, the project would also define her future, at least for the next decade, and perhaps beyond.

Her neighbors had told her that it was a "done deal," that powerful forces 150 miles to the west had made up their minds and that there was nothing to be done to stop it.

That kind of thinking was all too familiar in this part of Texas, which had always been considered by the locals to be the red-headed stepchild of two states, Texas and Arkansas. It was a well-worn bit of local wisdom that if you needed anything from the state, it was better to drive the hour and a half to Little Rock than it was to drive the four hours to your own state capitol in Austin because the answer would be same but you would have spent less money on gas before you got to "no."

Maybe it was the way the summer sunlight glided through the white oaks and the pecans on the far bank that late afternoon in 2000. But something deep inside Shirley that day whispered to her in words that she could then only barely make out, "*That's the kind of thinking that will get your land took from you.*"

It would be easy, particularly if you lived in those almost pristine woodlands in the Sulphur River Basin, to paint the powers that be as thoughtless, rapacious aggressors, bent on fueling the growth of their region with oil, with water, regardless of the consequences, so long as *they* didn't have to bear them. Easy, but wrong in many ways.

The truth is, it hadn't been that long, in the grand scheme of things—just over forty years since the drought of record—since Dallas had been on the precipice, coming within just a few days of running out of water from its primary aquifer.

"We never wanted anything like that to happen again," said Denis Qualls, now planning division manager at the City of Dallas Water Utilities Department.

And so, in the years after the drought, the city, along with neighboring Fort Worth, and the water utilities that not only served them but also carried water to growing municipalities in the region who bought their water from Dallas and its allied water utilities, began casting a wide net for alternative sources of water.

The same was true across much of the state. In the wake of that devastating drought, the state legislature established the TWDB, not only charged with developing statewide water plans but also empowered to set aside $200 million in general revenue bonds so that municipalities could borrow to gird themselves against future droughts.

Though the most ambitious of all those plans, the 1968 version championed by Marvin Nichols, had failed narrowly at the polls in the summer of 1969, that did not stop construction of dams and reservoirs. Between 1957 and 1980, more than 126 major reservoirs were constructed in the state, nearly doubling the number of major reservoirs that had existed before the drought. Among them were the Cedar Creek Reservoir on the Trinity River, constructed by the Tarrant County Water Control and Improvement District Number One, and slightly later, the Richland Chambers Reservoir, which would, under the supervision of Freese and Nichols, be linked to Benbrook Lake, a New Deal–era project that itself had been sort of grandiose in its conception. In addition to providing flood control, the project as originally envisioned would have created a shipping channel to carry oceangoing vessels from the Port of Houston 267 miles inland to Fort Worth, requiring the construction of twenty-six lock and dam projects along the way. The project never made it farther than Liberty, about forty miles upstream of Houston, and the water that would have floated those ships was later reallocated to slake the thirst of a growing Fort Worth.

The area that would be known as the Metroplex faced a peculiar challenge. Though it sat near or astride a few significant aquifers (the Trinity, which provides forty-one percent of the groundwater used in the district, as well as the Carrizo-Wilcox, the Woodbine, the Nacatoch, and the Queen City), on their best days those aquifers were simply not robust enough to meet the water needs of the region. In fact, they provided only about ten percent of the total 1.5 million acre-feet of water the region would demand each year by 2011, with ninety percent coming from surface water sources, reservoirs included, according to the region's (2016) water plan.[1] Even still, by 2001, water planners for the sixteen-county region known as Region C had already determined that "current use of groundwater exceeds the reliable long-term supply in many parts of Region C."

Then, as now, planners looked to conservation and reuse to make up part of their shortfall. As they put it in their 2001 report, "Over half of the water used for municipal supply in Region C is discharged as treated effluent from wastewater treatment plants, making wastewater reclamation and reuse a potentially significant source of additional water supply for the region."[2] But, they added, "at present, only a fraction of the region's treated wastewater is actually reclaimed and reused in the region. Many of the region's water suppliers are considering reuse projects, and it is clear that reuse of treated wastewater will be a significant part of future water planning for Region C."

For the time being, however, in order to make up for that dearth of groundwater, much of the rest had to come from surface water, most of that from the basins of the Red, the Brazos, the Sabine, and, yes, the Sulphur Rivers. And because those rivers, like all rivers in Texas, can be fickle, providing too little water in lean times and enough water to kill you in fat times, that meant that the region was largely dependent on reservoirs.

But the thirty-four reservoirs that served the region were already showing signs of stress trying to provide enough water for 4.9 million people—twenty-five percent of the state's population in 2000.

And that was before taking into account that the population in the region was expanding almost exponentially. By 2016, that 4.9 million people would become 6.4 million, and by 2070 that population was expected to double to more than 14.3 million people, most of them living in Dallas and Fort Worth.

Furthermore, there were additional demands for water that, as we will see, would soon fuel a developing industry, an industry that posed not inconsiderable risks to existing water supplies. At the turn of the twenty-first century, mining—a broad category of usage that includes oil and gas drilling—made up a comparatively small part of the region's water consumption, as little as four percent by some estimates.

The vast majority of water used in the region—as of 2017, more than 1.3 million acre-feet of it—went to municipal supplies, in other words, to the customers of the major water purveyors. That is still true today.

It may not have been entirely clear in the earliest days of Shirley Shumake's unlikely activism, but Fort Worth and the region in general were on the cusp of an energy revolution that by the mid to late part of the first decade of the twenty-first century would add an even greater sense of urgency to the battle for water. A few years earlier, in a remote Texas gas field, wildcatter George Mitchell had pioneered the technology that would come to be known as hydraulic fracturing. In essence, it is the process of pumping a mixture of sand, chemicals, and water—mostly water—deep into a gas well to exploit existing fractures in the gas-bearing rock, thereby unleashing previously unrecoverable stores of gas and oil. It is impossible to overstate the game-changing effect of that technological development on the nation's energy picture. Regions that since the 1970s had been considered energy backwaters were once again being mentioned in the same breath, and with the same breathless reverence among oil and gas analysts, as Saudi Arabia and Russia. Almost overnight, the United States, and Texas, had once again become energy-producing powerhouses. Strictly from an energy-producing standpoint, it was a development as historic as the drilling of the first Texas oil well at Spindletop one hundred years earlier.

And for a time, Fort Worth was ground zero. Beginning in about 2001 and running until about 2008, when the gas bust sparked by the Great Recession slowed growth to a trickle, some two thousand gas wells were drilled in Fort Worth alone. Every one of those wells used up to one million gallons of water, and at least some of that water, tainted by the chemicals used in the process and left underground or else disposed of in deep-injection wells, was lost forever.

In the grand scheme of things, it was still not a lot of water. According to a study done in 2012 by the Bureau of Economic Geology at the University of Texas in Austin, drillers used about 81,500 acre-feet of water—some 265 billion gallons—each year in Texas. As daunting as that sounds, it amounts to somewhere between two and six percent of the water demand statewide in Texas each year, though it can be considerably higher in some regions, and it pales in comparison to the estimated 2.2 million acre-feet a year sprayed on the state's lawns and golf courses.[3] In Region C, mining, the category that includes oil and gas drilling, accounts for about six percent of the total water consumed. And as the drilling process became more efficient, water planners estimated, it would eventually use less freshwater and rely more heavily on treated brine.

Of course, the amount of water consumed by fracking—as the process came to be called—wasn't the only problem. As pressure was being released at a breakneck pace from the gas-rich Barnett Shale beneath Fort Worth, pressure was mounting on the surface as environmentalists and just plain regular folks began to fret that spills on the surface and leaks beneath it, compounded by carelessness, recklessness, or just the luck of the draw, could contaminate both precious surface and groundwater supplies.

There was mounting evidence, in Oklahoma in particular, that the process of disposing of the wastewater through those deep-injection wells carried risks of its own. There was the same risk of surface contamination. Furthermore, earthquakes were being reported in places where they had been almost unheard of before. To be fair, that wasn't a problem just associated with fracking. If and when large-scale desalinization is ever considered a viable and cost-worthy option in Texas or elsewhere, the brine left over after the water is treated to drinking-water standards will still need to be disposed of, much of it probably in the same deep wells.

But even setting aside the obvious environmental effects, the gas boom in the Barnett certainly contributed to the already troubling trends with which Fort Worth and Dallas were contending. The boom by definition meant economic growth. And that meant more industry, manufacturing, and so on. And those businesses are notoriously thirsty. It is a measure of how thirsty the economic engines of the region were becoming that analysts in 2016 predicted that industry would gulp down an estimated 112,839 acre-feet in 2050, a dramatic increase from the 71,366 acre-feet sip the industry had taken in 1996.

It goes without saying that economic growth also means population growth.

All those new people were going to need water, and not just to water their lawns or wash their new cars. The people who were drawn to the region by a thriving economy would need energy—electricity—and that itself demanded water, and lots of it, over the next few decades, perhaps three times the fifty-two thousand acre-feet they were using in 1996. And a lot of that was going to have to be new water. Yes, they could expand reuse, develop the technology and the infrastructure to treat the water they were already using and use it again, though like everything else, there were downsides associated with that. Every gallon that was reused was a gallon that didn't flow downstream to another user or to meet basic environmental flows. And yes, they could expand their conservation efforts, or expand efforts at reducing demand, and take the sometimes-costly steps toward stanching all those leaky pipes and dripping faucets that cost Texans billions of wasted gallons every year.

Or they could expand their horizons and look elsewhere for water.

Their options were limited. As early as the late 1990s, the legendary oilman and entrepreneur T. Boone Pickens had recognized the pickle that Fort Worth and Dallas were likely to be in. Hardly a man hobbled by sentimentality, Pickens had early on recognized something that others were loath to acknowledge, at least out loud.

The simple fact, as he saw it, was that for all the talk about water as a priceless public resource, in Texas at least, it was a commodity no different than oil or gas or lignite.

Sitting on 150,000 acres on top of one of the largest privately held caches of groundwater in the state, albeit in the rapidly depleting Ogallala Aquifer, Pickens hit on a plan to exploit the rule of capture—that peculiar "whoever-has-the-biggest-pump-wins" twist in Texas water law—to make sure that he had the biggest pump and the pipelines necessary to haul his supply to water-starved cities like San Antonio, El Paso, and Dallas.

As we will see later, Pickens, a guy who seldom underestimated his foes, may have wildly underestimated the opposition his plan would provoke, even among people who had hitherto been staunch advocates of the idea that property rights trump all, even when it comes to water.

He also may have overestimated the appeal his proposal would have in places like Dallas. In fact, his water would have cost the city about $2.50 per thousand gallons, which, according to an analysis done by Freese and Nichols at the time, would have made it among the costliest options to provide new water to the city.

By 2010, Dallas decided to pass. The way Dallas water officials saw it, the city and the region still had a few other options. They could build a pipeline to carry water from the Toledo Bend Reservoir. They could take a bit more from Wright Patman. And high on their list was the reservoir to be constructed on the Sulphur River, to be named after the onetime senior partner of Freese and Nichols.

The new reservoir would be cheaper than Pickens's water, about half the cost, provided that the project didn't get bogged down as it made its way through the complex tangle of regulatory agencies, and that construction costs came in at or near budget.

And besides, it wasn't as if the Marvin Nichols Reservoir, to be built in a forgotten corner of the state, far from any center of political or economic power, was likely to face the kind of opposition that Pickens's plan was likely to generate.

At least that is what they thought until Shirley Shumake showed up on the scene.

"That's the kind of thinking," the lawyer drawled, "that will get your land took from you."

When Shirley Shumake, long-winded as she can be sometimes, put down her trusty chainsaw that afternoon and hurried inside the house to answer a call from a lawyer up in Texarkana, the last thing she expected was that the conversation she started that day would last at least fifteen years. She had no idea that it would thrust her into the center of a pitched battle between powerful people in a distant city and her neighbors who, the way the folks from the Metroplex saw it, were standing, bowlegged and insolent, in the way of progress. This self-described country girl who always had to be pried away from her woodpile to take any call from anyone never imagined that she would find herself allied with outsiders, environmental activists, and college professors on the one hand and honchos from the timber industry on the other, not to mention her own neighbors, on the front lines of that fight.

She thought the lawyer was calling about a deer lease.

And indeed, Ronald S. Burnett was interested in grabbing a few acres in the Sulphur River bottom in the hopes of tagging a buck and maybe a doe or two that coming fall. But that wasn't the only thing on Burnett's agenda that day.

In addition to his law practice, Burnett was, back then, an official for a small environmental organization called Friends United for a Safe Environment, FUSE for short, and a short time before, the group had gotten wind of the fact that the Marvin Nichols dam, long a favored project of the powers that be, seemed to be on the fast track.

The proponents of the project were saying it would take years to build. But there was mounting concern that the project was closer to being a reality than anyone in the Sulphur River Basin imagined.

"We could almost hear the bulldozers warming up," said Dr. James Presley, an author with a doctorate in history and a frequent lecturer on environmental issues who, together with Burnett, was one of the key players in FUSE.

It would be an understatement to say that FUSE was alarmed, Presley would later say. It wasn't just that the plans for the dam would sink tens of thousands of acres of environmentally valuable woodlands or that tens of thousands more would be taken out of circulation.

Those losses offended his sensibilities as an environmentalist. But what offended him most was that when he and three or four other members of the organization traveled to a meeting of the Sulphur River Basin Authority in Mt. Vernon, some seventy-five miles to the west of Texarkana, where the plans for the proposed dam were to be discussed, "the people that would be adversely affected immediately, there were none of them in the audience."

And so, a short time later, at a kind of gathering of the tribes of the environmental movement in East Texas, representatives of the local chapters of the Sierra Club and the National Wildlife Federation and Janice Bezanson, a onetime stay-at-home mom who had worked her way to the top of an organization now known as the Texas Conservation Alliance, discussed their options.

It was, in retrospect, kind of a glum meeting. It is true everywhere, but it is truest in deeply conservative East Texas: if an environmental group wants to build a movement to call attention to an environmental issue, simply having its facts aligned or being able to make a compelling argument isn't enough. Anything with the word "environmental" in its name smacks of big-city liberalism. Sometimes it is greeted with open hostility. Sometimes it is met with a yawn. Neither is helpful if you want to build a movement.

That was especially true in the Sulphur River Basin, where for hundreds of years people had gotten so used to being ignored or mistreated by whoever controlled that spit of land—be it the Spanish Crown or the French or the Mexicans or the Republic or the State of Texas—that they had developed a kind of stoic fatalism about almost everything, the Marvin Nichols dam included.

To mount any kind of opposition to the project, you had to enlist local support. And to hear the proponents of the dam tell it, opposition was going to be in short supply. Environmentalists who had discussed the matter with their higher-ups in Austin had been told by promoters of the dam that the people of the Sulphur River Basin were not just silent on the plan, that most of them were affirmatively in favor of the proposal.

The problem was no one in FUSE or in Bezanson's organization knew anyone in the region who could tell them any different. "The problem was nobody knew anybody in the affected area," Presley said. The Sierra Club didn't. The National Wildlife Federation didn't. Janice Bezanson didn't. "We're closer to it, and we didn't either," Presley said.

Call it an accident. Call it serendipity. But a friend of a friend of a neighbor's friend who had heard that Burnett was looking for a place to go hunting passed along Shirley Shumake's number.

And after discussing his needs and her terms for the deer lease, Burnett guided the conversation—as best as anyone can guide a conversation in which Shirley Shumake is a participant—toward the Marvin Nichols dam.

She allowed that she had heard about it but added that she had also heard that even if the permits were ultimately approved, it would be years before the dam would be built.

And then she expressed that fatalism that so often infects people in places like the Sulphur River Basin when confronting powerful forces from outside.

"It's a done deal," she told the lawyer. And when he replied, saying out loud the words that she had only whispered to herself, "*That's the kind of thinking that will get your land took from you*," it was as if a lightbulb had gone off.

"Do you want me to help you?" Burnett asked.

"Sure," she said.

Thirty minutes later she was on the phone with Presley, and an hour after that she was on the phone with Bezanson. "We talked for two hours," she recalled. And when they were done, Shirley Shumake, the country girl with the chain saw, had become an unlikely activist.

The first order of business was to recruit friends and family members to the cause. Her brother Max was among the first. And his first task was to assess the proponents' twin claims that the project was inevitable and that the people of the Sulphur River Basin were solidly behind the project.

"It was general knowledge this was a done deal," he recalled. "They said there was nothing you could do about it. The Sulphur

River Basin Authority . . . said that. Our regional planning board was of that opinion. In my opinion it was never a done deal. Just no one ever opposed it to speak of. They just thought, 'These old farmers and ranchers, you can tell 'em anything. We're gonna build a lake here. You guys get ready to sell out. That's the way it is.' We're up in the northeast. Arkansas is here. Oklahoma is here, and they just feel like our part of the state is Dallas's to do with what they want, to take what they want."

"They" he said, are the same people they have always been. "The money people in these cities."

He had, perhaps, always felt that silent resentment about being taken for granted by moneyed outsiders, but he had generally kept it to himself. But now, as he and his sister knocked on doors or buttonholed neighbors on the street, he was discovering that he was not alone. A lot of people in his neck of the woods had been nursing the same resentment, sometimes even longer than he had.

And it was while visiting with two land-rich old bachelor farmers, Olen and Seaby Love, both then in their eighties, on the front porch of the small, plain wood house where they had been born that he realized that the dam's boosters, perhaps, also had exaggerated the depth of the project's support in the neighborhood.

"Seaby, are you for it?" he asked.

"Nope. I'm not for it," Seaby replied.

"How 'bout you, Olen?"

"No, I'm not for it," Olen spat.

"Well, they say everybody's for it," Max Shumake muttered, and then, for the next several minutes, the three of them sat on that porch and rattled off the names of everyone they knew. "Nope. They're not for it either," they would say after each name, until finally, Shumake stammered, "Well, then, just who the hell *IS* for it?"

The two old men just scratched their heads. "I don't know who's for it."

It didn't take long for the Shumakes to break through that nearly two-hundred-year-old accretion of fatalism that had hardened the community into inaction. It wasn't easy, though. "You know how it is when you call people up on the phone and try to explain something like this," Shirley said. "They don't know what you're talking about." But she was persistent. And within a few weeks, she had enlisted dozens of people to what she was now considering a cause. She was starting to fear, however, that the hardcore cadre she assembled wouldn't be formidable or organized enough to challenge the big-money backers of the project.

She and Bezanson, together with a few regional environmental leaders, had called a meeting to discuss their options to block, or at least to stall, the dam, and as the deadline drew near, Shirley Shumake began to fret. When Bezanson walked into the meeting, Shirley cornered her, apologetically confessing, "There's thirty or forty people . . . I'm sorry I couldn't get no more than that."

Bezanson looked at her, stunned and then amused. "Get out of here, girl," she said finally. The wry smile of somebody who had, in her decades as an environmental activist in Texas, issued plenty of calls to arms that had gone utterly unheeded crossed her face as she surveyed the tiny army Shirley Shumake had mustered. "I've driven eight hundred miles and talked to two people before. I'm tickled to death."

At meeting after meeting, their numbers grew, Shumake recalled. And it wasn't just hay farmers and ranchers who were joining the campaign.

They say politics makes strange bedfellows. As opposition mounted to the proposed Marvin Nichols dam, the fellows in the bed of the Sulphur River were even stranger than usual. You had old-fashioned blue dog Democrats, cozying up to the same rock-ribbed right-wingers who would later swear allegiance to the Tea Party, and they were in turn sidling up to dyed-in-the-wool environmentalists, like Presley, Burnett, and Bezanson. And in a twist that the advocates of the dam could never have predicted and are to this day puzzled by, those same tree huggers were, by early 2001, proudly linking arms with executives of the nearly $30-billion-a-year timber industry in Texas, which had historically been centered in Northeast Texas.

International Paper, which operated a mill in the region that was almost entirely dependent on the pulp the local timber industry produced and on the flow of the river to get rid of its discharge, had lined up with the farmers and ranchers and tree huggers and ominously warned that if the project went through, it might just have to shut down operations there.

That, said Jim Thompson, a local lawyer who at the time also served as the chief financial officer for Ward Timber, could cost the region upward of three thousand jobs directly and indirectly. That might seem like a small number to people in a place like Fort Worth. But it didn't strike Thompson or Shumake or the others as fair that their neighborhood would have to lose not only their family farms but their jobs as well so that Fort Worth and Dallas and the growing suburbs that had been built using Sulphur River timber could keep growing.

And it wasn't as if the Metroplex didn't have other options, Bezanson told her hardy band of budding activists in what would, over time, become a well-polished recitation.

> There are reservoirs where there is enough water for them to get their water. Toledo Bend, Wright Patman, and Lake Texoma.
>
> In the case of Toledo Bend and Wright Patman, pipelines would have to be a little longer, but they wouldn't have to wipe out 50,000 to 70,000 acres of nice bottomland or take another 150,000 acres out of production for mitigation.
>
> But those aren't the most cost-effective either.
>
> The most cost-effective solution for the Dallas–Fort Worth area is to vastly increase the amount of the current municipal water supply that they recycle and reuse.
>
> Dallas–Fort Worth area water providers—North Texas Municipal, Dallas Utilities, Tarrant Regional—are doing some reuse. They have the potential readily to do enough to meet all of the gap between their current supply and their future demand at least through 2070. And that's as far as anybody's projected their future demand.

It may be true that in a state that uses 850,000 acre-feet of water—the effective annual yield of nearly two fully formed Marvin Nichols

Reservoirs—just to water its lawns, the concept of conservation, recycling, and reuse is a potent intellectual argument.[4]

But it is hardly the sort of thing that fires up the base. To do that, you need a touch of populism, an us-against-them message that inspires the kind of "come and take it" resistance that has defined Texans since Colonel Domingo de Ugartechea foolishly sent a corporal and five enlisted Mexican soldiers to Gonzales in 1835 to retrieve a small cannon the Mexican government had loaned to the Anglo colonists there, effectively triggering the revolution.

The opponents of the project found that populism in what they came to believe was the heavy-handed approach the Metroplex took in dealing with them.

Important men and women from the Metroplex could argue that the project was an essential element of their plans to help meet the very real needs of a growing metropolitan area, an area that had already made great strides in reducing its water consumption, reusing some, and identifying other sources of water in addition to the proposed Marvin Nichols.

But the way the folks in the Sulphur River Basin saw it was altogether different—an arrogant land grab that reflected, in their telling of the story, the covetous nature of powerful urban interests.

The engineering firm of Marvin Nichols itself was emblematic of that, according to Oren Caudle, a regional water planner and consultant from Texarkana who became kind of the Thomas Paine of the antireservoir movement. To a very great degree, Caudle and his fellow travelers argued, it was the engineering firm, as much as the local authorities and the heads of the utilities, that was driving the plan for the Marvin Nichols Reservoir.

Never mind that the firm was one of the oldest in the state, or one of only a handful that had the kind of background, experience, and expertise in water-related issues to tackle a multibillion-dollar project as complex as the Marvin Nichols dam. To Caudle and the growing cadre of opponents that Shirley Shumake had enlisted, the firm was part of a grand economic confederation—a "cartel" is the word they use—that, just like T. Boone Pickens, viewed water first and foremost as a commodity to be exploited, no different than oil. "It's the new gold" became a kind of rallying cry.

There was, the way they saw it, something questionable—maybe even unsavory—about the fact that Freese and Nichols's fingerprints could be found on every aspect of the proposal. It was the engineering firm that had guided the Region C water planners when they decided that it was essential to secure that region's water future, they said. It was Freese and Nichols who did the studies that affirmed that indeed it was a necessary project. And when the time came to build it, and to profit off the additional growth that would almost certainly take place in the ever-expanding Metroplex as a result of that assured additional water, Freese and Nichols would benefit just as surely as its partners and associates in the cities did.

To them, even the name of the reservoir reflected that kind of contempt the water purveyors and the cities and the engineering firms had always shown toward Northeast Texas, the same kind of contempt that distant elites had always shown to the residents of this "red-headed stepchild" region of the state. The fact that Freeze and Nichols, including Nichols's sons, had pushed so hard to have the reservoir redubbed not in honor of some regional grandee but as a monument to a man who was synonymous with a grandiose plan to reengineer the entire hydrology of the state, a plan that had been rejected by the voters three decades earlier, bordered on disrespectful.

"They're hell-bent on getting that reservoir built," Caudle said. "They want to build Marvin Nichols as a legacy for daddy . . . they've been trailing that ever since their daddy died."

Freese and Nichols and Fort Worth and its water purveyors would, in the years to come, emphatically rebut the suggestion that they were willing to spend more than $2 billion on what Caudle had described as a watery mausoleum for a failed big-government idea. In the years to come, as we will see later in this volume, they would churn out untold acre-feet of data supporting their contention that Marvin Nichols was an essential element of their plan to remain afloat in the dry years to come.

But the battle lines had been drawn. It would be a long battle indeed, as opponents of the plan persuaded their local officials and their regional water planners to join them in opposition to the project, while Region C continued to champion it. Both sides would wait in vain for the TWDB, charged with trying to balance the needs of a thirsty and affluent Metroplex with the more basic needs and wants of a rural region, to weigh in and pick one side or the other. And pretty soon, the conflict devolved into a kind of slow, grinding battle of inches. "World War I trench warfare," is how Jim Presley describes it.

Maybe someday a new technology would emerge that would reduce the Metroplex's thirst for water from the Sulphur River Basin, the opponents thought. Maybe the day would come when things would get bad enough that conservation would become a passion, as it would, years later in Melbourne, Australia, when a pernicious and lengthy drought threatened to run that city dry. Or maybe, as drought-stricken San Diego later would, Texans would figure out a cost-effective way to suck the salt out of billions of gallons of seawater from the Gulf and dispose of the brine that would be left behind without creating dead zones in the ocean or accidentally triggering earthquakes by injecting it—just as the oil and gas industry does with a portion of its waste—deep underground in regions potentially bisected by uncharted faults.

Perhaps someday, Texas would see its way clear to settle all the conflicts between regions with too much and too little groundwater, navigate between the property rights of landowners and the rights of their neighbors, funnel it all through the free market, and figure out a way to use more than ten percent of the estimated three to four billion gallons of water in the state's nine major and twenty-one minor aquifers.

But in the early 2000s, all of that was just a pipe dream, something that if it ever happened, would happen in a distant future. 2030. 2050. Maybe 2070.

And in the meantime, the folks in the Sulphur River Basin would try to just hold their ground.

They did.

And in the years to come, Shirley Shumake would often wander along the banks of the Sulphur River near that grand old oak tree, sixteen feet around, that had been there before her great-grandmother had first set foot in this part of the country. She still fretted that there might come a time when she would "get her land took from her." But at least she had changed her thinking. And what she had at first thought was a done deal was anything but.

MT
WY
SD
MN
NE
IA
CO
KS
MO
NM
OK
AR
TX
MEXICO
COLORADO
KANSAS
OKLAHOMA
Dumas
Canadian
Red
OGALLALA AQUIFER
NEW MEXICO
Lubbock
Brazos
Hobbs
Midland
Odessa
Colorado
El Paso
Pecos
TEXAS
Rio Grande
Comanche Springs (Fort Stockton)
Williams' ranch
MEXICO
0
50
100 mi

THE LAST STRAW

A STIFF BREEZE blows down from the north, hot and dry across the tawny prairie grass of the High Plains. If you listen closely, you can almost hear the old steel fan blades moan and whirr. You can almost feel the deep, dull clank of an iron piston struggling to lift itself, rising and falling, rising and falling.

Peer across the expanse and you can still find a few of them, almost comically frail, these spindly skeletons with heads like sunflowers that rise up here and there from the plains, slowly pumping water, a few dozen gallons at a time, into corrugated aluminum water tanks.

There are more than a few of them still in service. In fact, a company in San Angelo still makes about a thousand of them a year. They are as much a part of the iconography of Texas as hand-tooled saddles, waxed lariats, and ten-gallon hats, as much a part of the mythical landscape of Texas as longhorn cattle. And in their own way, they are just as obsolete as those leathery beasts. Compared with the gigantic wind turbines, thousands of them that march in a phalanx across the plains, generating electricity—a dry electricity at that, that doesn't require vast amounts of cooling water or steam to run turbines—they seem ridiculously small and insignificant. They have been supplanted in their primary purpose—to pump life-giving water from the aquifers below this parched land—by industrial-strength diesel or electric pumps that can produce thousands of gallons a day.

But once upon a time, those old, creaky windmills marked the furthest boundary of technology. Had it not been for a craftsman and inventor from Connecticut who invented the iconic windmill in 1854, the arid plains of the Panhandle would be as unforgiving today as they were when Comanches used to snake along the edge of the prairie from water hole to water hole, unaware that their horses were walking just a few hundred feet from a seemingly boundless freshwater sea buried underground.

The windmills provided the water that allowed steam locomotives to bring progress—and immigrants from the Midwest and East—to the Panhandle, lured there by the promise that "rain followed the plow" and the conviction that if, from time to time, that promise went unfulfilled, the windmills would carry them through.

Those windmills allowed those farmers to begin irrigating, raising corn and grains on land that previously yielded only dry-land crops, and those only reluctantly.

The High Plains blossomed and bloomed. And for a time it seemed that the water beneath the ground would last forever.

It won't.

We just don't know for sure how long we have until the water runs out.

Sprawling underground beneath 174,000 square miles of land from South Dakota south into the arid easternmost edge of New Mexico, an ocean is buried—the Ogallala Aquifer, the largest subterranean water supply in America, one of the largest in the world. Its size and scope are staggering. As author William Ashworth put it in his book, *Ogallala Blue*, imagine nine Lake Eries stacked on top of each other and hidden deep below the surface of the land, and you can begin to get a picture of the immensity of the Ogallala. If you emptied every drop and dumped it out on the continental United States, you could create a swimming pool, a foot and half deep, that would stretch from New York to California.

As it is, it supports a $20-billion-a-year agricultural economy in eight states. By some estimates, one-fifth of the total agricultural output of the United States—corn, cotton, sunflowers, feed for cattle, and the cattle themselves—owes its very existence to the largesse of the Ogallala. In the sixteen-county Panhandle region of Texas alone, water pumped from the aquifer supports a $3-billion-a-year agricultural industry. Nearly half of the corn and three-quarters of the hogs produced in Texas every year depend on water pumped from the Ogallala.

Just a little more than half a century ago that was not the case. For most of the recorded history of Texas, the Ogallala Aquifer was one of nature's most jealously guarded secrets. When Coronado and his thirsty band of treasure hunters trudged across this parched landscape in 1541, they had no idea that there was an empire of water beneath them, hidden from them. It would still be hidden hundreds of years later, when in dry years cowboys on long cattle drives would watch in horror and pity as their herds weakened and died while foraging their way through this parched land. And in the 1930s, when sodbusters watched their land blow away in the great roiling dust storms, they could hardly have imagined that their salvation lay just out of reach a few hundred feet below them.

It wasn't until the modern era, in the years immediately after World War II, that the full bounty of the Ogallala was unleashed. Small wind-powered wells that had struggled to fill small cattle tanks gave way first to mechanized pumps operated by repurposed car engines, which in turn gave way to the industrial-strength, diesel powered pumps that in the space of a few short years turned the arid High Plains into a garden. All across the Ogallala, tinder-dry prairie grass gave way to cash crops as center-pivot irrigation systems orbited in the fields. As Jane Braxton Little, writing in *Scientific American* in 2009, put it, "The number of irrigation wells in West Texas alone exploded from 1,166 in 1937 to more than 66,000 in 1971. By 1977, one of the poorest farming regions in the country had had been transformed into one of the wealthiest, raising much of the nation's agricultural exports and fattening 40 percent of its grain-fed beef."

By the end of the end of the twentieth century the Ogallala was said to produce nearly thirty percent of all the water used for irrigation in the United States.

That bounty, however, had an expiration date. The nation's largest aquifer is also one of its most endangered. Most of the water in it is ancient, thousands upon thousands of years old. "Fossil water" scientists call it, snowmelt from eons ago that ran down from the Rocky Mountains and was trapped when the aquifer formed. It is slow to recharge, and most of that happens when water collecting in small, seasonal ponds, called "playas," in the High Plains slowly— excruciatingly slowly—percolates through the soil and down into the aquifer, which is buried in some places more than eight hundred feet deep.

As early as the 1960s, water experts were beginning to become concerned about the future of the Ogallala. Replenishing the Ogallala was one of the key reasons why men like Marvin Nichols advocated pumping vast amounts of water from the Mississippi River uphill across the northern reaches of Texas. By 1980, that concern turned to outright alarm, as reports began to circulate that water levels across the aquifer had plunged by an average of ten feet.

A deep dive into the aquifer's statistics by the US Geological Survey in the years that followed found that, indeed, the aquifer was being drained at a rate that far exceeded the rate at which it could possibly be recharged. In a good year, the Ogallala recharges at a rate of about half an inch a year. At the same time, farmers and ranchers, who used ninety percent of Ogallala water, by the mid-1970s were taking out, in some cases, five times as much as they had in 1949. By the middle of the first decade of this century, as much as eleven percent of the original aquifer had been used.

Nor was overpumping the only threat the Ogallala faced. In some places the same technology that had allowed the Ogallala to be exploited on an industrial scale in the first place now posed a separate risk. It was diesel-powered pumps that opened the aquifer to widespread development, and thousands of miles of pipelines that carry the crude oil to provide the raw material for that diesel, or in some cases the refined fuels themselves, cut through the Ogallala in Wyoming, Colorado, Kansas, Nebraska, Oklahoma, and Texas. Environmentalists have warned that undetected leaks or a catastrophic rupture of one of those pipelines could permanently contaminate the already beleaguered aquifer. There are concerns, too, that the by-products of the agricultural revolution the Ogallala created also may take their toll, as chemicals from fertilizers and other sources of pollution from farms and ranches trickle into an aquifer that becomes less and less able to dilute them as it is drawn down. And then there is the impact of a changing climate—dry places getting drier, as most scientists warn, meaning that the already glacial pace of recharge will become even slower and more sporadic.

Even without a catastrophic event, there is little doubt that the days of seemingly boundless water from the Ogallala are numbered. In fact, the decline has already begun. By 1990, the rate at which the water levels in the aquifer declined, which had been a loss of ten feet a year, had been reduced to about one and one-half feet. It is still draining at a rate far faster than it can possibly be refilled, but now it is ambling toward extinction rather than lurching headlong.

There is a reason for that. As water from the Ogallala has become scarcer, the demand for it has fallen. By 1994, the number of irrigated acres in the Texas High Plains had dropped from a high of 3.95 million to 2.7 million. And it will drop further, as the region's water planners reported in their 2017 submission to the state water plan. Statewide, by 2070, planners expect the amount of water demanded by irrigation to decline by eighteen percent, with much of that coming as a result of less water from, and greater restrictions on, the Ogallala.

Some of that, of course, will come from farmers who just give up altogether. Some will come from farmers returning to the ways of their grandparents, to dry-land farming and small-scale irrigation.

But much of that reduction will come as a result of greater efficiency, says Jason Coleman, general manager of the High Plains Water District, which has jurisdiction over the aquifer in that part of the state. New developments in irrigation technology have helped some farmers squeeze more crops out of less water. They are experimenting with genetically modified crops from companies like Monsanto and Pioneer, strains of corn, for example, that are less thirsty and more resistant to periods of drought. They have altered when they plant in an effort to take advantage of the natural growth cycles of their crops, learning through trial and error, for example, that corn planted earlier in the year seems to use about four inches less water per acre than corn planted later. And they are changing how they plant, plowing less before they put their seeds in the ground and leaving a stubble after harvest that catches more rain and draws less from the overburdened aquifer.

You can see these changes on David Ford's seven thousand acres of corn and cotton and hay outside Dumas, Texas. At the height of the last drought, Ford began adapting his practices to a drier future. He quadrupled the amount of cotton he raised to twelve hundred pounds—and has sought out less thirsty varieties of the stuff. He cut back on the corn he planted, he said in a 2013 interview.

Those techniques are, by necessity, being replicated across the Panhandle.

"We're seeing a lot more of that kind of stuff," Coleman says.

But even that kind of conservation comes at a cost. Less water sprayed on crops means that there is less runoff, so less water makes its way to the playas. Those playas account for up to ninety-five percent of the water that finds its way to the Ogallala, and thus, in places the already slow recharge of the Ogallala is slowed further.

Efforts are under way to slow the inexorable decline. In an effort to make sure that the aquifer in the region is depleted by no more than half by 2060, the local High Plains Water District has placed restrictions on the amount of groundwater that can be pumped out of the Ogallala—farmers are restricted to pumping one and one-half acre-foot of water per year for every acre farmed. That is about the amount of water needed to raise an acre of corn. But in a state where groundwater is considered an inalienable property right, where the rally cry has always been whoever has the biggest pump wins, even that modest restriction was met with some grumbling. That grumbling turned into outright defiance when the district tried to tell the farmers that they needed to install water meters, which could cost up to $2,000 apiece.

As Brad Heffington, a local cotton grower, told the *Texas Tribune* at the time, the whole idea—not just the notion of limiting the rule of capture but requiring the meters—was an affront to all that Texans hold sacred. "It's very emotional when you try to tell people what to do with their own property," he said.[1]

Fearing that its efforts at regulation would not survive a court challenge—particularly not at a time when the courts increasingly favor the farmers in such cases—the water district sought a truce. "We sat down with ninety-plus stakeholders," Coleman said, and hammered out an agreement. The farmers would still be limited to a one and one-half acre-foot of water per acre, but they were provided with alternatives—six of them—to installing meters, most of the alternatives relying on the good faith of the farmers. The two sides averted a showdown. "It was determined to be a reasonable solution."

It doesn't seem quite so reasonable if you cross the state's boundary line with New Mexico, near the parched city of Hobbs in Lea County, where a shallow finger of the Ogallala rests. There you will find those who look on Texas's rule of capture with disgust and envy in equal measure.

Dennis Holmberg, the former county manager for Lea County, is one of those. His complaints echo those you hear from residents in those states that share the Ogallala with Texas. For decades, Holmberg says, he has watched in horror as farmers right across the state line suck water out of the rapidly depleting aquifer at a breakneck pace. The new regulations in the Panhandle, he says, have done little to stanch that flow, thanks to the rule of capture. On the New Mexico side, meanwhile, where laws restrict the amount of water that can be pumped, the residents can do nothing.

It is the same land, the same aquifer below it, but on one side, he said, it is lush and green and on the other it is desert. "We have no surface water," he says. "All our water comes from the Ogallala."

And much of it is going to Texas. "If you were to fly along the border," he says, "you'd see circle irrigation systems in Texas. That's the rule of capture. As big a well as you could get, as big a well as you could drill, that's what you could pump to water your crops. And there are circles for as far as the eye could see. Yet when you got to the state line the circles dropped off. There aren't nearly as many."

It is not, he says, because some natural force arbitrarily had decreed that water would flow on one side of the divide and not the other, he says. "It wasn't because that line was the difference between having water and having no water. That was a political boundary. The issue was the political-ness of how water rights were managed."

The way he describes it, it is as if the aquifer in this region is a gigantic soup bowl, and Texans have for generations tilted it toward themselves and are slurping greedily right down to the dregs.

That is why for years now, Holmberg and others, so far without success, have been lobbying officials in Santa Fe to carve out a water-pumping free-fire zone along the border with Texas, where the rule of capture would apply equally on both sides.

It is hardly an optimal solution, Holmberg admits. The ideal solution, he said, would be to forget about the political boundaries and work jointly to preserve the Ogallala for as long as possible for the benefit of as many people as possible.

But that is not likely to happen any time soon, he says. For now, he contends, the rush for what is left in the Ogallala is summed up by this phrase: "If we're gonna have a race to the bottom of the barrel, we might as well get there first."

Coarse as it is, that formulation is to a great extent the prevailing sentiment in much of the Ogallala, where for many there is a sense that time—and water—will eventually run out.

It would hardly be the first time Texans had pumped a place dry.

Take Comanche Springs, for example.

It is pretty much a dry hole now.

But not so very long ago, this dry expanse of Pecos County that sits atop four aquifers was a sparkling oasis, a magical place where crystal clear and cool water that had rained down upon the Glass

Mountains fifty miles to the south would bubble up here. There were softshell turtles aplenty. And fish, the endangered Comanche Springs pupfish among them.

For thousands of years, nomadic Native Americans traveling across the high desert would stop here. The Spanish explorer Coronado watered his horses and his men here as early as 1540.

More than 230 years later, the explorer John C. Reid described the water erupting from the ground as "a sea monster." The Comanches called the place "Awache"—white water. The Anglos called it "Comanche Springs."

Seen as a vital strategic location by the military, both to protect settlers heading west and to deprive the Indians of a vital resource on their well-worn raiding path south to Mexico, it became the site of a significant military base, Fort Stockton. Once it was secure, the southern branch of the transcontinental railroad followed, and the railroad brought immigrants.

Farms, irrigated by those small windmills, began sprouting up in the broad arid depression—a giant crater, actually, left behind after an ancient meteor strike—between the mountains to the south and the mesa where Interstate 10 now runs. And still the springs flowed as clear and clean and strong as ever.

That is the way it was in the late 1890s when a sickly, young Massachusetts lawyer with breathing problems, Clayton Williams, first stepped off the train. Williams, according to his grandson, Jeff, had come west for the air. He stayed for the water.

"My great grandfather was a Harvard-educated lawyer who came down with—I think it was tuberculosis—and they told him, 'Well, go to the desert.' So he went to Dallas. He couldn't find work so he ended up hiring on with a survey crew and ended up here in Fort Stockton. They were surveying all of this part of Texas."

Clayton Williams wasn't looking for water when he came to Fort Stockton, Jeff Williams says. He was looking for oil.

But he understood enough about geology to understand that the karst aquifer—a kind of fast-filling limestone reservoir—underneath the region could itself be a source of riches for a man who could grasp the mysterious and occult nature of the water belowground, how the Edwards-Trinity Aquifer, as well as the Rustler and the Capitan, flowed together in that place to make a seemingly boundless reservoir. And so Clayton Williams Sr. began quietly amassing land west of town. He farmed. He ranched. And others joined him.

"At one point, I think there was 130,000 acres being farmed here. Cotton. They also laid in alfalfa and some other crops," Jeff Williams recalled.

For a while, it seemed like the bounty would never end. In some places, from time to time, the water table would drop, and farmers at the edge of the developing agricultural zone would see their wells run dry because their neighbor with a more powerful pump was sucking the water out from beneath them faster than nature could recharge it. But there was nothing to be done about that. The law said whoever had the biggest pump won, and so the only solution was to suck it up, or get a bigger pump and suck up even more of it.

For decades, the springs at Fort Stockton continued to flow. In fact, the springs and the canals they flooded became a kind of tourist attraction. In 1936, the residents of Fort Stockton established an annual Water Carnival. Two years later, a pavilion was built to provide shelter to pleasure seekers who would paddle and splash in the seventy-two-degree water, sometimes traveling as much as fifteen miles out of town on the easy currents in the canals. It was, for this dusty Pecos County town, a chance to spend a few hours each year basking in the limelight. In 1947, for example, after the city fathers shelled out $1,500 to an Ohio-based theatrical producer to throw a lavish party—the equivalent of $17,000 today—the *Fort Stockton Pioneer* crowed about how the town had lured Governor Coke Stevens to lead "a big street parade," before "a dazzling stage show" was presented at that year's Aquacade. "An added feature of the Saturday night 'Aquacade' will be the All Southwestern Bathing Revue to select 'Miss Southwest of 1947,' with a beautiful loving cup and a trip to Hollywood, Cal. as the prize for the first place winner."[2]

But then, in 1951, Clayton Williams, his brother J.C., and a few other big farmers brought out the big guns, massive diesel pumps that sucked water from ten new wells drilled into the karst with such breathtaking efficiency that within just a few hours of flipping the switches, Comanche springs all but dried up. The pupfish vanished. So did the turtles. And so did most of the tourists. To the east, 108 farmers ran out of water. As the *Fort Stockton Pioneer* reported on August 14, 1952, local water officials decried the loss of the once free-flowing springs as "a serious economic problem to . . . landowners [and] a tragedy to the citizens of the county in general because it has deprived them of the wonderful recreation spot enjoyed for so many years and . . . a threat to the public health of the City of Fort Stockton by the creation of stagnant and polluted water."[3]

Gunnar M. Brune, in his landmark book, *Springs of Texas*, volume one, put it a bit more poetically. "After uncounted thousands of years of beneficial use by mankind, these beautiful springs have been sacrificed in the name of progress."[4]

But Clayton Williams and his associates to the west of town had all the water they wanted.

The Pecos County Water Control and Improvement District Number One sued, of course. And of course, in 1954, they lost. On June 21, 1954, the Texas Court of Civil Appeals ruled that indeed groundwater was too mysterious, too occult to regulate and that the law in Texas truly was whoever has the biggest pump wins.

But two generations later, Jeff Williams would find himself in court and in a pitched battle to decide whether there were indeed some limits to the rule of capture.

CHAPTER 5

RICE IN THE DESERT

JUST WEST OF FORT STOCKTON, as it hugs the edges of Interstate 10, farm-to-market road 2732 is as smooth as glass, rising and falling like ripples on a mill pond as it passes by the Williams place.

On the right side of the road, on a hot mid-October morning, the land looks pretty much the way it always has, the way it did when Clayton Williams Sr. first stepped off the train near here more than 120 years ago. It is sparse and dry. There are patches of Russian thistle, better known as tumbleweeds, a thirsty and invasive species that followed the first settlers here and stayed without quite staying put. There is mesquite, dropped here in the dung of passing herds of Mexican cattle a long, long time ago. A few cows still graze in the distance. A llama, seemingly out of place, scans the horizon side-eyed, keeping watch for coyotes.

Look to the left, though, and it is another world. Lush and green, a carpet of alfalfa as far as the eye can see, and other crops beyond that. It was Clayton Williams, and his son, Claytie Jr., and now his grandson, Jeff, who turned those fields green. And it was their pumps. And the rule of capture.

According to the Texas Cooperative Extension at Texas A&M University, it takes about six or seven inches of water to grow a ton of alfalfa, a little more perhaps out here in usually dry Pecos County.

The Williamses produce thousands of tons of it a year, growing it, harvesting it, shipping it out to places as far away as drought-stricken California or perennially damp Florida. In a way, they are exporting tens of thousands of gallons of Pecos County water every year. They are just doing it by the bale, rather than by the gallon. But that is all right. They have plenty of it.

Forty-seven thousand four hundred twelve acre-feet of it a year, to be precise. That is what the Williamses are permitted, based on their historical or existing use, to suck out of the underground reservoirs beneath the land they own or rent outside Fort Stockton. It is, by some estimates, the largest privately held groundwater permit in the state of Texas, and Jeff Williams and his father draw up every drop from thirty-two pumps arrayed more or less in a straight line across the middle of the land they control, drilled right into the sweetest spot of the aquifers that run below it, each one pumping between twenty-five and thirty-five hundred gallons a minute.

"Anything less than twenty-two hundred gallons per minute is not considered commercial," Jeff Williams notes. Most of the time, there is plenty of water left over when the pumps shut off, he says. Most of the time the water levels in the wells remain fairly constant. "There isn't much drawdown," he says casually as his big old Ford pickup rattles over a washboard farm road running along the line of wells. As a general rule, the water levels rise and fall within a fairly narrow range. Most years, he says, "the static water level is basically 120 to 140 foot. And there's very little drawdown when we pump. The one that draws down the most I think is twenty foot. Eight to fifteen is about max you're going to expect."

The truth is, most of the time, they don't even need all the water they are entitled to. "This year, we'll probably use about 20,000 acre-feet," Williams says.

They will use it on the crops like alfalfa and cotton and Teff grass that Jeff, with his data-driven approach to farming, determines will fetch the best price in any given year. He can rattle off those prices and the amount of water each crop will need with ease.

That is the kind of farmer he is.

Jeff Williams is not his father. There is none of that crude, sometimes abrasive style—the characteristics that doomed his father's bid for the governor's mansion against Ann Richards. The old man helped erase a double-digit lead over Richards in the 1990 election with one of the most ill-considered comments ever made about rape—"If it's inevitable, just relax and enjoy it."

Jeff Williams is far more measured in his speech. With a mop of straw-colored hair and the open expression of a forty-something schoolboy, there is something self-effacing about him. He knows that his father made a lot of enemies in Texas. He knows that his father and grandfather made a lot of enemies around Fort Stockton. Stop in at a local motel with concrete teepees in back, a throwback to the days when Fort Stockton was a postcard mill for tourists, or chat with the Comanche woman behind the counter at the gift shop at the fort itself, mention the Williams name, and see how long it takes before somebody mentions what happened to Comanche Springs. Jeff Williams recognizes that there are a lot of people who still hold a grudge against his father and grandfather. He guesses that they include him in that too. But most people, he says, "seem pretty friendly to me."

It is only recently that he returned to these lands. For most of his adult life, he lived in Austin. In fact, though there have been Williamses in this region since the 1890s, for a quarter of a century none of them farmed.

It wasn't long after Comanche Springs dried up, in fact, that Clayton Sr. and Claytie abandoned farming. Jeff's grandfather sold the farm. "He sold it when my dad was in college, which is just about the time the springs quit flowing and the lawsuit started," Jeff recalls. "My dad likes to say that he was out of a job because he was planning on coming back to farming. So then he had to go wait tables and sold insurance and learned the oil and gas business on the side."

That foray into oil and gas made Claytie Williams a very rich man, rich enough that by the 1970s he began quietly amassing land—and the rights to the water underneath it—until he had recovered all of his father's land and then some. In those days, it was easy to pick up the land in that flat stretch of the northern Chihuahuan Desert known as the Belding Draw. The mysterious and occult nature of international commodity prices had caused fuel prices to rise and cotton prices to fall, which together put a lot of farmers on the brink of financial ruin, meaning that deals could be made.

Since he returned here a few years ago, Jeff Williams has run the farm with a kind of flinty, merciless, and market-savvy practicality. It is a business, and first and foremost Jeff Williams is a business-man, albeit one dressed in Carhardts, not pinstripes. He watches the markets like a hawk, and each year he adjusts his crops accordingly. More cotton one year. More alfalfa the next. "Soybeans don't do well here, for some reason," he says, though he has tried several varieties. Under his stewardship, for the first time since his father began rebuilding the landholdings, the farm recently turned a profit. At least for now, the farm needs no subsidy from the Williams family oil and gas business.

But through it all, Jeff Williams and his father both know that the most lucrative product that land can yield, more valuable than all the cotton or hay they could ever grow, is water. "To come back and try to put a lot of this farmland back into production, well, you're not gonna do that with straight farming," he says.

Water is, the way he sees it, a crop—a commodity to be traded like hog bellies or corn or oil on the free market.

They are certainly not the first to try to commoditize water—in effect to maintain ownership of the resource at its source and sell it—the same way they might sell oil or gas to a targeted end user. Nor are they first to find that such an arrangement is easier said than done. In the early part of this century, for example, oil and gas magnate T. Boone Pickens found that his legendary deal-making skills were not enough to counter the headwinds he encountered when he tried to begin a wholesale mining operation of the water that sat below his roughly 211,000 acres of land in Roberts County, seventy miles or so from Amarillo, above the Ogallala Aquifer. His plan, as he sketched it out back then, was to build a multibillion-dollar pipeline to carry the water to thirsty cities like San Antonio and El Paso and Dallas.

It was the rule of capture that permitted him to envision such a scheme, but that same rule also applied to others, and Pickens soon found he had some stiff competition. The Canadian River Municipal Water Authority had already purchased 42,765 acres of land near Pickens's ranch with plans to mine the water beneath it and ship it thirty-five miles to the west to Lake Meredith. The city of Amarillo bought another 71,000 or so acres, with the idea of eventually mining the water.

The competition, the controversy, and the opposition—local and regional—eventually persuaded Pickens to throw in the towel. In 2011, Pickens struck a deal with the Canadian River Municipal Water Authority to buy outright the water rights to his land.

It wasn't a total loss for Pickens. He walked away with $103 million.

The way Jeff Williams sees it, T. Boone Pickens was on to something when he recognized that water, perhaps even more than oil or gas, is well on its way to being the hot new commodity. Texas, he says, has changed and is going to continue to change. Farmers and ranchers are having a hard time making a go of it, even in comparatively wet times, while cities and oil-patch towns, often riding the waves of boom and bust cycles, are the future.

But whereas Pickens gave up, Jeff and Claytie Williams are still pressing their case.

That is why, beginning in 2009, the Williams family had been in a pitched battle with the Middle Pecos Groundwater Conservation District, which regulates, within the limits imposed upon it by the rule of capture, the portion of the Edwards-Trinity Aquifer that lies beneath them. For years, the Williams family had been stymied in their bid to export some significant portion of the 47,412 acre-feet of water they are permitted to pump across county lines, out of the basin, to the growing, thirsty oil-patch towns of Odessa and Midland, as well as to help support a proposed "clean-coal" power plant nearby. To get it to those cities, they had planned to build, through their Fort Stockton Land Holdings Company, a hundred-mile pipeline. More than a few local residents have noted with rueful irony that in order to finish the pipeline to pump their private water to a public utility, some other people's private property likely would have to be taken through eminent domain. But such is the price of progress.

To Jeff Williams and his father, it was a no-brainer. During the last drought, he points out, those cities were in dire straits. Their principal sources of surface water were in danger of drying out. By 2012, Lake Ivie, the largest of three reservoirs that serve the region, had dropped to less than one-third of its capacity, and the two smaller reservoirs were at risk of drying up altogether. And while they have rebounded since then, the risk, particularly in a changing climate, when dry spells can be expected to be longer, deeper, and closer together, has remained very much on the minds of water planners.

It is not that the thirty-five thousand gallons a day that the Williams family pumps from the aquifer during the growing season would all have gone to Odessa and Midland under their proposal. They probably still would use the twenty to twenty-five thousand acre-feet a year to continue their own farming operations, he says. What they would like to do in addition to that, however, is change the historical and expected-use designation for the water that is left over, so they could still protect their inalienable property right, as they see it, to nearly fifty thousand acre-feet of groundwater every year and sell a portion of the water they don't use to the cities.

To be fair, the cities of Odessa and Midland had not claimed that they needed it, at least not at first. Jeff Williams, however, insisted that they did and, more to the point, that they certainly will in the future. Those cities, like cities all over the state, are growing, he says. And this is Texas. There is always a drought on the horizon. In time, the cities came around to Jeff Williams's point of view.

What is more, he insisted, he and his father would be agreeable to some restrictions. Sensitive to allegations that they are trying to double-permit—in essence, that they are plotting to keep their permit to pump for agricultural purposes and secure a permit to pump separately for export, a practice he says they have no intention of doing—Jeff Williams says he and his father agreed to permit careful monitoring of their water usage. To prove that they wouldn't be double-dipping, he says, the groundwater district could meter their wells. "You could put meters on the well. You'd know how much I pump because in the contract it says whoever the purchaser . . . and they're going to say 'I want that amount of water,' and so that tells me what I have left over to farm with. But we were accused of double-permitting—trying to double the amount of water we could use. And that is not the case by any stretch of the imagination."

The local groundwater district saw things entirely differently. As Mike Gershon, the lawyer who represents the Middle Pecos Groundwater Conservation District, puts it, there are certainly concerns that if the Williams family pumped their entire allotment, rather than the roughly half they historically have used, and pump it out of the region, that could, particularly in hard, dry times, deplete the aquifer and leave neighbors wanting. Williams disputes that.

But more to the point, Gershon contends, as far as the groundwater district is concerned, Claytie and Jeff Williams have not demonstrated that the risk is even necessary. As part of the district's due diligence, officials contacted Williams's potential water customers, not just in Odessa and Midland but also in all twenty-two counties of Region F. Most had developed alternate plans to provide for their coming water needs, he said. Not a single one said that it was inevitable that they would need to buy water from Fort Stockton at some point. "They're all telling us that it's NOT inevitable that they're taking the water. Most of them don't want the water. Most of them say it's not economically feasible to get it to them because they've told us that they have cheaper water that they can get access to," Gershon recalled. "And so we went down the list, I remember taking the highlighter or the pen out and saying, 'Look, highlight the ones that you think you're gonna sell to and then let's talk about it.'"

The district repeatedly rejected Williams's application. Williams took them to court, and the case continues to wend its way through the system. In the meantime, the Williams family joined forces with Republic Water Company and filed a second application. This time, they are asking for the district's blessing to export about 28,000 acre-feet. And the city of Odessa has signed on to the application.

In July of 2017, the groundwater district ultimately relented, allowing Williams to funnel about twenty-five million gallons of water a day—some twenty-eight thousand acre-feet a year—to the thirsty oil-patch cities.

It still will take years before the water starts flowing—the pipeline still must be built. And while the years-long battle between Williams and the groundwater conservation district may have drawn to a close, issues that underlie it loom as large as ever.

To some degree, the battle over what the Williams family can and cannot do with its water underscores just how murky and complicated groundwater rights have become in Texas. There is no question that the legislature is partly to blame. In 1997, the legislature approved Senate Bill 1, which in effect declared that groundwater districts, local authorities, were the state's preferred method for regulating groundwater. The law also authorized districts to require permits for transferring water out of the district. A few years later, in 2001, the legislature adopted Senate Bill 2, which among other things gave the districts more authority to regulate water within their districts but also scaled back their authority to limit transfers out of the district. In effect, the two bills together were an attempt by lawmakers in Austin to straddle the tiger. In a general way, lawmakers have acceded to the idea that groundwater can be regulated by local authorities while at the same time holding fast to the principle enshrined in the *East* decision 115 years earlier that groundwater is a mysterious and occult thing that can be exploited by whoever happens to own the land on top of it. It is, critics say, an unsustainable balance.

But politicians are nothing if not survivors, and rather than risk alienating any voting bloc, they have left it to local groundwater districts, nearly one hundred fiefdoms, to effectively set the ground rules for groundwater. That has led to a couple of problems. First, there is the perennial problem of parochialism—that perfectly understandable tendency to view water as a local resource first, summed up by the lawyer who said of water in Texas, "if I'm pumping it's mine, if you're pumping it, it's ours, and if it's polluted, it's yours."

Then there is the problem that while groundwater districts have expanded greatly over the past several years, there are still vast swaths of Texas where none exist, and often those Wild West regions butt up against groundwater districts over the same aquifer, setting the stage for conflict as water purveyors, denied access to the riches underlying the district's jurisdiction, simply move a few miles away, where they can be entitled to pump to their heart's content.

In 2014, for example, landowners in an unregulated portion of Hays County were shocked to learn that some of their neighbors had struck a deal with the Houston-based water purveyor Electro Purification to draw five million gallons of water a day from Trinity Aquifer. They filed suit, directing the court's attention to the 1917 Conservation Amendment to the Texas Constitution, which declares that "the preservation and conservation of all . . . natural resources of the state," was a public right and duty. That duty, they argued, outweighed the rule of capture. "The time has come for the court to recognize that the rule of capture . . . is no longer valid," the plaintiffs argued. The court never got to decide that one. After months of behind-the-scenes arm-twisting, the legislature quietly placed the disputed region under the jurisdiction of the Barton Springs–Edwards Aquifer Groundwater District. The lawsuit went away, as did the deal, though Electro Purification continues to pursue exporting water from the region.

In fact, in the absence of clear leadership from lawmakers, developing groundwater policy in Texas has increasingly been a triumph of litigation over legislation.

Further complicating matters is that while, as matter of law, you can easily separate groundwater and surface water, in the real world the distinctions are not always so clear.

There is a term for the inevitable interplay between the waters that ebb and flow below the surface and those that bubble up above it. It is called *conjunctive use*. Water planners in Texas have long recognized that managing that interplay, as privately owned groundwater becomes publicly owned surface water and often becomes privately owned groundwater again somewhere downstream, would have to include some kind of conjunctive management component. The problem is that when the Texas Court of Civil Appeals ruled in 1954 in favor of Clayton Williams's big diesel pumps and against the interests that had grown dependent on the water bubbling up from Comanche Springs, it effectively ruled that there was no such thing as conjunctive management in Texas.

"There is no conjunctive use in Texas, and to me that's a huge problem," said Robert Gulley, who before he joined the Texas Comptroller's Office, where he is in charge of endangered species programs, served as the mediator for the Edwards Aquifer Recovery Implementation Program (about which we will read more later). "What makes it worse is this: Texas did say it recognized the value of conjunctive management, but right now because we have surface water owned by the state, groundwater owned in place by the surface owner, under the threat of a takings claim [in essence, a charge that the state has unlawfully taken an individual's property] you'll never get conjunctive use or be able to come in and regulate the groundwater to protect surface users."

What is more, he added, "I don't think you're ever gonna have that tool, but I think it's a very important tool."

The notions of what water law is and what it should be are maddeningly complex and often conflicting. And they have turned groundwater policy in Texas into a kind of full employment program for lawyers with a background in water. Now, more than the legislature, it is the courts in Texas that have been driving water law, and their various decisions, in recent years, have become increasingly deferential to the rule of capture.

To be fair, it's not that courts haven't expressed reservations about both the rule of capture and their unwelcome role in defining its limits.

In 1999, in the landmark decision in *Sipriano v. Great Springs Water*, the company that sells Ozarka bottled water was sued when it began pumping 90,000 gallons of water a day from land it held in Henderson County, drying up its neighbors' water wells. The court sided with Ozarka and found that the rule of capture prevailed. But the justices also made it clear that they'd like to see some changes.

"By constitutional amendment, Texas voters made groundwater regulation a duty of the legislature. And by Senate Bill 1, the legislature has chosen a process that permits the people most affected by groundwater regulation in particular areas to participate in democratic solutions to their groundwater issues. It would be improper for courts to intercede at this time by changing the common-law framework within which the legislature has attempted to craft regulations to meet the state's groundwater conservation needs. Given the legislature's recent actions to improve Texas's groundwater management, we are reluctant to make so drastic a change as abandoning our rule of capture and moving into the arena of water-use regulation by judicial fiat," the court declared.[1]

In a blistering shot across the bow of the state legislature, Justice Craig Enoch added, "In the past several decades it has become clear, if it was not before, that it is not regulation that threatens progress, but the lack of it."

And in case that wasn't clear enough, the justice continued, the rule of capture had outlived its usefulness. "It is revolting," he wrote in the court's unanimous opinion, "to have no better reason for a rule of a law than that it was laid down in the time of Henry IV. It is still more revolting if the grounds upon which it was laid down have vanished long since, and the rule simply persists from blind imitation of the past."

That is not to say that the court hasn't tried to find a balance.

In 2008, that same court again reaffirmed the rule of capture but tried to define, at least in part, the authority of local groundwater districts in the case of *Guitar Holding Company v. Hudspeth*. In that case, the Guitar family of Abilene owned thirty-eight thousand acres of land, and while the property had fifteen existing wells on it, ten of which were large irrigation wells, none of them had ever been used much. And so, when the Guitar family made a deal to sell their unused groundwater to the growing, thirsty desert city of El Paso, they ran up against the Hudspeth County Underground Water District's interpretation of its authority under Senate Bill 2. The district believed that it had the right to establish a permitting system under which all existing groundwater users would be entitled to at least four acre-feet of water per irrigated acre based on historical and existing usage as demonstrated by their usage over the ten previous years. Those existing users, if they wished, could export their water. But the district's rules also meant that it could prevent those who hadn't been using their wells from exporting water. That effectively left the Guitar family out in the cold. Some of their wells hadn't operated at all in twenty years. And so they sued. And the high court, in 2008, agreed with the plaintiffs that the district's rules favored those who were already pumping over those who weren't. The court concluded that, indeed, the groundwater district had the right to regulate pumping. But the court ruled that it had to consider not just how much water had been used historically but also how that water would be used. "Both must be considered when a groundwater conservation district issues a permit preserving historic or existing use."[2] In effect, the court found that the Guitar family had just as much right to pump its water as any of its neighbors and for the same purposes as its neighbors. But if that purpose changed—if, say, water for irrigation was to diverted to export—then those rights could be restricted. But even in a case such as that, as the Williams's application demonstrates, there are some gray areas, and it will be up to the courts to decide whether by maintaining their rights to their agricultural pumping rights, and converting only that portion of it that they don't use for farming to municipal use, the Williams can stay within the letter of the law. Jeff Williams believed they could. The groundwater district believed otherwise.

What is more, there have been subsequent decisions that seem to make the authority of groundwater districts and similar agencies to regulate groundwater even more tenuous. To be sure, justices, elected in Texas in partisan races, are not immune to political winds, and it is possible that the courts have in recent years begun reflecting the prevailing political attitude toward private property rights. Or perhaps they have simply been trying to suss out the attitudes of the legislature. Whatever the case, major decisions increasingly have favored the rights of the landowner over the authority of local groundwater districts, observers say.

The decision in what has come to be known as the *Day/McDaniel* case is a prime example. That case, which was closely watched and in fact encouraged and supported by advocates on both sides of the groundwater issue, began when a pair of farmers above the Edwards Aquifer sought and were denied a permit from the Edwards Aquifer

Authority (EAA) to pump seven hundred acre-feet a year to irrigate their lands. Though they had used that much in the past, it previously had been drawn from surface water, and the authority determined that drawing the water from the aquifer was different and rejected the application. The farmers sued. In 2012, the Texas Supreme Court ruled that while groundwater districts like the EAA may have a right to regulate groundwater usage, and to do it based on historical usage, under some circumstances those regulations could amount to a taking of private property for which owners would have to be compensated.

A year later, in the Bragg case, the Fourth Court of Appeals found that exactly that sort of taking had occurred when the EAA restricted a couple of farmers who had invested $2 million into their operation from pumping sufficient water to maintain their crop. The court, in a decision that most observers had expected to favor the EAA, surprised nearly everyone and ruled that Glenn and JoLynn Bragg owned their groundwater, and their right to it outweighed "the importance of protecting terrestrial and aquatic life, domestic and municipal water supplies, the operation of existing industries and the economic development of the state."[3]

But it went even further, in essence defining the Braggs' right *as a right to the water in place*, meaning it was theirs even before they used it. It was, one wag noted, the hydrological equivalent of declaring that life begins at conception.

The high court let that decision stand. And while the fallout from those decisions is still unclear, critics of the state's jury-rigged, court-driven approach to settling such sweeping groundwater issues contend that, taken together, the decisions do nothing to solve the conundrum that bedevils the entire system. But what would you expect, when the defining feature of the system—the rule of capture—is not so much a policy, as one water expert put it, as it is a tort principle? However, so far the legislature has been willing to let it remain so and to let the courts sort it out on a case-by-case basis.

That is almost as frustrating to Jeff Williams as it is to the EAA and the Middle Pecos Groundwater Conservation District. He wouldn't mind seeing the legislature take a more active role in defining groundwater rules and regulations, streamlining them perhaps, or at least making them less contradictory and easier for a landowner to navigate without a team of high-priced water attorneys and paid experts.

That is why, at the height of his legal battle with the groundwater district, on a small patch of land deep on his property, only a few acres really, he carved out a small plot to try out an experimental crop.

Jeff Williams will tell you that the rice he planted is only slightly thirstier than the corn or the alfalfa he grows elsewhere on the place. That is the kind of farmer he is. "Corn, alfalfa, they're probably going to take five and a half or six acre-feet of water a year," he says. "The rice takes maybe eight acre-feet."

And there was, toward the end of the last drought, a small opening—also the result of the state's byzantine water regulations—that gave a little extra incentive for Jeff Williams to consider the incongruous crop. That was when rice farmers in eastern Texas, locked in a competition with the city of Austin and the recreational communities on the lakes in the Hill Country over surface water from the Colorado River, found themselves cut back by the river authority there and had to lay some forty thousand acres fallow for a time. "For four or five years, they were kind of cut off from water. They weren't able to farm. So I kind of got to start thinking, 'I wonder if I can grow rice?' If they kept getting cut off then maybe the rice prices get to the point where it's worth farming it," he says.

Even still, he knew almost certainly that rice would be a money loser for him. Unlike East Texas, which has over more than a century developed an agricultural infrastructure to support rice planters, and to process the crop when it is harvested, Fort Stockton is remote from any such amenities. "The problem with grain—any grain—in this part of the world is that you have to truck it," he says. "You either have to truck it in or truck it out. And that hits you in the knees every time."

For a guy like Jeff Williams, who prides himself on having been able to turn a profit on the farm over recent years, that should have been to be a deal breaker. But it wasn't. That is because he didn't plant rice at the edge of the Chihuahuan Desert to make money. He planted it to make waves, to make the point that in the absence of a clear, consistent policy governing groundwater, what has emerged is a baffling, complex, and absurd patchwork of often contradictory imperatives that can lead to ridiculous results. Like growing rice in the desert.

"It was . . . a little bit of a protest," he said at the time. "They say we can't sell water? You know what? I can grow rice. And they can't do anything about it."

In the end, he says, the rice was his way of showing the powers that be from Fort Stockton to Austin that "the system that they created that they think is so fantastic is already broken."

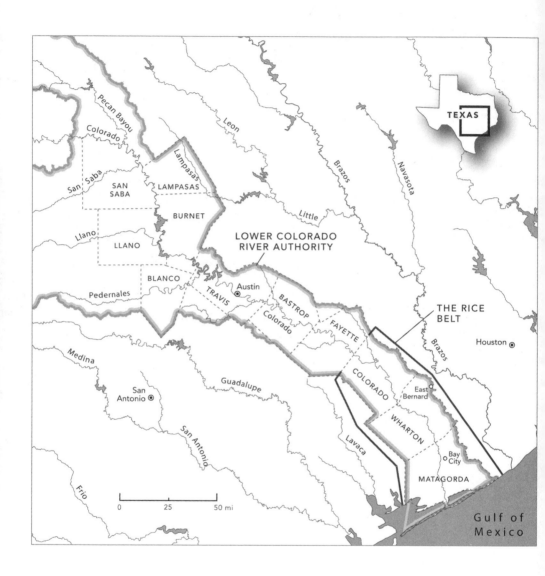

TEXAS

Pecan Bayou

Colorado

San Saba

Lampasas

SAN SABA

LAMPASAS

BURNET

Llano

LLANO

BLANCO

Pedernales

Leon

Brazos

Navasota

Little

LOWER COLORADO
RIVER AUTHORITY

TRAVIS

Austin

BASTROP

Colorado

FAYETTE

THE RICE
BELT

Brazos

Houston

Medina

Guadalupe

San
Antonio

San Antonio

Frio

COLORADO

East
Bernard

WHARTON

Lavaca

Bay
City

MATAGORDA

Gulf of
Mexico

0   25   50 mi

CHAPTER 6

WHAT MAKES THE DOLLAR FLIP

IT IS EASY TO MISS if you have become inured to it, if you have lived all your life in a contrived, ever-growing world of modern conveniences like fast-food joints and housing developments and strip malls. If you were raised to believe that that sprawling world is the way things always were and always will be, it can be almost invisible to you. The drumbeat of the development is just the metronomic regularity of progress, rendered in faux brick and plaster, a sound as steady as the waves on a beach, a sound you are so accustomed to that you don't even know that you hear it anymore.

But if you haven't been raised in that kind of world, then the drive southwest from the sprawling metropolis of Houston toward El Campo and on down to Bay City can be a jarring experience. It almost might feel like you are riding the crest of a wave, a tsunami of development rushing downhill toward the low-lying rice fields and farms along the Gulf Coast, bent on sweeping you away. Bobbing atop the crest of that wave are all the icons of now: grand housing developments around Richmond and Rosenberg full of McMansions with odd, mass-produced, and vaguely French details. Ride the wave a little farther and you are awash in retail outlets, some sprawling, some cloyingly fashioned to evoke some artificial memory of a small-town square in a place you have never been and will never visit.

Not far from the highway, there is a grand fountain spraying water insolently into the air, and a few hundred yards beyond it, across a jammed parking lot, there is a Texas Roadhouse, a crude corporate parody of what some high-paid restaurant designer thought Texas used to be.

Stand in the center of the wide and empty boulevards in El Campo, built wide enough for an old farm wagon with a team of mules to make a U-turn back in the days when there were still enough of them to matter, or along a farm road in Lissey, and that ever-encroaching wave seems portentous, even ominous.

"It's what makes the dollar flip," says Ronald Gertson, a third-generation rice farmer, who has for years now been watching with a measure of resignation and alarm as each year the leading edge of a creeping metropolis creeps closer. "It's growth, urban growth in particular." Sitting in his well-appointed office overlooking his farm in East Bernard in Wharton County, Gertson almost can feel the ground slipping, as if the backwash from that looming wave already was pulling it out from underneath him. Once upon a time, he says, and not so terribly long ago that there aren't people still around who remember it, this region of the state was an economic and political powerhouse, a center of commerce fattened on a precious grain— rice. Back then, agriculture, not just on these flatlands one hundred miles west of the Gulf Coast but almost everywhere in Texas, was the political center of gravity. Decisions made in Austin were made with the input and approval of a powerful agricultural lobby or they weren't made at all. But in recent decades, he continues, that political center of gravity has shifted. Now the power belongs to those who believe that growth in development, in housing and in retail, is all.

That was driven home to him recently, Gertson says, when he was chatting with the mayor of a nearby midsize Texas city who told him that if his city "isn't growing, it's dying."

"That's the philosophy," he says. "Now granted, me as a rural guy, I think, 'What's wrong with remaining the same?' I live in a community here, East Bernard, that's been roughly twenty-five hundred persons for all my life. We're not dying. We're healthy. We're a good, healthy, rural community. We don't have to grow to survive. But the mentality of those folks who are elected in our urban metropolises is, it's grow or die."

Already, he says, the first reverberations of that tectonic shift are being felt in places like East Bernard. You can see it in the price of an acre of land, which used to be valued on the basis of what you could grow on it. Increasingly, he says, the price is determined by what somebody else can build on it. And land for development is always more valuable than farmland.

But the issue on which the fate of rural communities like those in this part of Texas are most precariously poised is the issue of water. The unchecked growth that these farmers see as a looming, almost existential, threat is fueled as much by water as were the steam locomotives that turned Texas into an empire more than a century ago. And the battle over it has pitted these farmers against residents of ever-expanding cities like Austin and the lake communities north and west of them.

"There is no limit on growth and there's virtually no way to connect available water to growth, to say you can only grow this much because this is how much water we have," says Gertson. "Instead it's grow, and somehow we'll squeeze the water from somewhere."

It is more than simply finding enough water in the dry times, of course. As those who have been riding that crest of development southward from Houston learned in late August of 2017, when the waters of Hurricane Harvey, which dumped enough rain on Texas in the space of just a few days to slake the thirst of every man, woman and child in America for forty-two days, turned their streets into raging rivers contaminated in some cases by the toxins of modern suburban life, the rainy times are just as dangerous. And yet, as of now, there is no statewide flood plan, nothing comparable even to the state water plan. Indeed, it was only after Hurricane Harvey that the state began the process of developing one, based on the same ground-up model as the water plan.

And when those state flood planners are finally ready to collect the observations of the farmers down here, it is a safe bet that the farmers will tell them that the experts can argue until the cows swim home about how much a changing climate has affected the nature of the storms, whether hurricanes like Harvey and Irma, which devastated the Caribbean and much of Florida a week later, or Maria, which visited ruin on Puerto Rico two weeks after that, are stronger and more deadly than ever before. They cannot argue, however, that the storms are not more devastating. The storms are more ruinous, the farmers will tell them, because there is simply so much more to ruin.

A century's worth of virtually unchecked growth, the farmers will tell you, has brought prosperity to many. But it also has altered the landscape in ways that have made both the droughts and the floods more destructive and made that prosperity fleeting. Much of the region sits atop the overtaxed Gulf Coast Aquifer, and though efforts have been made over the last forty years to limit withdrawals from it, enough water has been sucked out of it that the ground still subsides in some places, altering runoff patterns and allowing floodwaters to gather.

What is more, those millions of newcomers to the region are living in houses and driving on roads and shopping in stores built atop what once was prairie that could have absorbed at least some of the fury of this flood and the next. What once was land that might have softened the storm's blow is now, in many cases, collateral damage in what could turn out to be a $190-billion-plus disaster.

Those are the kinds of insights that take root in these fields and grow in those hard years when little else can.

To some degree, the story of how the rice farms in this part of Texas began, how they grew in power and prestige, and how they began a long, slow, and inexorable decline, at least the way the farmers tell it, is analogous to the story of Texas as a whole. It is analogous, in fact, to the story of the nation. It is, they say, a story of grit and determination, of individualism in service of a sense of community, a tale of vision and adaptability to changing circumstances. But it is also a story of unforeseen consequences and of the inevitability of change.

Around here, most people will tell you, Haskell Simon, a soft-spoken but verbose man, is the keeper of that story, the rice belt's unofficial historian.

He's now in his eighties, genteel, with an easy, classically southern manner. If you can't find Simon in his rice paddies you can usually find him in his office in Bay City, a place that, like the man himself, is at once staid and quietly chaotic, where overstuffed filing cabinets stand cheek by jowl with barrister boxes loaded with documents, the minutia of a century or more of rice farming and water issues. It is a place lined with bookshelves that groan under the weight of a lifetime's worth of treatises on everything from the history of the Lower Colorado River Authority (LCRA) to a dog-eared copy of Rabbi Adin Steinsaltz's translation of the first volume of the Talmud. He draws on all of them, he will tell you.

"I'm sure they warned you," he says. "If you ask me the time, I'll tell you how to build a watch."

To a great extent, the history of the Simon family parallels the history of the rice belt, and the arc of the story, Haskell Simon will tell you, is very much the same. There have been Simons in this part of Texas since the end of the nineteenth century. That's when his father, a Russian Jewish immigrant fleeing the oppression and anti-Semitism of the czar, a peddler by trade but with that ancient Jewish yearning to be tied somehow to the land, made a left turn on the road south from Houston and ended up here. Had he made a right, he might have found himself in a place better suited to more traditional crops—corn, cotton. But here in Bay City, he found himself on land above a shallow pan of clay, the kind of ground that spells death for dry-footed deep-rooted crops.

Serendipitously for him, at the time that he arrived, a new crop was taking root in the region. Long a staple of the Old South, rice had been planted in the Carolinas as early as the 1600s, and for the better part of two centuries it thrived there. It was, along with indigo and tobacco, a chief export of the colonies and, later, a source of great wealth for antebellum plantation owners. There are some who attribute its decline in the Carolinas in the latter part of the nineteenth century to the end of slavery, the loss of a cheap labor force. Others blame it on the vagaries of climate, to a series of powerful storms and hurricanes that lashed the region toward the end of the century, overrunning and destroying the primitive, tidal-driven irrigation system on which the old planters relied.

It was, most likely, a combination of those and other factors, including the availability of land and water, that pushed rice westward, and it did so with a vengeance. By the turn of the twentieth century, the vast majority of rice grown in the United States was produced in two states, Louisiana and Texas; in Texas, because of that hard clay pan just below the surface, most of it was produced in just three counties: Matagorda, Colorado, and Wharton. To this day, though its share of the market has declined, the region remains one of the most productive rice-growing regions in the nation, along with parts of Louisiana, Arkansas, Mississippi, Missouri, and California.

The region was, in many respects, ideally suited to rice farming. Hot and humid with abundant rain—Wharton County gets an average of nearly four feet of rain every year. Although there were sporadic droughts, growers could more often than not count on water enough to raise two crops most years, a regular crop, which they would flood to "keep its feet wet" and kill off weeds that might otherwise strangle the budding plants, and a second—or ratoon—crop grown from the cut stubble of the first.

As rice took root in the area, so too did small, often competing canal and irrigation companies, allocating water to those who claimed under law their rights to it—not always without conflict—in times of normal rainfall and in droughts. The first pumping station along that stretch of the river was built in 1901 in Colorado County, and it gave rise to the town of Garwood. Within fifteen years, hundreds of miles of canals snaked through the region. The system was not without conflict, Simon notes, and from time to time it was not unheard of for one irrigation company to use underhanded tactics—sometimes even escalating to the use of explosives—to poach scarce water from another. As one old-timer recalled in the book *Corralling the Colorado*, by Jimmy Banks and John E. Babcock, "These companies tried to cut one another's throats. . . . They'd go out and dynamite their flumes and other structures . . . they'd have to shut down to make repairs and while they were shut down this other canal system would get their acreage watered up."[1]

But there was also something unpredictable and dangerous about the weather patterns in the area. State records show that there were, indeed, periods of drought that would pit farmers against each other as the water in the Colorado River slowed to a trickle. Then there were the floods. This land, some of the youngest in the state, was itself formed by savage storms in the far distant past that washed soil down along the Colorado onto these lowlands from the Hill Country. This lush corner of the state, part of the original land grant from Mexico to Stephen Austin, had always been prone to floods. Indeed, before the relentless rains of Hurricane Harvey swelled the river to an almost unfathomable crest of 51.4 feet in August of 2017, perhaps the most spectacular was a flood in July 1869 that sent the waters of the Colorado surging down through Austin toward the lowlands at a rate twice as fast as Niagara Falls and twenty-five feet above flood stage. As Frank Brown, then a minor official in Travis County, wrote years later, eyewitnesses described a scene of horror. "The rise was estimated at 46 feet," he wrote. "The waters rushed down from the narrow and confined channels between the mountains above . . . with such fearful velocity that the middle of the stream was higher than the sides and the aspect it presented was appalling."[2]

But the periodic floods created a greater and more immediate threat. While there had been efforts to control those floods, they had generally been unsuccessful. Repeated efforts had been made to dam the Colorado River, beginning in 1854, when Adam Johnson proposed building one near the current site of Lake Buchanan. It wasn't until the 1930s, with the creation of the LCRA, that a full-scale push to tame the river was undertaken, and to a very great extent, Simon says, that happened at the behest of the downstream rice farmers.

Somewhere, tucked away in one of those filing cabinets in his office, Simon has a yellowing newspaper clipping from the 1930s, with a picture of his father and some of his neighbors as they loaded themselves into a car for the bone-rattling daylong ride to Austin to discuss the creation of an authority that would give them the means to smooth out the rough edges between drought and flood and to turn the Colorado into a reliable and reliably consistent water source for agriculture.

By that time, despite his origins, Simon's father had become a respected member of the community. Though he had arrived in Bay City virtually penniless, he was a born businessman and a natural polyglot, which allowed him to move seamlessly among the diverse ethnic communities—Spanish, Swedish, and English speaking—that had put down roots in the region. With the assistance of his older brother, whom he had brought over from Russia, he became a successful merchant, Simon said. In time, he became a kind of unofficial ambassador between the communities. "He had a wonderful sense of humor," Simon recalls, even if, from time to time, he had to deploy it in his own defense, against the accidental prejudices of his neighbors. One of his favorite stories was how a frantic young mother, a devout Catholic, burst into his store one day and in breathless Spanish pleaded, "Oh, Don Simon, you have to come with me to the priest because my baby's dying, and we have to go to the priest so he can bless him and baptize him." The young merchant tried to beg off. "He said, well I can't leave the store right now," Simon recalls. "She said, 'Oh, please go with me. Otherwise, he'll die a Jew.'"

It was, in fact, a consequence of his heritage—though an unanticipated one—that Simon's father became a farmer. Under ancient Jewish law, a law that nowadays is much more honored in the breach, when his older brother died, Simon's father was obliged to marry his brother's widow. Instead, he married a woman he met while on a business trip to Europe. That so outraged his sister-in-law that she demanded her rightful half of all the brothers had amassed in Texas. "He had to sell off the businesses. But he kept the land. That was what he had always wanted to do anyway." As the old man used to put it, "Abraham, Isaac, and Jacob were farmers too. I guess I'm a throwback."

Few people, and fewer historians, would dispute how critical the support of the farmers, Haskell Simon's father included, was to the genesis and the early evolution of the LCRA and that body's efforts to control the flows along the Colorado. It was an example of the muscle farming interests could muster at the time. But they had allies as well, some of whom nowadays would seem to be strange bedfellows. The City of Austin was one.

For decades the city, which by the mid-1930s had grown from a sleepy little village to a good-size town of about sixty thousand, had been trying to defend itself against the periodic river rampages with little luck and with sometimes disastrous results. In 1893, after years of political intrigue, the city opened a massive dam that was, at the time, a significant enough feat of engineering to merit a feature story in *Scientific American*. What would come to be known as Lake McDonald began filling up. The project, its boosters insisted, would do more than simply contain the river when it got rambunctious. It also would be used to provide water for city residents and create the city-operated hydroelectric power plant that the city fathers were certain would run its lights and its trolleys and catapult Austin into the twentieth century—and do it all at a cost far less than what private companies could charge.

In the years that followed, it almost seemed as if the plan might pay off. Lake McDonald became a local recreation center almost unparalleled in the nation. Pleasure seekers bathed in its waters or toured the lake in paddle wheelers. At night, the electricity generated by the dam fired massive arc lamps mounted atop thirty-one towers, each 165 feet tall, casting Austin in an otherworldly glow. Seventeen of these "moontowers" still remain.

But almost immediately after the dam was constructed, trouble began. Within thirty days of its completion, the dam had begun to leak from beneath, and the city moved quickly to correct the problem. As Banks and Babcock put it, that was only the first "in a series of misfortunes."

From the beginning, it seemed, engineers had wildly overestimated the flow of the Colorado in most years and had particularly underestimated how low that flow could go in dry years. By 1899, one of those dry years, the water levels in the lake had dropped low enough that city leaders switched off the moontowers, sidetracked the electric trolleys and replaced them with teams of mules, and told pleasure seekers and ratepayers alike that they wouldn't be switched back on until the rains came.

And then the rains came, and in typical Texas fashion, they came with a vengeance. What made matters worse was that as wildly optimistic as the engineers had been about the consistency of the average annual flows of the river, they had been just as egregious in their underestimation of how dangerous silting could be. That had reduced the capacity of the lake by thirty-eight percent in its first four years.

At about 1 p.m. on April 6, 1900, the rain began, the worst rainstorm the region had seen since the 1869 flood, and by the next morning the floodwaters had risen ten feet above the top of the dam. At 11:20 a.m. on April 7, the dam gave way. One eyewitness whose account was unearthed by Babcock and Thompson reported that the river had simply shouldered the dam out of its way, first shunting a 300-foot-wide section off its foundation, then "two sections—each about 250 feet long—were shoved or pushed about 60 feet from their former positions. There was not the slightest overturning." It was as if the river had simply kicked open a door.

For the next several years, the city made a few vain attempts to rebuild the dam, but the occasional rampages of the river scuttled those efforts that didn't fail because of political infighting. It wasn't until the 1930s that Austin found, in the rice farmers downriver, and in the infant LCRA, the allies it needed to at last tame the river.

History, Haskell Simon will tell you, has a way of turning on you. It is rife with examples of how unintended consequences turn allies into adversaries, and never is that more evident than in cases in which it looks as if things are turning out just as planned.

The final conquest of the irascible Colorado River, he says, is just such a case. Within fifteen years of his father's car trip to Austin, in a triumph of the farmers' persistence coupled with political savvy, the river had been completely transformed—by the can-do spirit of the rice farmers, the city officials in Austin and elsewhere along the banks of the river, and the not-so-gentle nudging of powerful politicians, among them Alvin Wirtz and Lyndon B. Johnson, a man who, it was said, had never met a dam he or his backers in the engineering and construction industries didn't like.

Johnson had come by his passion for dam building honestly, in the political sense of the word. As a young man he had been mentored by Wirtz, a Democratic power broker, later undersecretary of the Department of the Interior under Franklin Roosevelt. Wirtz was a major supporter of dam construction and the man chiefly responsible for marshaling those downstream rice farmers and organizing the LCRA in the first place. Though the power of Texas's seventeen quasi-governmental river authorities is supposedly limited—they don't have the authority to levy taxes, and their revenues come largely from the sale of the water they govern and the hydroelectricity that it can generate—in fact, such authorities often have a broad portfolio.

They are charged with not only managing and conserving the water resources they supervise but promoting them as well. And working with federal agencies—the Army Corps of Engineers and the Bureau of Reclamation principally—they manage many of the state's reservoirs. All but one—the San Antonio River Authority—have their boards appointed rather than elected. Therefore, they are considered by critics to be unaccountable, and in the ninety years since the first one was established along the Brazos River, this arrangement has caused some chafing between the authorities and the various other stakeholders.

Such trifling concerns about political accountability, however, did little to dampen Johnson's enthusiasm for river authorities in general and the LCRA in particular. As a congressman and later a US senator in the years after World War II, Johnson encouraged the LCRA to take full advantage of that mandate to promote water resources and he used all his considerable wiles to shunt whatever federal resources he could get his hands on in its direction. If some of that largesse made its way to the coffers of his friends and supporters in the engineering industry and the trades, well, that was just icing on the cake. Indeed, by 1951, six reservoirs had been constructed north of Austin, creating a chain of reservoirs that now provide the bulk of irrigation water to Simon and his fellow rice farmers and also provide drinking water to well over one million people in central Texas.

But that regular source of water also fueled growth. Austin, in the decades that followed, exploded, and by 1999 the city had grown to 629,729 people, well on its way to nearly one million just within the city limits today. Moreover, it sparked an industry in the Highland Lakes. Recreation and tourism flourished there, driven not just by the descendants of those same pleasure seekers who had once frolicked under the moontowers of Austin a century ago but by immigrants from the north and east and California, immigrants who, in many cases, differed from Haskell Simon's father in that they never entertained any notion of returning to the land.

And yet, for decades, in dry times and rainy seasons, a kind of balance was achieved and maintained based in large part on the terms of the original agreement. As the years passed, the LCRA acquired rights to much of the water that flowed downstream from the Highland Lakes, even acquiring the oldest and thus highest priority rights, the ones that led to the establishment of Garwood. While city dwellers and business owners paid a fee comparable to other municipal water customers elsewhere in the state, largely because they were footing the bill for the infrastructure that made it all possible, farmers like Simon paid more or less the same rates they had paid before the dams were built. Although there was some grumbling at the end of the month in a lot of Austin households, in general the water flowed, the taps in Austin never ran dry, and the farmers downstream received billions of gallons of river water each year at a fraction of the price that municipal customers did.

Even in the drought of record, and in a less severe but nonetheless drought in the 1980s, that precarious balance was maintained.

But then, in the 1990s, things began to change. Call it evidence of climate change, call it an unusual natural phase, but a little less than two decades ago, Texas in general and Austin in particular entered a period of dramatic wet and dry cycles. The single driest year Texas ever experienced was 2011, a year in which Lake Travis fell to forty-one feet below normal. That year, the rice farmers, the children and grandchildren of the individuals who had demanded that those lakes be built in the first place, turned one hundred billion gallons of water loose on their rice fields, just as they had for the better part of a century.

But it would be the last time they did that for several years.

Those who still remember the drought of record in the 1950s contend that the drought that gripped Texas from 2010 until the deadly rains of 2015 broke it was in some respects worse. That, says L. G. Raum, a rice farmer from El Campo, has less to do with the severity of the droughts than with the fact that there are just so many more people in Texas than there were in the 1950s. "We've gone from a state of fourteen million to twenty-eight million without building a major reservoir in this state," he says.

Most of that growth has taken place in the cities, and in the ever-expanding collar of suburbs that spread out from them, and with that shift came a quiet but seismic shift in the clout of guys like Raum and Simon. As early as 1989, it became clear that that balance of power was shifting. That was when, prodded by the ballooning city of Austin and memorialized by a court settlement, the LCRA altered its policy and declared that municipalities like Austin had a guaranteed right to a share of the water from the Highland Lakes and that in dry times, water deliveries to the farmers would be considered "interruptible." In an extreme case, they could be cut off altogether.

In 2012, that is what happened.

By that point, the thirsty cities and suburbs had already implemented water restrictions on their municipal users, ultimately reducing lawn watering to once a week and with the threat of stiffer action if the drought persisted. Upriver, the impact of the drought was even worse. As writer Kate Galbraith noted during a visit to Lake Travis at the time, the lakefront was littered "with the grim trappings of lake life . . . a dock that had been moved so it could stay in the shrinking lake . . . a boat ramp that ended far above the water . . . restaurants threatened with bankruptcy . . . a huge sign that read 'Slow Your Boat.' It stood dozens of feet above the water line."[3]

What galled the lake residents and business people, and the residents of Austin and its environs, was the knowledge that had the farmers not taken their 452,000 acre-feet of water the year before, that lake would have been thirteen feet higher.

And so, in March 2012, by then facing a drought so severe that the lakes were down to thirty-eight percent capacity, forcing everyone to operate under a drought emergency plan, the LCRA announced that for the first time since the agency was established in large part to serve the farmers in the coastal lowlands of the state, those farmers would lose their annual allotment.

Those who could, like Ron Gertson, turned to other sources of water to compensate for what, until then, they had seen as their birthright. The Gulf Coast Aquifer, severely restricted in other parts of the region because of the historic ground subsidence overpumping had caused, provided some water, he said. But it was costly and not enough.

Across the region, some fifty thousand acres that would have otherwise been planted were left fallow. But at what cost? Gertson asks. "I did some figures," he says, "and the rice production that was lost in this area just from the loss of river water from the Colorado would provide one hundred percent of the calorie consumption for about 1.2 million people for a year. Which is roughly the broader population of the city of Austin and the suburbs."

It is perhaps a measure of how convoluted, mysterious, and occult—how Talmudic in its complicated permutations—water policy can be that an action taken in one place, say, cutting off water to rice farmers along the Colorado River in central and eastern Texas, can produce unintended consequences hundreds of miles away, says Haskell Simon. Like in Fort Stockton, for example, where a guy like Jeff Williams, bent on making a political point about his own use of water, can decide that maybe growing rice in the desert isn't such a bad idea after all.

By the spring of 2015, the drought had broken. But more than that, an old way of doing things, a way of thinking—a kind of certainty borne out by a century of rice farming in the region that agriculture was and always would be a political force to be reckoned with in Texas—had also dried up and blown away in the drought.

The conflict between the lake residents and their allies in the city and the rice farmers had cast into the sharpest relief the battle between rural interests, the id of Texas in many respects, and its ever-growing urban ego.

You can see that battle playing out elsewhere in Texas. You can see it in the struggle between small towns and farms and places like San Antonio as that city struggles against local opposition to build a massive $3 billion pipeline, the Vista Ridge Project, a 140-mile-long conduit to carry sixteen billion gallons of water from rural Burleson to the city's residents. The pipeline comes with a cost to the residents of San Antonio. By 2020, according to a report in the *Texas Tribune*, homeowners who pay about $54 a month as of 2016 could see their monthly bills rise to $82, with about twenty percent of that increase directly attributable to the construction costs of the pipeline. And the rest is earmarked for mandated improvements to the city's water system, including the construction of a brackish water desalinization plant.

But rural landowners, those who would find themselves competing with San Antonio for the water in the Carrizo-Wilcox Aquifer and those whose land would be taken through eminent domain to make way for the pipeline, contend that their interests are being ignored to slake the thirst of a growing metropolis.

In their complaints, there is an echo of the same complaints you hear in the Sulfur River Basin, where rural residents have banded together to try to stop or at least to delay the construction of the Marvin Nichols dam. You can hear the complaints along the Colorado River from the rice farmers who fear that their way of life is losing ground every day to increasing urbanization.

And if you listen really closely, you can hear a sense of inevitability in all of it.

For now, Simon and his fellow farmers are surviving. They don't believe they have seen their last drought, or even their worst. In that they agree with the scientists who warn that in years to come the droughts will get deeper and longer, and as Hurricane Harvey so brutally demonstrated, the floods, when they come, will grow more violent and destructive.

And they know that they have lost the clout they once held, and so they are trying to find ways to slow the inevitable. They are experimenting with different techniques, different strains of rice that can use less water. And they are casting about for allies in their efforts to stay afloat. They have found a few, surprisingly among the environmental community, which has sided with them in their conflict because the environmentalists realize that the water that flows into and through the rice paddies one hundred miles inland from the Gulf of Mexico provides desperately needed freshwater inflows to help keep coastal bays and wetlands healthy. Though even there, there are conflicts. Simon, for example, is an advocate of building an off-channel reservoir closer to the rice farms, so they at least can store rainwater when it comes. Some environmentalists object, he says, fearing that such a proposal would reduce the very freshwater inflows to the coast they are hoping to protect.

Still, attempts are being made to find common ground. Haskell Simon can describe all those efforts in excruciating detail. Ask him the time, he will say, and he will tell you how to build a watch.

And what that watch tells him is that for him, and a lot of guys just like him, time, and water, are eventually going to run out. He only need look north on the road to Houston to see what is coming. That slow-moving tidal wave of development, of strip malls with insolent fountains and McMansions with broad, thirsty lawns, rolling south and washing away, he believes, everything in its path.

CHAPTER 7

DOW BY LAW

TIME, at least the way Haskell Simon measures it, runs in a straight line. Rivers don't. Nor does the seemingly inexorable shift in the balance of power between the rural interests of the state of Texas and the urban centers.

To be sure, the combined forces of Austin and the Highland Lakes region exerted significant pressure on the LCRA, and that, in turn, placed pressure on the rice farms of the lowlands.

But it is worth noting that at the same time that Simon and his neighbors were grappling with the consequences of having to cut back dramatically on the water they drew from the Colorado, just a few miles away on the Brazos River a critical court battle was playing out, pitting farmers and ranchers, as well as one of the largest manufacturers in the state, against the tens of thousands of residents of thirteen of Galveston County's fourteen municipalities, more residents of Fort Bend and Brazoria Counties, and the Texas Commission on Environmental Quality (TCEQ).

In the end, the farmers and Dow Chemical won. In many respects, water experts say, the case of *TCEQ v. Texas Farm Bureau* underscores the challenge of trying to manage surface water rights in a state where those rights are often in conflict—not just with each other but with the nature of surface water in an environment where devastating droughts are common and perhaps becoming increasingly more

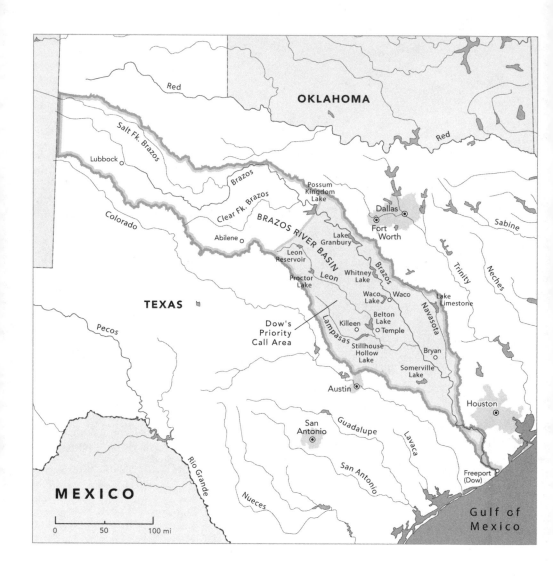

so. It is not just in times of drought, of course, that the state must face the challenge of protecting water sources that have been and are being used by so many competing users for so many seemingly incompatible purposes. As we will see later in this volume, floods, like during Hurricane Harvey, which turned the normally shallow Brazos River into a 52.6-foot monster,[1] can also threaten the precarious balance, overwhelming water treatment plants and tainting the source water with a host of contaminants and chemicals, many of them toxic.

But it is often in times of drought that the conflicts can be seen most clearly.

That struggle between the farmers, ranchers, and Dow Chemical, by far the biggest water user and owner of the oldest—and thus most senior—water along the 840-mile-long Brazos River, against the state is a case in point that sheds some light on how limited the state's options might be in the face of an even more extreme dry spell.

It began not with the farmers but with the chemical manufacturing giant setting up shop along the banks of the river in 1940 to extract manganese from seawater. Dow's operation is a thirsty one, demanding one hundred thousand gallons of freshwater a minute, and the company had a long history of taking extreme steps to guarantee its supply. More than fifty years ago, just after the drought of record, the plant catapulted itself onto front pages and the front lines of the technological battle to develop alternative sources of water when President John F. Kennedy flipped a switch and turned on what was then one of the largest desalination facilities in the nation. But there were limits to how much water the sea could provide, and the chemical giant remains heavily dependent on the Brazos River. So do farmers and ranchers and residents of the fast-growing communities from Galveston to the suburbs of Houston.

Because of that ever-increasing demand over the years, the stretch of the Brazos from Possum Kingdom Reservoir to the Gulf—once an untamed run of water that John Graves, in his 1957 emotionally charged *Goodbye to a River*, beheld with "enraged awe"—had been thoroughly domesticated by a series of reservoirs and concretized channels.

Lost was the raw spirit of the river, on whose banks Austin set up his first colony. But the march of progress did much to reduce the impact of drought and to assure those who depended on the river that it would be there when they needed it. Indeed, to this day there has been no repeat of what those Brazos River denizens still old enough to remember call the "big dry-up" during the drought of record, when the river all but dried up and its forty-two-thousand-acre watershed turned into parched hardpan.

There were, of course, moments of contention between the various stakeholders along the lower stretch of the river in the years that followed. But it wasn't until 2009 that those tensions began to turn truly acrimonious.

It was then, toward the beginning of the 2011 drought, when water flows along the river dropped to the point at which Dow's pumps no longer worked efficiently, that the company flexed its muscle. It demanded that the state step in and cut back junior water users, including not only farmers and ranchers but also fast-developing urban areas.

Dow had that right under the law. But that same law also could be interpreted to require the TCEQ to take extraordinary steps in the interest of public health and safety to protect water supplies to municipalities and power generators, and so when the agency finally did partially accede to Dow's request, it did so in a way that cut off water to some junior users, curtailing forty-six billion gallons of water to downstream farmers and ranchers, for instance, but not other users. In 2012, the agency formally adopted rules protecting the rights of those municipalities and utilities. So the TCEQ was in a bind. Once upon a time, municipalities, through eminent domain, could just take the water they needed, but in 1997 the state legislature stripped them of that authority. That meant that it was up to the TCEQ to take action. "I was one of the commissioners that voted to not curtail every single junior water right, only because of the public health crisis that would have created," said Carlos Rubenstein, then a TCEQ commissioner.

The TCEQ's decision didn't please the rural interests, and it didn't please Dow either, which didn't see any increase whatsoever in the water flowing past its pumps. In fact, to the farmers from Brazoria County who saw themselves cut off from their traditional source of surface water, the move was tantamount to a declaration of war on their property rights.

As Rick Lowerre, one of the lawyers representing landowners along the Brazos, put it, "What Texas tried to do in that case—with the Farm Bureau versus TCEQ—is say we have a system that has historically been what every other western state is. 'First in time, first in right.' And we cut back on those junior rights before we cut back on those senior rights. And they said we're not going to do that anymore. We're going to protect municipal or industrial or steam electric or whoever, regardless of the priority dates."

The chemical company objected. So did more than a few environmentalists. "Environmentalists were on Dow's side in the Farm Bureau case because . . . the environmental community was concerned that what the TCEQ was doing would basically mean that any rights for an environmental use would also become—regardless of what their priority was—sacrificed without really doing any real process. Some of the environmental water rights were senior rights," Lowerre said. And in yet another of those strange-bedfellow circumstances that are so common in water disputes in Texas, the Farm Bureau filed a state suit in which it agreed with Dow and the environmental community.

The courts agreed too. After losing in the lower court, the TCEQ took the case to the Thirteenth Court of Appeals in Corpus Christi, which also rejected the state agency's argument. And it did so in a way that underscored what increasingly has been the mantra of the courts in all water issues, the notion that while the state has a right to manage water, that authority must bend to the idea that water is, perhaps first and foremost, an inviolate property right. "None of the statutes or constitutional provisions give the agency the general authority to suspend water rights after they have been issued," the court wrote. "While we recognize TCEQ's authority to manage and regulate the state's scarce water resources, such authority must not exceed its express legislative mandate."[2]

In February 2016, the Texas Supreme Court declined to hear the case, which left the lower court's decision intact.

The Farm Bureau hailed the decision as a victory for property rights. The TCEQ saw it differently. As spokesman Terry Clawson told the *Texas Tribune*, the decision limited the agency's ability to "protect public welfare during drought conditions."

In the years since, the state appointed a "watermaster" for the lower Brazos—one of four in the state—at least in part in an effort to avoid that kind of showdown when the next drought rolls around. That too, has proved to be controversial. Rubenstein, who was himself watermaster for the Rio Grande, was not surprised by backlash to the creation of the post. Though he says he expects to see more watermasters appointed elsewhere in the state in the years to come, he believes there will remain stiff opposition to the whole idea. "We're a very red state, and in a red state you don't mess with . . . additional regulation. The legislature resists creating additional regulatory schemes such as watermasters."

Indeed, as former state senator Troy Fraser, R-Horseshoe Bay, then chairman of the Senate Natural Resources Committee, told the *Texas Tribune* in 2014, "I . . . generally am opposed to more watermasters. I'm concerned that we're giving too much power to one person."[3]

Just how much power that one person will have to avert a replay of the Brazos River standoff in the next major drought remains unclear. The TCEQ declined to make the watermaster available for an interview.

What made the Dow case even more complicated, and to some degree more representative of the myriad intersecting issues that water policy has become, was that over the years many of those municipal water customers had turned to sources like the Brazos and the Trinity so that they could cut back on their use of the Gulf Coast Aquifer. There was good reason for that, said Mike Turco, executive director of the groundwater district in Harris and Galveston Counties. As early as 1929, toward the beginning of the water-intensive oil boom in Texas, users of the Gulf Coast Aquifer began to see an ominous phenomenon. In some places, the land above overpumped aquifers started to sink.

"Over the next fifty years or so you began to see the same thing going on elsewhere in the area with subsidence, but in those areas it wasn't related to oil and gas," Turco said. "It was municipal supply and industrial withdrawal of groundwater. So any kind of shallow fluid withdrawal, really, if you pull on it long enough and hard enough, you're going to see in the aquifer subsidence at the surface."

As a result, he said, those users turned increasingly toward surface water. "We were created in '75 to deal with that issue and have regulated groundwater ever since then . . . We've gone through a progression from groundwater to surface water," he said. "There's a lot of data out there that shows where we've regulated people from one hundred percent of their supply being groundwater down to ten percent being groundwater," with the bulk of their supply coming from the Trinity and the overallocated Brazos River basins. "We've seen water levels come up, and we've seen subsidence rates change or go back to zero," he said. "The only exception being during the 2011 drought, when water was scarce." Thanks at least in part to the same circumstances that created the conflict between Dow, the farmers, and the TCEQ, "a lot more groundwater had to be pumped."

To a great extent, says Dr. Robert Mace, deputy executive administrator for the TWDB and the guy generally regarded as the state's point man on all issues water related, the Whac-A-Mole nature of the dispute between the Farm Bureau and the TCEQ is not unique to that corner of the state. All over Texas, water planners find that if they address a problem that threatens billions of dollars worth of infrastructure in one place, for example, the subsidence-prone land above a portion of the Gulf Coast Aquifer, they inadvertently help trigger a water war between a major industry, a motivated army of disgruntled farmers and ranchers, and a phalanx of growing and thirsty municipalities.

That would be challenging enough anywhere in the Western world, but it is especially challenging in Texas, where both property rights and the idea of local control over most things—from what is taught in the local elementary school to how precious water resources are allocated—are articles of faith, and where the idea of centralized planning of almost any sort, at least nowadays, is considered heresy.

That is the tightrope that policy makers have to walk in trying to articulate the state's goal for its water plan. Not only do they have to address the needs of competing stakeholders, but the principal tool they have to do it with is a plan that percolates from the ground up rather than from the top down. Critics have charged that the state water plan is less a comprehensive vehicle for addressing the state's looming water needs than it is—as Lowerre puts it—"sixteen wish lists that nobody thinks is a plan. It's not a plan. It's a justification for some water development. It's an encouragement for some conservation. But when the plan can include pumping more water OUT of the Ogallala than is IN the Ogallala, that's not a plan."

Mace disagrees with Lowerre's assessment. To be sure, he said, there are drawbacks to the state's approach, delegating to parochial interests an issue critical to the future of the state as a whole, but he insisted that the approach had, at least thus far, been generally successful.

"One thing I like to point to in the regional water planning process that the state has undertaken . . . is that in [the drought of 1996] we had small communities actually run out of water. Folks were having to truck in bottled water to these communities. Now we're fortunate that we didn't have a larger city run out of water. But nonetheless, we still had a few communities run out of water," he said. "We just went through . . . a five-year drought" he said, referring to the drought of 2011. "And we did not have a single community run out of water," though he added that one community, Spicewood Beach, did see the water levels drop so low that water briefly had to be trucked in. "But . . . nobody actually ran out of water, and in my opinion that's directly related to the state water planning process and other innovations that our legislature put in place in 1997 after the previous drought.

The Drought Preparedness Council, state agencies working together to actively respond to communities, to work as hard as possible to prevent them from running out of water. That's something I would point to."

There are serious challenges looming, Mace said. "I think when you look at the 2017 plan you see that we're not ready for a repeat of the drought of record," he said.

But individual regions have developed plans at least to move in the direction of girding themselves against future droughts. In West Texas, places from Odessa to El Paso have moved in the direction of conjunctive use, of dealing with groundwater and surface water together and conserving both accordingly, he said. "What those folks have done is put into place projects and water management strategies that are conjunctive . . . they're diversified, and it has made them far stronger going into the future. By managing it conjunctively they think they can have their groundwater supply for, I want to say, three hundred years."

And there are also sources of so-called new water that could be brought online as the need arises. Though costly, they are out there, he said. And he insisted that with the help of a $4 billion fund that voters in Texas overwhelmingly approved in 2013 to make state loans and grants available to those communities and entities that can afford to take on additional debt—a kitty that Mace believes can be leveraged into $27 billion in buying power—they can be brought online.

It has been nearly six decades since the first large-scale desalination plant came online in Texas, and in recent years the technology has taken root in various corners of the state where groundwater tends to be brackish, though, as we'll see later in the volume, not without cost and some resistance from customers. Still, Mace believes taht the technology can, will, and perhps *must* be expanded.

In the more immediate term, the plan also envisions a greater reliance on surface water, which would require the construction of reservoirs as well. According to the plan, "surface water resources, including new reservoirs, compose the greatest portion of the recommended water management strategy supplies in 2070 at approximately forty-five percent."

But like everything else in the confoundedly complicated world of water in Texas, calling for a new reservoir and actually getting it built are two different things.

Cost is certainly a factor, Mace said. "But it would be lovely if that was the only issue."

It is not. In many respects, all the issues that confront water planners in the state are cast in stark relief in the debate over new reservoirs. Not only do planners have to struggle through the various levels of state and federal regulations to acquire the appropriate permits to build one, but before they even can get to that point they have to run a gantlet of conflicting interests. There are cities, places like the Dallas–Fort Worth Metroplex, that must find a way to articulate their needs and find a way to pay for it, and then there are the various interests in the places where reservoirs, like the proposed Marvin Nichols project along the Sulfur River, would be built. "There's environmental considerations," Mace said. And then there is the one issue that, as we have seen, bedevils water planners all over Texas. "Property rights are . . . one of the obstacles . . . impacting . . . the construction of reservoirs," he said.

Environmental concerns and property rights.

As we will see in the next chapter, in Dallas and Fort Worth, where for a decade and a half the plan to build the Marvin Nichols Reservoir has been on hold, those two issues have proper names: Janice Bezanson and Shirley Shumake.

CHAPTER 8

AN OAK WITH ITS ROOTS IN THE RIVER, REDUX

IT HAD BEEN MORE THAN fifteen years since she had first heard the rumblings about plans to build the Marvin Nichols dam, and yet the old oak tree at the edge of Shirley Shumake's place was still standing on the river bank.

Shirley was still standing, too.

So were her neighbors, and the timber company, and the local officials who sit on the planning commission for Region D.

But the dam, which hadn't been built and, under the proponents' most optimistic scenario, wouldn't be for decades, still managed to cast a long shadow across the bottomlands of the Sulphur River by the late winter of 2015. After years of grassroots action and legal wrangling—some of it seeming at times like hand-to-hand combat the TWDB announced that the proposed dam still remained a key goal of many officials in the Dallas–Fort Worth Metroplex and would remain a part of the state's latest water development plan.

And it still remained an existential threat to the homes and livelihoods and ways of life of Shumake and her allies. In short, it had become "a David and Goliath situation," as Dr. James Presley, the historian and activist, put it. "And there are a lot of little Davids out there."

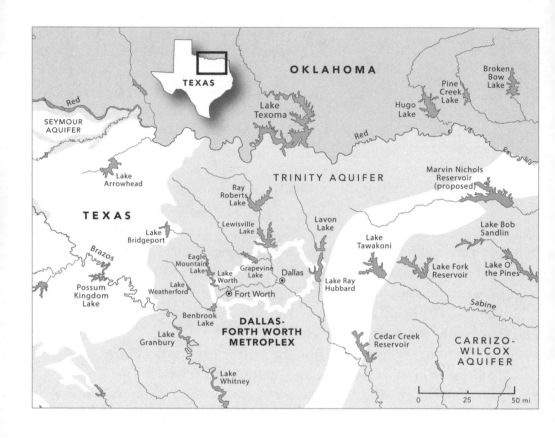

OKLAHOMA

TEXAS

SEYMOUR AQUIFER

Red

Lake Texoma

Red

Hugo Lake

Pine Creek Lake

Broken Bow Lake

TRINITY AQUIFER

Marvin Nichols Reservoir (proposed)

Lake Arrowhead

Ray Roberts Lake

Lake Bob Sandlin

TEXAS

Lewisville Lake

Lavon Lake

Lake Bridgeport

Lake Tawakoni

Lake Fork Reservoir

Lake O' the Pines

Brazos

Eagle Mountain Lake

Grapevine Lake

Dallas

Possum Kingdom Lake

Lake Worth

Lake Weatherford

Fort Worth

Lake Ray Hubbard

Sabine

Benbrook Lake

DALLAS-FORTH WORTH METROPLEX

CARRIZO-WILCOX AQUIFER

Lake Granbury

Cedar Creek Reservoir

Lake Whitney

0   25   50 mi

Granted, the insurgents in the Sulphur River Basin had exacted a price. They had managed to persuade some of the officials in favor of the dam to consider shrinking the footprint of the reservoir, from about seventy thousand acres to perhaps less than forty thousand acres. But it was by no means certain that would happen, and even if it did, it would still mean that tens of thousands of acres of timber and ranchlands would be lost, Shumake said, and tens of thousands more would have to be surrendered.

In a contentious court battle, they had managed to persuade the Texas Court of Appeals in Eastland to order the TWDB to step in and resolve the conflict between the water planning board in the Metroplex and the planners representing their part of the basin. "The board is in a position to resolve the conflict in the manner that is most consistent with protecting the state's agricultural and natural resources," Justice Terry McCall wrote in a 2013 decision.[1]

The TWDB, however, continued to delay a decision, though it did instruct water planners in the Metroplex to file a statement measuring the impacts of the proposed reservoir. Though those planners concluded that the reservoir would affect a comparatively small percentage of timberland—about "5.2 percent of the forested wetlands, 2.4 percent of the bottomland hardwood forests, and 0.4 percent of the upland forests in Region D"[2]—they acknowledged it would have a measurable impact on wildlife habitat and cultural resources, including several pre-Columbian Native American sites.

Apparently, however, the idea of building a 199-billion-gallon reservoir atop a Native American graveyard was not a deal breaker for Region C water planners or for the TWDB. Nor was the notion of placing that much water—83 million tons—atop the little-understood and long fault line.

Travel east from Fort Worth across the so-called Pine Curtain that divides the water-rich counties of East Texas from the sprawling Metroplex of Dallas and Tarrant Counties and beyond, and you are following the path of a fault line: the Mexia-Talco Fault Zone that arcs like an inverted fish hook from the Rio Grande Valley to the Arkansas border. It was formed tens of millions of years ago as the sea retreated under a relentless assault from an ever-growing land mass, leaving deposits of salt behind that, over millions of years, strained and finally fractured under the crushing weight of geological change.

It has been, for eons, a stable fault as such things go. Though moderate earthquakes have from time to time rattled other areas of Texas, from El Paso to the Panhandle to the suburbs of Dallas, the Mexia-Talco fault line has remained comparatively quiet.[3] Indeed, as far as geologists can tell, there may never have been a significant quake along the fault line.

At least not so far. There are those who contend that the proposed Marvin Nichols dam could awaken the slumbering fault line that divides rural Northeast Texas, the hardwood bottomlands and the farms and ranches of the Sulfur River Basin, from the rest of Texas. There are fears that damming the river and loading eighty-five million tons of water atop a known fault, over time, could cause the fault to buckle, even if it didn't trigger an outright earthquake. Those fears have been exacerbated in recent years as a series of unpredicted earthquakes—most of them minor but all of them alarming—have been reported in otherwise seismically quiet areas of Texas (and elsewhere) in connection with the fracking boom that has helped fuel the growth of places like Fort Worth. Adding to the concern is, to some degree, that there is precedent: cases in which dam builders suddenly have found themselves standing on very shaky ground. In 1985, for example, as crews were relocating the cemeteries of two long-abandoned ghost towns north of Dallas to make way for the construction of the twenty-nine-thousand-acre-foot Ray Roberts Lake, a magnitude 3.3 earthquake shook the ground. It did not shake the resolve of the dam builders, however, and a year later, Ray Roberts Lake was completed, with the assurance of the Army Corps of Engineers that the dam was strong enough to withstand a similar tremor if such an event ever occurred.

Taken together, the existence of the fault and the limits of our understanding of the mechanics of their seismicity may be reason enough to ensure that the project is never built. "What do you think will happen when you stack up 30,000 acres of new overburden [lake water] plus a new dam" atop the fault line? geologist William Crowder wrote in a blistering 2014 letter to the TWDB during the height of the debate over the Marvin Nichols. "Not only will you introduce a new overburden, your new dam and lake will allow old surface faults to come into direct contact with lake water. Will the old fault planes become re-hydrated and lubricated such that they are re-activated? Someone has to ask these questions."

For their part, the proponents of the dam point to assurances from the project's engineers, Freese and Nichols, that the proposed dam and the massive lake behind it would not be threatened by the fractures below the surface.

In effect, the proposed Marvin Nichols dam, at least as of 2015, remained what it had always been: its own kind of fault line, dividing two tectonic forces, the ever-expanding urban centers of the Metroplex on the one side and the motivated rural communities of the Sulphur basin on the other.

And while the Mexia-Talco fault had been dormant for a hundred years, things had not been as quiet along the fault line that runs roughly along the course of the Sulphur River. There the pressure continued to build.

It is not that the Metroplex doesn't have other places it can find water, says Jim Thompson, the lawyer appointed by Region D to respond to what it perceived as the Metroplex's water poaching. There are existing reservoirs, such as the Toledo Bend Reservoir, he said, that could be tapped. The 185,000-acre lake, the largest in the south, the fifth-largest in the United States, was created in 1966 across the Sabine River on the border between Texas and Louisiana and has for decades been a sportsperson's paradise. Managed jointly by the Sabine River Authority in Texas and its sister agency in Louisiana, Toledo Bend's nearly 4.5 million acre-feet of storage has been doled out sparingly over the years, primarily to spin the turbines of a hydropower plant, and only then are the 1.8 million gallons a day that pass through the turbines made available to municipalities and industries in both states.

Though there certainly would be costs and perhaps even environmental consequences associated with tapping into Toledo Bend, those would pale in comparison to the havoc that would be wreaked by the construction of the Marvin Nichols project, Thompson said. With Toledo Bend, they "have a vast amount of unused water that's already impounded. That land has already been taken and accounted for. And they're looking to sell water out of Toledo Bend," he said.

Nor is it their only option, he argued. Another option would be raising water levels and increasing consumption from the Wright Patman Reservoir, the 20,300-acre reservoir on the Sulfur River that currently provides about 14,570 acre-feet of water a year to Texarkana, on both the Arkansas and Texas sides of the boundary. "That would give additional water and wouldn't have the impacts that Marvin Nichols would have," Thompson said. "And, of course, there's always the matter of how much water they use compared to statewide averages and so forth, and they could certainly do more on the conservation side."

Indeed, the per capita water consumption in the Metroplex historically exceeds the statewide average—in 2008, for example, Dallas consumers used an average of 213 gallons a day, according to state officials, compared with 171 in Austin and 149 in San Antonio,[4] though the region has been making strides in reducing that discrepancy.

Still, some environmentalists, Bezanson among them, contend that the Metroplex could do more, and they maintain that a more aggressive reuse regimen would maximize the impact of what is essentially happening anyway—a kind of impromptu interbasin water transfer in which water is collected from a variety of sources, used, and then flushed downstream. Rather than diminish flows to downstream consumers, maximizing the process in effect could create additional water supplies for communities downstream on the Trinity River.

"They have the potential readily to do enough to meet all of the gap between their current supply and their future demand at least through 2070. And that's as far as anybody's projected their future demand. They could do all of that with reuse. And they don't really have to. I mean there are other sources they could combine it with," Bezanson said.

"They're already bringing a lot of water from the Red River, the Sulphur River, the Sabine River, and they're about to be bringing some from the Neches River. All of that water is already going down the Trinity. It's an *interbasin transfer*. The result is that the Trinity right now already has more water going down it than it historically did."

In fact, aggressively reusing such existing water supplies—as long as they aren't used primarily for watering lawns or filling swimming pools in Dallas—could go a long way to reducing the bane of Texas water planners, evaporation, and mean that even more water would flow downstream, she contends.

"The water that goes on your lawn or goes in your swimming pool, anything that evaporates to the sky, that water is lost to the local system. It blows away in the wind and comes down somewhere else, she said. "But all the water that goes down the drain winds up back in the river system. So you're not reducing the downstream flows by bringing water out and using it or reusing it or re-reusing it as long as you're releasing it to go down the drain. It's when you put it on your lawn that you're losing it."

Manicured lawns and in-ground swimming pools aside, the way Thompson and Bezanson see it, the Metroplex, and Region C in its entirety, have largely overlooked those significant options other than the Marvin Nichols. And why? It is because, as Thompson and Bezanson see it, the dispute between the two sides is not really a battle over water for the future.

"It's a power struggle," Thompson says.

"I have argued for years that this is NOT about water," Thompson said. "It's about the power and the control and the money involved in the water. If it was just about water—obtaining the water for the Dallas–Ft. Worth entities that they needed—this problem would have been gone a long time ago.

"But it's about them wanting the power, the control, and getting the absolute one hundred percent value for their money and becoming stronger and even more viable in the future."

It might surprise Thompson to learn that on that singular point—that the dispute is about something more than just water—there are those on the other side who might agree with him.

It is easy to lose sight of it in the daily urban bustle of a metropolis like Dallas. You could be forgiven for being distracted by the modern, honking, impatient rhythms of Fort Worth. But there is, for those whose job it is to make sure that there will be enough water for the Metroplex down the road, always a sense of almost painful urgency. Talk to them long enough and you begin to hear between their words a kind of persistent, low-level humming anxiety. In a way, it is not different from the aura that surrounded the so-called Depression babies, who were born into hardship and never forgot it.

It is a "never again" kind of feeling. In fact, that is the very phrase they often use. "You probably heard that when we came so close to being out of water and we were rationing water in the fifties, our city leaders said 'never again,'" Denis Qualls, who oversees the planning division for the City of Dallas's Water Utilities Department, said before even beginning a discussion on the future of the Marvin Nichols project.

It is odd in a way. Few if any of those officials are old enough to remember the drought of record with any clarity, if they are old enough to remember it all. And yet in much the same way that the rural ethos of the Sulphur River Basin has, over the years, been woven into the DNA of people like Shirley Shumake and Gary Cheatwood Jr., the officials in the Metroplex are steeped in the lore of that long and vicious dry spell.

Many Texans are steeped in it, of course, though for most it is often imagined as a predominantly rural catastrophe. But it was a particularly hard time for the growing urban areas as well, and what would become the Dallas–Fort Worth Metroplex had as hard a time as any place in the state.

It was certainly not the first drought to savage the region. Dry as it was, it was not as dry as a virtually uninterrupted generation-spanning drought that the region experienced in the period between 1697 and 1725, according to the scant records that exist. And that paled in comparison to the forty-year dry spell that plagued the region at the end of the fifteenth century.

The difference was, few people lived in the area at that time. But by the time the drought of record came along, the region had blossomed into a major metropolitan center.

It is perhaps a measure of how drastically the region had changed since the 1400s—and perhaps a metaphor for it as well—that among the victims of the relentless heat and remorseless drought were the penguins that perished at what was then called the Marsalis Zoo.[5]

If the penguins were ill-prepared to face the drought and heat, the city was as well. By the end of the first year of the drought, the East Fork of the Trinity River had gone dry. Soon afterward, Lake Dallas, now known as Lake Lewisville, dropped to eleven percent of capacity. By 1956, city officials had begun pumping water, water that for many was considered far too salty to drink, from the Red River in Oklahoma. But in those days before the advent of desalinization, there were concerns not only about the taste of the water but about the dangers it posed to people with preexisting medical conditions, such as kidney problems, not to mention the havoc it could wreak on old iron pipes.

As the surface water slowed to a trickle, or in the case of White Rock Lake, dried up altogether, the residents turned to other sources, like old, underused wells. The *Dallas Morning News* reported on October 16, 1956,[6] that desperate city officials had reopened a long-abandoned well that had been drilled into the sand beneath a school thirty years earlier. Heavily laden with iron after all those years of disuse, the well was run for a few days, in the hopes that it would clear up. Parched neighbors watched as in the middle of the worst drought in memory, thousands of gallons of water went to waste, forming pools and small lakes on the street. It didn't take long before one enterprising neighbor, appalled by the waste, took matters into his own hands, building a small dam and hooking up a pump to siphon off enough water to meet his own needs, with enough left over to share with a few of his neighbors, at least until the city took over the pumping duties.

All over the region, drillers worked overtime, and, according to reports from the time, more than a few do-it-yourselfers headed into their backyards with pickaxes and determination, hoping to strike water before they collapsed from the oppressive heat. Some found water. Others had to take even more drastic steps.

Those with less faith in themselves or more faith in Providence—pastors and their congregations, even a few politicians who found in the drought their "come to Jesus" moment—prayed fervently, and fruitlessly, for rain. There were reports of people wandering around behind houses, holding dousing sticks and witching for water.

In 1956, long before the bottled water craze that took hold across America in the 1980s, residents of what would become the Metroplex were paying the equivalent of $4.41 today for water sold to them in what looked like repurposed milk cartons.

But despite all of that, the drought continued, unabated, until the rains finally came in early 1957. By the time they did, the city and its neighbors were perhaps within days of running out of water altogether.

It is therefore not surprising that in the aftermath of that drought, the Metroplex, independently at first and now increasingly as a regional unit, embarked on a massive campaign to augment its water supplies and to do it in a way that facilitated the continued growth of the region's economic might.

As of 2016, there are thirty-four major reservoirs, each holding in excess of five thousand acre-feet, that serve the sixteen-county region known to state water planners as Region C, which stretches from the Trinity River Basin in Cook County in the northwest to Freestone County along the Brazos River in the south. But those reservoirs, which provide about ninety percent of the water used in the region, are carrying a heavy load. Twenty-six percent of the state's population lives in Region C, with most of them living in communities of more than twenty thousand people, and more than half of them—sixty-four percent, according to the region's 2016 water plan—live in the area generally accepted as the Metroplex, roughly defined as Dallas and Tarrant Counties. In all, more than 6.7 million people call those two counties home, and a lot of them are relative newcomers, with more than 1.5 million of them having shown up since the year 2000. By 2040, another 2.1 million people are expected to live in the region. By 2070, the year in which the Marvin Nichols Reservoir is now expected to be built, planners expect there to be more than 14.3 million people in the region, with more of that growth expected in the counties that collar Dallas–Fort Worth.

These are, by far, the most prodigious consumers of water in the region. Though the region as a whole uses only about 8.3 percent of the water consumed in the state each year, about 90 percent of it is used by those business and urban dwellers in the Metroplex. And they are going to need more of it as the years go by, from about 1.7 million acre-feet available now to about 2.9 million acre-feet by 2070, meaning that the region is going to have to come up with that additional 1.2 million acre-feet of water someplace.

That is why they have been covetously eyeing the land that Shirley Shumake calls home.

It is, to be sure, not the only source of water they have been hoping to acquire, nor is it the only strategy they are pursuing. In fact, they contend that through various strategies, they have identified almost 1.8 million acre-feet of water per year, enough not only to meet their projected needs but to do so with a little bit left over just in case the climate scientists are right and the future holds warmer and significantly drier years than the past. To that end, the region is already pushing conservation aggressively—everything from stanching leaky pipes to urging consumers to use less, especially in dry times—and by 2070, they expect those initiatives to pay off to the tune of about 136,000 acre-feet a year, about a fifth of what the Metroplex could expect to see from the Marvin Nichols Reservoir if the project is ever built.

Treatment and reuse of much of the millions of acre-feet that would otherwise go down the drain (replenishing the Trinity River in the process) is also expected to play a critical role in years to come. Still, according to the region's 2016 plan (prepared, it should be noted, by Freese and Nichols), expanded surface water supplies are by far the largest target for the region in the coming decades. And the largest chunk of that, some half million acre-feet a year, is without question the Sulphur River Basin and the proposed Marvin Nichols dam project.

For the moment, that project effectively is stuck in the mud, thanks to the surprisingly effective campaign that Janice Bezanson, Shirley Shumake, and her neighbors have waged to stop it, or at least to slow it down.

The stalemate to which the two sides have fought each other would be frustrating enough on its own, says Martin Rochelle, a partner in Mike Gershon's law firm who, as the attorney for the North Texas Municipal Water District, has spent years arguing the case for the Marvin Nichols project. But what makes it even more maddening is that there is, after all, a clock ticking.

"As we look at a fifty-year planning cycle under our regional and state planning processes, there is an envelope of need that is coming to the Metroplex," he says. "The Metroplex is a huge economic engine for our state and our country. And it has to be fed. It doesn't have to be fed so that people can have—you know—St. Augustine lawns. But it sure has to be fed so that there's . . . the opportunity . . . for continued economic development. Economic development requires water. And the population growth that results from economic development requires water."

But even if the objections of the Sulphur River residents could be overcome, or brushed aside, that would be a beginning, not an end. It would trigger a whole new round of time-consuming bureaucratic challenges that could take years—decades perhaps—to clear before water from the Marvin Nichols Reservoir even could begin to trickle into the Dallas–Fort Worth area, Rochelle says.

That, too, is part of a profound political and cultural shift that has occurred since the heyday of dam building in the west, the days when Marvin Nichols and others could envision replumbing the entire state and building a cascading network of giant reservoirs from the Mississippi River all the way across the Llano Estacado. Back in those days, there was no federal Environmental Protection

Agency (EPA) that needed to sign off on a major project, and the state and federal authorities who oversaw such projects, the Army Corps of Engineers and the Bureau of Reclamation, were loaded cheek by jowl with gung ho dam builders who had really thin rule books and a reservoir full of experience.

But it has been forty years since President Jimmy Carter reined in the Bureau of Reclamation and the golden age of dam building ended. It has been more than thirty years since a major lake—Lake Allen Henry, outside Lubbock—was approved by the Corps, Rochelle notes.

And in that time, the expertise, the experience, and to some degree even the will among regulators to dive into such major projects have come perilously close to running dry.

"I'm working . . . on . . . five reservoir projects right now around the state, all smaller than Marvin Nichols. Some appreciably smaller," Rochelle says. "The biggest one of those projects is about 350,000 acre-feet of storage and it's about 125,000 acre-feet of yield—that's Lower Bois d'Arc. And that project [also beset by challenges from residents and environmentalists] has been on the mill for a decade at the state and federal level. The state permitting has been issued. The federal permitting drags on . . . because of the inefficiencies of the federal government.

"To be fair—even to the federal government—there's no staff at the Corps office in Tulsa or staff at the EPA office in Dallas who have ever really worked on a reservoir project. Since the '60s and '70s, there really haven't been reservoir projects."

As a result, he believes, even if the time does come when the opposition to the Marvin Nichols dam is quelled, or at least quieted, it could still take a lifetime for the permits to be issued. And it is not at all clear that the expanding Metroplex, and its increasing number of residents, can wait that long.

Perhaps, he says, if the gulf between the folks who live in the Sulphur River Basin and those in the Metroplex could be bridged sooner, the Marvin Nichols dam would have a fighting chance of getting through that federal maze.

But if you listen closely to Rochelle, or to others in the debate, you begin to get a sense that that is unlikely. There is a sense of resignation in his voice, a feeling that many of the people in the Sulphur River Basin never will sell their land willingly, and that if the time comes to take it, it will be through eminent domain.

And in that, you begin to sense that the divide isn't really between those who need the water and those who have it. It is not even primarily a battle between rural and urban interests, though that is part of it.

Instead, you get the sense that it is about something bigger: a battle between two cultures, each with its own mythology, be it the ancient roots pioneers laid down beside a giant old oak tree, sixteen feet around, on the banks of the Sulphur River, or the echo of a distant memory of the driest time in Dallas when the penguins at the zoo died and the lakes ran nearly empty. It is about two different ways of looking at the world. In one, the world looks a lot like it used to. In the other, it looks a lot like Dallas when it finally grows up.

Rochelle, who grew up in Northeast Texas on a farm that had been in his family since before Stephen Austin got a land grant from Mexico, says he understands both points of view. He still remembers the day when the man from the utility company showed up and told his daddy he would have to give up a chunk of his land—whether he wanted to or not—so that a gas pipeline could be built.

"It shook me as a kid to think that this for-profit oil and gas company could do that. But you know. That's the law," he said. "And I would say this: it's tragic sometimes that private property has to be taken for public purposes. But I would encourage people to think about how much it would cost to build a road from Texarkana to Dallas without eminent domain. How long that road would be if there were one hundred landowners out of the ten thousand between those two points that just decided this is granddaddy's land, or I just don't want to sell it?

"This public purpose is really for everybody. It's for economic development. It's for truckers. It's so my grandmother can get to the hospital in Dallas in a timely way. It's so commerce can go. It's just so people, normal people, can go visit Dallas or drive to Texarkana if they wanted to without them having to go through North Carolina.

"What benefit to the public would be enough for the guys who complain about eminent domain or condemnation to start thinking, well maybe it's not that bad. Sometimes. Or is it just that it's my ox that's gettin' gored as opposed to the guy down the street that I don't know?"

It is, he said, a sad but inescapable fact of life that "every reservoir in the state, every highway in the state, virtually every public building in the state of any size may have involved the taking of private property.

"So I don't like it. I get it. Eminent domain is a Big Brother deal. But it is a necessity that we can't do without," he says. "I get the emotional part. I felt it, too. I wouldn't like it either, but I can be objective enough to see that it's a necessary evil if you want to call it evil. It's just necessary."

Necessary, perhaps, but for now at least, the process to acquire by whatever means necessary the right to build the Marvin Nichols dam is in limbo. Region C continues to insist that it will be needed. Region D insists that it is not, and in its 2016 state water plan, the TWDB magnanimously has decided to give both positions equal weight.

In any event, an agreement between the combatants has guaranteed that if anything ever does come of the proposal, if the last great reservoir ever to be built in Texas is indeed built, it won't be before 2070.

And in the near term, that means that Metroplex will have to rely more heavily on other options, much as Thompson has demanded. "Water supply planning is very opportunistic," Denis Qualls said. That is not a pejorative, he says. It is just a fact of life. And that is why, at least in the city of Dallas, they are hedging their bets on the future of the Marvin Nichols project. "In Dallas's long-range water supply plan, Marvin Nichols . . . is not one of our primary or recommended strategies. It's an alternate strategy.

"Now, we have other suppliers in the region . . . it is one of their recommended strategies," he says. "And if they were to move forward, and if the permitting came through and *IF IF IF IF* it became available and it looked as though something was going to be done, well then we would jump in. That's what I mean by opportunistic. Certain things come up and we're like, 'Whoa, hey!'"

But frankly, he says, he's far from certain that it will happen. Like Rochelle, he lays part of the blame at the doorstep of the federal agencies charged with permitting reservoir projects. Simply put, "it is becoming more and more and more difficult with federal regulation—and some state regulation—to develop a large surface water supply." And like Rochelle, he believes that a lack of experience after a thirty-year dry spell with regard to construction of major surface water projects has contributed to the problem among regulators at both the state and federal levels.

But those problems, perhaps, could be managed. Savvy water officials, cunning lawyers, and motivated politicians often can find a way to bargain with bureaucrats if the political winds are favorable.

But there is a more intractable problem, one for which there is no easy answer and which, by its very nature, exacerbates the divisions between people from one region of the state and those from another. And that is that, like it or not, water is a commodity. It has a price. It costs billions, Qualls says, to provide water supplies and to develop and maintain the infrastructure to deliver it on demand, something people, even in rain-starved portions of Texas, have come to expect.

To be sure, Qualls embraces Thompson's and Bezanson's call for greater conservation. In fact, as in most of the state's regional water plans, conservation plays a key role in the region's water strategy, both now and in the future. Water planners in Region C estimate that by demanding more efficiency from its users, for example, by using low-flow fixtures and more efficient water-using appliances, and by aggressively pursuing reuse strategies, the Metroplex and surrounding counties could see "a total conservation and reuse supply of over 1.16 million acre-feet per year by 2070,"[7] roughly the equivalent of all the water pulled on behalf of millions of people each year from the Gulf Coast Aquifer (which stretches from Florida to Mexico).

But such dramatic conservation measures can carry you only so far, he says. "You can't conserve your way all the way into the future," he says. "You can't conserve your way out of your problems. You can postpone your problems, if you want to call it that. But . . . there's only so much water conservation that can occur before you have to have something new."

But the phrase "something new" is, in a way, misleading. Scientists will tell you that there isn't a single drop of water on the planet that hasn't been here in the beginning. All the water we will ever have is right here, right now. It is just that in places like Dallas and Fort Worth, and the ever-expanding cities around them, it is not where they have decreed it is needed. It is in the Gulf of Mexico, still out of reach by available and affordable technology. It is in riverbeds that snake past other people's homes far from the Metroplex. Some of the water that the Metroplex craves now runs slowly past Shirley Shumake's homestead.

Families depend on that water in the Sulphur River Basin. So do businesses, like the timber industry. They see their future reflected in the slow-moving waters of the Sulphur River. But there are families in Dallas and Fort Worth as well. It is a blunt instrument, to be sure, but the 2016 Region C water plan warns darkly that if the mounting water needs in the region are not met, "the annual combined lost income in 2070 would be $34.6 billion and that 2070 employment would be reduced by over 373,000 jobs."[8]

Not providing that water would carry an awful cost for the people of the Metroplex. Providing it would carry an awful cost for the people of the Sulphur River Basin.

"So here's the question," Qualls says. "Jane Doe in East Texas . . . does her job and her lifestyle have more value than, you know, Jane Jones in Dallas? The answer is probably no. But that doesn't mean that she's not important. How do you weigh those things?"

It is, he says, a complicated question, far more complicated, in a way, than the massive engineering challenges associated with building a dam or the logistical problems of moving massive amounts of water from one place to the next. It is more complicated because it is a human problem. And it is not just one problem. It is hundreds. Thousands. And all of them have proper names, like Shirley

Shumake or Janice Bezanson. Those problems are more complicated because those people have needs and ties to a community of people just like them.

You can't simply tally costs and measure them against benefits and come up with an easy answer.

And in the grand scheme of things, you can't solve the challenges of providing enough water for all of Texas—not just the Metroplex, but all those thirsty cities and suburbs and hubs of industry that are growing across the state—without first addressing that prickly human question. "These are the kinds of things that we have to deal with. Is there a good way to deal with them? I don't know. I'm sure there is. Have we found it yet? Probably not," Qualls says. "But we're looking."

For now, the status quo remains. The old cemeteries still slumber under the live oaks along the Sulphur River, no longer used to bury people but still tended by those who are linked by blood to those first settlers to this region. The ancient graves do not yet need to be disturbed. The local volunteer fire department will, at least for the foreseeable future, still hold its annual fund-raising fish fry and pie auction to raise money to keep itself afloat. The department raised $15,000 the last time it was held, says Gary Cheatwood Jr., and in his eyes, that is a testament to the people of the region and to the culture of self-sufficiency and the spirit of community that have always been a hallmark of this part of Texas. "People here don't give to bump themselves up or show off," he says. "They do it to support their community. We have a cemetery fund-raiser, too. It's the same way. People love each other. They love their community. It never ceases to amaze me."

The thought that it might all be washed away to serve the needs of a distant city, where most of the residents couldn't find Cass County with a Geiger counter, motivated this community, Cheatwood said. It turned ordinary people like Shirley and Max Shumake and Cheatwood's father, Gary Sr., into activists. "My dad, and Max Shumake, these two guys are always out there on the front line. They're at every meeting. They're gathering all the facts. I mean they're like warriors. And they're just country boys," Cheatwood says. "Just country boys."

It might seem odd to think that in a place where tradition and "country" and everything that word conjures run so deep, where ancient mistrust of the distant cities almost seems to be imprinted on the DNA of the locals at birth, there would be such an abiding faith in the future of technology. But when you ask the locals like Shirley Shumake and Gary Cheatwood Sr. what they believe will ultimately save their homes, they will point to the stunning advancements in technology that are, in their minds, looming just over the horizon.

They point to advancements in small-scale technology that could, if properly funded and fully implemented, dramatically reduce the amount of water Dallas or Forth Worth or Austin or Houston consumes, thus making projects like the Marvin Nichols dam seem a little less necessary.

"That's where the future is," says Janice Bezanson, the environmental organizer who first enlisted the locals in the battle to block the dam nearly two decades ago.

With leadership from the state, Bezanson argues, emerging technologies could be blended. Some of the same techniques used to desalinate brackish groundwater could be used to add an additional layer of treatment to reclaim wastewater, she says.

Leadership from the state could also pave the way for aquifer storage and recovery, the same technology championed by State Representative Lyle Larson as a more cost-effective way of preserving one hundred percent of the water captured from existing sources. As noted by Larson in the previous chapter, developing such a facility in the depleted aquifer under Dallas could make the Marvin Nichols project unnecessary or at least less attractive to the Metroplex on a cost-per-gallon basis.

Oren Caudle, the self-appointed Thomas Paine of the Sulphur River revolutionaries, says that that proposal alone has made Larson a kind of folk hero in the Sulphur River revolution—no small feat, in Caudle's eyes, for a Republican from San Antonio.

And if all those technologies and techniques aren't enough, there is always the sea and the saltwater beneath the earth.

But each of those approaches requires more than just technology. For a water strategy that would be able to meet the growing needs of Texas in an increasingly volatile climate to be fully and reliably developed in a way that would benefit interests on all sides of the ever-expanding fault lines that snake through Texas, it would require an almost seismic shake-up. The state, which has thus far deferred to local interests, would have to take an active role in developing a true statewide water plan, one that recognized that the state is not a collection of nearly one hundred local groundwater districts or dozens of river basins but is a single entity. As Larson has put it, it would require recognition that "either we're all Texans or we're not."

If the stalemate over the Marvin Nichols dam proves anything, it is that so far the people of the state of Texas have not yet accepted what water planners have known since at least as far back as 1968, when they were frustrated in their attempt to rechannel the mighty Mississippi so they could water the High Plains and the Rio Grande Valley. The future of the state, not just the continued growth and prosperity of its urban centers but also the fate of its traditional agricultural communities, depends on making sure that water flows from where it is to where it is needed. And in order for that to happen, everyone is going to have make a few sacrifices.

It will happen. It may not happen behind the bulwark of the Marvin Nichols dam. Shirley Shumake is not the only resident of the hardwood bottomlands to claim that the Marvin Nichols will "never get built as long as I'm alive." But dig a little deeper and Shumake and her neighbors in the Sulphur River Basin will tell you that they understand that nothing lasts forever, that there will eventually come a time when the growth in Dallas, or at least a shadow of it, will come to their neck of the woods. There may come a time when water from the Sulphur River is transferred to the Metroplex, perhaps from the Wright Patman Reservoir. What they are hoping is that when that time comes, conservation and the development of alternative sources of water will mean that the Metroplex can take less of their water and they can keep more of their land, more of their legacy, more of their traditional way of life. And they insist that when that time does come, those changes happen on their terms, or at least with the proper deference and respect to their needs.

As rancher, farmer, and reluctant activist Gary Cheatwood Sr. put it, "We just don't believe that somebody from outside ought to be able to come in here and just roll over us like a steam engine and take everything we've got and worked for."

"We know the world's changing," said his son, Gary Jr. "That's true. But you can't forget the rural people, or the urban people won't have anything to eat. And they may not have any water. You've got to take the rural people along for the ride. And acknowledge them.

"We're not outside the realm of working with people. Like I say, we're not stingy people. When we see people in need, we help. That's part of the community here. We help people. But we don't like to be told what to do.

"If we see somebody in need, we're going to help them. If our brothers in Dallas are thirsty, we'll help 'em out. But don't run over us. Let's talk about it."

The world is indeed changing. Dallas is growing, as are most of the major cities in Texas. And rural communities from the rainy woods of East Texas to the fallow fields outside Presidio are finding themselves challenged in ways they never could have imagined a few decades ago. If the scientists who study such things are to be believed, there will be more droughts and deeper ones in the decades to come, and one way or another, Texans are going to have to find a way to talk about it to each other.

The question is whether Texans, a stiff-necked people, whether they hail from the suburbs or the prairies or the coarse sandy scree of the Rio Grande Valley, can prod themselves to begin talking now, when there is still time to develop the systems and technologies to avert disaster or whether it will take a sudden earthquake triggered by one of those droughts that come along in Texas every century to shake Texas to its senses.

For now, that remains an open question.

CHAPTER 9

OLD MEN SHOUTING AT THE CLOUDS

HE CUT A DASHING FIGURE that early autumn morning as he strutted outside the Argyle Hotel in San Antonio. A crowd had gathered. That was no surprise. In the early 1890s, crowds always attended the man whom a fawning East Coast press reverently called "General R. G. Dyrenforth." He was a celebrity, a man with a military bearing and a polished European manner who, at least according to the newspapers, easily straddled the chasm between magic and science.

But they were also drawn by the promise of one hell of a fireworks display. In the hours before, Dyrenforth and his men had arranged a battery of mortars, all of them pointing toward the sky. A nearby mesquite tree had been festooned with explosives. At Dyrenforth's order, the explosives would be detonated, the mortars would be fired, and, he assured the crowd, the rains would indeed fall: the drought that had begun to spread through the entire Southwest would be stopped dead in its tracks.

And so the crowd waited. Eagerly. Anxiously.

For as long as there have been people in Texas, there have been attempts to alter and control the forces of nature that do battle there. The ancient Native Americans who re-created creation in the caves above the Pecos River did so with the hope that their precious personal sacrifices would ensure the continued cycle of rain and sun upon which their lives depended. Thousands of years later, Marvin

Nichols and the other modern men who dreamed of reengineering the entire state so that the waters of the Mississippi would fill the playas in the Panhandle believed, as humans always have, that there was a way that humans—through magic, or faith, or more recently through science—could bend nature to their will. It is a conviction that persists to this day. You see it in the emerging debate over geo-engineering, the controversial idea that by changing the way the clouds move or by altering the way the oceans absorb heat or carbon, perhaps we can slow or even reverse the climate-altering cascade of events that we accidentally triggered with two centuries of burning fossil fuels. In Texas, you see it every time a pilot climbs into the cockpit of an airplane and flies off to seed the clouds with silver nitrate in the hopes that the pilot can trigger a rainfall above the Ogallala or the Edwards Aquifers.

We don't call it magic or faith anymore. We call it weather modification. But it remains a part of our creed. Though the science remains inconclusive, as we will see later in this chapter, our faith in it is as strong as ever. In the state's 2017 water plan, for example, officials optimistically predict that within the next fifty years, billions of gallons of water will be coaxed from the sky by weather modification techniques.

Perhaps it will.

And if it does, it will be the latest chapter in a long history of charlatans, madmen, and visionaries shaking their fists at the clouds and ordering the heavens to do as they are told.

It is perhaps poetic that almost from the beginning, at least among Western cultures, the notion of summoning the rain has often been infused with the notion of conquest, of violence, linked in a way with war, or the tools of war, and with destruction.

As far back as the second century, Plutarch observed that rain often followed great battles. A man ahead of his time, Plutarch posited two potential reasons for the phenomenon. The first was that the cries of dying men had so touched the hearts of the gods that the heavens wept.

The second was a bit less theological.

Plutarch opined that in the carnage left on the field after a battle, "moist and heavy evaporations, steaming forth from the blood and corruption, thicken the air, which naturally is subject to alteration from the smallest causes."[1]

It was an idea that persisted, though by the sixteenth century, as cannon and musketry played a bigger role on the battlefield, it became common wisdom that gun smoke triggered rain. This idea was embraced wholeheartedly by Napoleon Bonaparte, who, ironically perhaps, lost the battle of Waterloo and his empire in no small part because his army got mired in the mud caused by a torrential downpour BEFORE the battle. As Victor Hugo would later write in *Les Misérables*, "A few drops of water, more or less, decided the downfall of Napoleon."

In the years after the Civil War, veterans noted that at least a little rain had fallen after most of the major battles of that conflict. That, of course, might have been because most of those battles were fought in the usually rainy East during the spring and summer months, when rainfall was expected.

By the end of the nineteenth century, the whole idea that the skies could be forced by military means to release their rain had taken on the patina of science. Edward Powers, a leading proponent of the emerging field, by then dubbed "concussionism," published a treatise on the phenomenon, *War and Weather*, and used that, his charm, and his political connections to wrangle $2,000 from the US Congress to conduct a feasibility study on the technique in 1891.

He enlisted Dyrenforth to carry out the experiments.

A tall, handsome, and slightly mysterious man with a prodigious mustache that dangled to his chin and a hint of a foreign accent—he had been born in Germany in 1844 and educated at a military college there—Dyrenforth had two critical qualifications for the job. First, he was an avid concussionist, having been converted to the faith while working for the US Patent Office. He had become convinced that, properly deployed and detonated, explosive charges could create whirling vortexes of air, moving upward like an invisible cyclone and sucking in moisture from surrounding areas in such copious quantities that the clouds would have to release it. He was, without question, a true believer. Second, and more importantly, perhaps, he was a shameless self-promoter who was not above padding his resume when it suited his purposes.

Though he had been dubbed "General" by the press, and enthusiastically embraced the title, he never rose above the rank of major during his years of service in the army. He had no real expertise with explosives, nor did he have any specific scientific training of which to speak. But he had, by all accounts, a remarkable talent for convincing people that he was who they wanted him to be, and he managed to leverage that talent to persuade Congress, with Powers's help, to make him a special agent of the US Department of Agriculture, give him thousands of dollars in taxpayer money, arm him with enough explosives to blow up a significant portion of the state, and dispatch him to Texas to do battle with the looming drought.

His first battles with the skies took place in August 1891 just northwest of Midland, where he showed up with a trainload full of munitions: cannons, mortars, gunpowder, dynamite, and rackarock explosives, a mixture of potassium chlorate and nitrobenzene that had to be whipped up on the spot, as well as kites to carry the stuff skyward.

For two weeks he waged furious battle against the sky, issuing regular press releases along the way, claiming immense success. As S. C. Gwynne recounted in his 2003 story for *Texas Monthly*, "Rain of Error," the national press lapped it up. The *New York Sun* dubbed him "Cloud Compelling Dyrenforth," describing him, with the kind of poetic license permitted at the time, as a virtual wizard who could "call the clouds together with a load of dynamite."

As it turned, however, he couldn't. The early experiments were effectively a bust. But Dyrenforth, with the kind of bald-faced chutzpah that would make P. T. Barnum blush, branded them a success. He touted his achievements himself in the *North American Review* in an article titled "Can We Make It Rain?" in which he claimed that he had indeed made it rain dozens of times.

Citing the aftermath of one particularly intensive barrage, for example, Dyrenforth breathlessly claimed that he had triggered a deluge—"a drenching rain [that] fell in torrents for two and a half hours" and flooded the roads between his camp and Midland under several inches of water.[2] The *Chicago Herald*, in its report from afar, did him one better, claiming that Dyrenforth had unleashed a "rain of six hours duration, breaking a drouth of many months." Actually, according to his own meteorologist, about two-tenths of an inch of rain—a hefty dew but far less than the 2.1 inches of rain Midland usually gets in August—collected on the parched grass around the time of the experiments, and eyewitnesses would later note that much of that fell before Dyrenforth's men hoisted their first kite or lit their first fuse.

As the year drew to a close, the gullible national media was beginning to suspect that Dyrenforth was a con man. That largely resulted from some good old-fashioned shoe-leather reporting by two small publications, *Farm Implement News* and *Texas Farm and Ranch*, which actually had sent reporters to cover the fireworks. What they saw was a disaster. The unskilled, disorganized amateurs who made up the bulk of Dyrenforth's team couldn't keep kites bearing explosives from being blown off-course or ripped to shreds in the wild West Texas wind. Devices exploded prematurely, in some cases triggering fires, or didn't explode at all. And even when everything did function as designed, not much happened.

By January 1892, *Scientific American* magazine had decided to call Dyrenforth's bluff, indicting his antics as "foolish fireworks" and judging that his hyperbolic press releases were "in most instances grossly exaggerated and in some cases wholly destitute of truth."[3]

By all accounts, Dyrenforth was unbowed. He dashed back to Washington to see if he could "make it rain," at least figuratively, there and buttonholed increasingly skeptical lawmakers in the hopes of wringing more money—a lot more money—out of them. They gave him another $10,000.

This time, though, they wanted to see proof.

And so, in November 1892, he swept into San Antonio. He was, according to accounts at the time, still well enough regarded there that the local hoi polloi feted him with a sumptuous dinner at which the champagne flowed freely.

The bonhomie was short-lived. Unlike his previous experiments, which had taken place largely far from most prying eyes, the disaster that greeted his efforts in San Antonio was in full public view. It was carried out with the same kind of inept bungling as the previous experiments, but this time there was an audience that watched in horror as he blew up a mesquite tree and shattered most of the windows in the Argyle Hotel. And while the shards of glass rained down on the streets of San Antonio, virtually nothing else did.

For four days he blasted away at the heavens, and when he was done with his "constant bombardment, not enough rain fell to lay the dust," the *Austin Weekly Statesman* reported at the time.

The man who had parlayed his proud bearing and his conviction that he could bully the heavens had become a laughingstock, mocked for the rest of his life by the nickname "General Dry-Henceforth."

It would be easy to imagine that such a humiliating end to Dyrenforth's misadventures would have been the death knell for attempts to "shoot up a rain."

It wasn't.

In 1910, the same year that Dyrenforth died, the eccentric, erratic, and irascible cereal magnate C. W. Post decided it was his turn to declare war on the skies.

Though a midwesterner, born and raised in Springfield, Illinois, Charles William Post had a long history with Texas and, it appears, an equally long history of mental instability. In fact, it was not long after his first nervous breakdown in 1885 that he turned up outside Forth Worth, in 1886, presumably to recover.

Instead, his first sojourn in Texas may have contributed to his second nervous breakdown. A business venture with local real estate investors who had planned to build a three-hundred-acre development dubbed "Riverside" on the eastern part of town hadn't quite worked out the way Post had hoped. Neither did a two-hundred-acre subdivision he planned on his own.

This time, he found himself admitted to the Battle Creek Sanitarium in Michigan, where for a time he was under the care of Dr. John Harvey Kellogg, an equally eccentric man who was an early and enthusiastic proponent of "hydrotherapy," the psychiatric equivalent of concussionism. Kellogg subscribed to the notion that you could be cured of whatever ailed your psyche by the regular application of enemas.

It is not at all clear from the historical record whether Kellogg's treatments had any significant effect on Post's mental health. Post remained as prone as ever to manic bursts of intense inventiveness and creativity and deep troughs of depression—melancholia, as his family called it—for the rest of his life. But there is little question that Kellogg, who would later become Post's chief competitor in the cereal business, may have done much to influence Post's fortunes. Both men were convinced with that kind of scientific certainty that often afflicted men of their era that a diet of toasted grain and an avoidance of coffee was the path to a healthy life. That belief led Post to develop both the first cornflakes and Postum, a coffee substitute that was based on a recipe Post had learned from farm wives in Texas.[4] It also made him a millionaire at a time when that still meant something.

In 1906, he used a small part of those millions to buy two hundred thousand acres of bone-dry ranchland south of Lubbock and laid out what he expected to be the perfect utopian community, a mix of dairy farm and dry-land cotton and grain farms arrayed in meticulous order around a small town that would bear his name.

He would soon discover, however, that the climate around Post, Texas, had other ideas. By 1908, much of the state of Texas was entering a prolonged four-year drought. It threatened the crops from the first of the experimental farms Post had laid out, and it made a mockery of the reservoir the community was building nearby.

Post was not the sort of man to take that kind of thing lying down. As a boy during and after the Civil War, he too had heard the tales of torrential rains following major battles, and like Dyrenforth, he became intrigued by the notion that the skies could be compelled by force to yield. He was not a true believer, not in the sense that Dyrenforth was. "I did not undertake the task of rainmaking as a disciple of science," he later told a researcher, "but because the crops . . . needed rain and needed it badly."[5]

Unlike his humiliated predecessor, Post was in the unique position of being able to self-fund his experiments. Between 1910 and 1913, Post spent $50,000—$1.2 million in 2017 dollars—waging a relentless battle against the clouds, first sending up a kite loaded with dynamite and then, when that proved unsatisfying, detonating fourteen-pound bundles of dynamite spaced fifty feet apart on the ground of the Caprock, on thirteen separate occasions. Just one of those "rain battles" as he called them involved twelve tons of explosives.

The results were, to put it charitably, inconclusive, and what little rain did fall afterward critics credited to nature rather than to Post. He gave up and in 1913 sold off his interests in the utopian community he had founded. He never returned to Post. He committed suicide a year later.

There is an odd coda to the Post story. Three years after his death, in the midst of the Great War, a war that among other things led scientists finally to conclude that concussionism was a dry hole, the outskirts of Post were the site of a spectacular final send-off for the theory and for the town's namesake.

Fearing that German agents would somehow find their way to Garza County and use the twenty-four thousand pounds of dynamite Post had left behind in a grand act of sabotage, the town leaders of Post obtained permission to blow it all up. On April 17, 1917, in the throes of yet another deadly drought that gripped most of Texas, the town of Post was rocked, as the *Corsica Daily Sun* would later put it, by "a tremendous explosion," that "sounded requiem for the rainmaker's experiments."[6]

The skies were not impressed. That year was the third driest in the state's history.

Though the spectacular flameouts of Dyrenforth and Post, and the studies conducted over the battlefields of France during World War I, doused the last flickering embers of ardor for the pseudoscience of concussionism, they did not extinguish completely the burning desire among people to find a way to make it rain.

It was clear that the clouds couldn't be beaten into submission. But maybe they could be seduced.

It took a high school dropout from Schenectady, New York, a motivated autodidact who had an uncommon fascination with snowflakes, to figure out the mystery that had confounded philosophers and scientists for thousands of years, to find a way to tickle the clouds to rain.

"Well-trained men wouldn't do the things I do," Vincent J. Schaefer, the self-taught chemist who invented cloud seeding, once quipped. "If I found anything, it's most likely because I didn't know better."[7]

A natural tinkerer with a naturalist's eye, he was, according to those who knew him, a guy with a sharp mind and a talent for making friends. According to a biography that was kept among his papers in the archives of the State University of New York at Albany's M. E. Grenander School, he reluctantly had dropped out of school when he was just fifteen, in no small part because his family needed his help to support his four brothers and sisters. He tried his hand at a couple of things. He worked a drill press for General Electric and found that not to his liking. He spent some time working as a tree surgeon and apprentice gardener, but that didn't hold his interest either.

Through one of his other interests—he was an avid hiker and an amateur archaeologist who studied the pre-Columbian artifacts of his beloved Adirondack Mountains—he had cultivated some powerful friends among the upper crust of Schenectady society, among them the Nobel prize–winning chemist at General Electric, Irving Langmuir.

Langmuir clearly saw something in the young man, and not long after Schaefer returned to General Electric, this time as a model maker in the research department, Langmuir took him under his wing. By the time he was twenty-six, Schaefer had worked his way up to becoming a research assistant, and by 1938, he had published a sufficient number of papers on complex issues that he was made a research associate, working throughout World War II on military technology, including finding ways to create artificial fog to blind an enemy.

It was a boyhood fascination of his—the unique nature of individual snowflakes and the mystery of how they formed—that led to

Schaefer's most significant achievement. He had already found a way to preserve the images of snowflakes, instantaneously and before they melted. He would capture them on a strip of treated plastic of his own invention called Formvar. That gave him a deep understanding of their architecture. It also made him a bit of a celebrity. National magazines, amused by the novelty of Schaefer's discovery, wrote laudatory articles, and schoolchildren badgered him with letters to see if he could help them win their local science fairs.

But he was still no closer to figuring out how to make snowflakes.

As much on a lark as anything, he had rigged an old freezer at General Electric, and he would breathe into the freezer, shining a light on his condensed breath and then sprinkle a variety of substances on it in the hopes that they would be the nuclei around which a snowflake would form. He tried household chemicals, salt and talcum powder, and even sand.

Nothing really worked.

Not even the freezer.

On one particularly hot day in July 1946, while Schaefer was conducting an experiment, the freezer started to fail. Quickly, he grabbed some dry ice and stuffed it inside to cool things down. His next breath triggered a breathtaking display as thousands of ice nuclei, each containing a prism, formed.

He had made it snow in that little box.

A few months later, in November, Schaefer tried the experiment again, this time in the world outside the laboratory. Flying above the Berkshires in western Massachusetts, he released six pounds of dry ice into the sky. "It seemed as if the cloud almost exploded," he wrote in his notebook at the time.[8] A steady snow began to fall.

A short time later, a colleague of his, Dr. Bernard Vonnegut, refined the process, swapping out the dry ice for silver iodide, and together they discovered that if you could make it snow, you could also make it rain.

So it was that a high school dropout and failed gardener with a faulty freezer unraveled the mystery of rainmaking and launched the modern age of weather modification. Or, as Dr. Vonnegut's brother, the late writer Kurt, might have put it, "so it goes."

Schaefer and Vonnegut had high hopes for their discovery. They had imagined that their process would evolve to the point at which we could conjure thunderheads at will, breaking droughts, or that we could target them precisely enough to douse raging forest fires. Conversely, they believed that if you could seed the clouds before a major hailstorm formed—a bane of farmers, homeowners, and anyone with a windshield in Texas, where more insurance claims for hail damage were filed than anywhere else in the nation between 2013 and 2015[9]—you could urge the storm to make a constellation of far smaller hailstones that would melt and evaporate before they hit the ground, reducing damage.

Indeed, for the next twenty years, between the 1950s and the 1970s, weather modification entered a kind of golden age. Experiments, funded by both the states and the federal government, were carried out across the American West—the High Plains of Texas were considered a particularly promising testing ground.

While the results of those experiments remain cloudy, the US military apparently had enough faith in the process to draft it during the Vietnam conflict. Between 1967 and 1972, in an effort to deny the North Vietnamese army the use of the Ho Chi Minh trail, the Department of Defense launched a top-secret plan dubbed "Operation Popeye," dispatching the US Air Force's 54th Weather Reconnaissance Squadron to "make mud, not war," sprinkling the clouds above the trail with silver iodide in the hopes of extending the monsoon season and flooding the road.[10] Though the United States has since signed a treaty banning the use of weather modification, back then the military considered the operation a success.

In the decades since, weather modification techniques have been deployed around the world by desperate governments and agencies in water-starved regions. In one year alone, 2011, the Chinese government spent $150 million on a single cloud-seeding experiment, and in 2008 that government claimed that it used the technology successfully to force clouds to release their rains early, so rain would not mar the opening and closing ceremonies of the Beijing Olympics.[11]

So far, however, it remains unclear just how effective all those efforts have been.

While there is a growing body of evidence that the technology can increase precipitation, the question remains—can it be done predictably and on a sufficiently large enough scale to provide a reliable source of water? As Dr. Rob Jackson, an environmental researcher from Stanford, put it in a May 30, 2016, interview with *Chemical and Engineering News*, "I think you can squeeze out a little more snow or rain in some places under some conditions, but that's quite different from a program claiming to reliably increase precipitation."

And there are also environmental questions raised by the practice. While there is no evidence that lacing the skies with silver iodide has led to unhealthy levels of the stuff settling on the ground after a rainfall, there are concerns that if the practice were expanded, it could.

There also is the question, Whose rain is it anyway? If there is only so much precipitation that can be wrung from a wandering cloud, and it is wrung out in one place, does that mean it is stolen from others downwind who might have been counting on it?

Leave it to litigious Texans to tackle that question. In 1958, a group of farmers in Jeff Davis County, lamenting their climatological misfortune, sued Southwest Weather Research, one of several early companies that had spring up to exploit Schaefer's discovery, after the farmers spotted the company's pilots flying around trying to suppress hail. The farmers feared that the operation would not just suppress hail but also limit the rains that fell. The local court granted a temporary injunction against the company. On appeal, later upheld by the Texas Supreme Court, the Texas Court of Appeals ruled that as a point of law, the farmers had the same rights to the resources that floated above their land as they had to those—like groundwater—that collected below it. "We believe that the landowner is entitled . . . to such rainfall as may come from clouds over his own property that Nature in her caprice may provide."[12]

That ruling—that the rule of capture applies as much to heaven as to earth—did little to stop cloud seeding in Texas, though now the law does stipulate that only licensed companies can seed the clouds and that before they do, they have to warn the neighbors, once a week for three weeks in the local newspaper of record.

After spending $11.5 million in seed money between 1997 and 2004 to get cloud-seeding programs around the state started and another $1.5 million to study the results, the state no longer funds cloud-seeding projects. But they continue apace.

In fact, according to the Texas Department of Licensing and Regulation, in 2016 there were six cloud-seeding operations in the skies over about one-sixth of the state, 28.2 million acres in northwest and south Texas. The chemicals and compounds now used go far beyond silver iodide, says George Bomar, a meteorologist who manages the Texas Department of Licensing and Regulation's regulatory program for weather modification. Pilots in the West Texas Weather Modification Area in San Angelo, the South Texas Weather Modification Association south of San Antonio, those working for the EAA, the Trans Pecos Weather Modification Association, the Rolling Plains operation, and the Panhandle Groundwater Conservation District all carry skyward a mixture designed specifically to attack the clouds in each region. And they have all seen promising results. "While it's true we've not gotten to the point of providing undeniable proof that cloud seeding is a sure bet," Bomar says, "the available evidence, as it continues to accumulate, is highly suggestive of a positive impact."

How positive? An analysis of those six regional operations in 2015 concluded that seeded thunderstorms appeared to have lasted an average of twenty minutes longer and produced 137 percent more rain than those that had not been seeded.

That optimistic assessment has been embraced in the 2017 state water plan. "About 22,000 acre-feet per year of supply from weather modification strategies is recommended in 2070," the water plan concludes. That may seem a staggering amount. But in fact, in a state that expects its water demand to increase to 21.6 million acre-feet a year by 2070 at the same time that available water supplies decline from the 13.6 million acre-feet currently available, it is a drop in the bucket—about the amount of water the state's largest utilities deliver every month to their major industrial customers.[13]

Clearly, blasting the skies with artillery and munitions, or seeding the clouds with silver iodide, is never going to be a silver bullet for Texas's water woes. For that, you would need a vision as wide and deep as the Gulf of Mexico. You need to peer as deep as the alkaline aquifers of West Texas.

Travel even further back in history than Plautus and the Greeks, and you will find that humans have always dreamed of turning salt-water sweet. And there are scores of examples where by either dint of luck or divine intervention, they did, at least on a small scale.

In the *Book of Exodus*, for example, after wandering for three days without water, the Israelites stumble across an oasis with water unfit to drink. They call it Marah—the Hebrew word for "bitter." Some biblical scholars have speculated that the spring was located in either the Suez or south of Beersheba in southern Israel, areas which to this day contain a number of brackish aquifers. True to form, the Bible tells us, the Israelites grumbled. "The people mur-mured against Moses, saying, 'What shall we drink?' And he cried unto the Lord; and the Lord shewed him a tree," and in what may be the first recorded example of brackish water desalinization, when Moses tossed the tree into the spring, "the waters were made sweet."[14]

More than two thousand years ago, there were unconfirmed reports that ancient Chinese experimenters had come up with a way to filter saltwater through treated bamboo sheets in earthenware jugs to produce potable water, though thus far little evidence has been found to support the legend.[15]

And Aristotle himself speculated that saltwater could be turned fresh through a similar process, writing "if one plunges a watertight vessel of wax into the ocean, it will hold after twenty-four hours a certain quantity of water that filtered into it through the waxen walls, and this water will be found to be potable, because the earthy and salty components have been sieved off."

While these early references to desalination—particularly in China and Greece—seem to presage the modern techniques of osmosis and reverse osmosis used to desalinate large quantities of water, there is no evidence that they were ever employed to any great extent. Instead, for most of the next two millennia, desalination remained a small, strictly retail operation. Sailors at sea, looking for freshwater, would use the most primitive technique to get it. They would simply gather up a few gallons of seawater, built a fire aboard ship, and boil off the water, collecting it as it distilled.

It would take centuries before anyone stumbled across a way to treat saltwater on an industrial scale, and, like so many other aspects of humans' long and convoluted struggle to find enough water, it was an unintended consequence, the result of an attempt to solve an entirely different problem.

Engineer and inventor Norbert Rillieux, a Creole from New Orleans, wasn't trying to freshen the seas when he invented the multistage evaporator in the 1830s. He was trying to lessen the workload and the danger for slaves on Louisiana's sugar plantations. At the time, the process of refining sugar was primitive: it involved boiling vats of cane juice and letting the syrup thicken, transferring the scalding-hot liquid repeatedly into smaller and smaller vessels as it thickened.

Rillieux developed a process in which cane juice boiled in one chamber produced enough steam to boil the juice again as it collected in a second chamber, at lower pressure and thus at a lower temperature, and then again in a third and so on. The process consumed a lot less time, used a lot less energy, and left a lot fewer cane workers with burns and scalds. It was hailed as a triumph for the sugar industry.

It took another fifty years or so before anybody figured out that there might be other applications for the process. By the end of the nineteenth century, however, a modified version of Rillieux's contraption had found its way aboard steamships as a means of bettering the Greeks in terms of desalting seawater, and a few experimental distilleries were built in the Middle East.

By the 1950s the technology had morphed, and the multistage flash process had come into vogue. By means of intense heat in the first stage, salty or brackish water is passed through a series of chambers, again at lower pressure, in which some of the water evaporates and freshwater condenses at the top while increasingly brinish water collects at the bottom of the chamber. That process was further refined and gave rise to the Multi-Effect Distillation System, currently in use in the US Virgin Islands and other places in the Caribbean where freshwater is scarce and seawater abounds, and it pretty much does the same thing as the multistage process but more efficiently and at a lower temperature.

By the 1960s, however, new and far more effective means of coaxing freshwater out of seawater had emerged, and in a way, these methods drew on the beliefs that had buoyed the ancient Chinese and intrigued Aristotle. In the 1950s, the US government, through the Office of Saline Water, began funding research into ways to desalinate large quantities of seawater or to reclaim brackish water found in aquifers throughout the American West. Researchers discovered that through the process of osmosis, highly saline water on one side of a membrane would be drawn to less salty water on the other, and that the result would be a less salty solution on both sides. Researchers further speculated that if the process was reversed, if the saltier solution were placed under greater pressure, that more of the freshwater would slip through the membrane and that a more concentrated brine would be left behind. In 1960, researchers at the University of California at Los Angeles figured out how to do just that, and the modern age of desalination began.

It is worth noting that back in the early days of large-scale desalination, Texas was on the cutting edge. One of the world's first demonstration plants for Multi-Stage Flash Distillation was built by Dow Chemical at Freeport as part of a joint program between the federal government and the chemical manufacturer. When the million-gallon-a-day plant opened on June 21, 1961, Vice President Lyndon Johnson was on hand. But it fell to the president, John F. Kennedy, to flip the switch from the Oval Office. In a speech to mark the occasion, Kennedy said, "No water resources program is of greater long-range importance than our efforts to convert water from the world's greatest and cheapest natural resources—our oceans—into water fit for our homes and industry. Such a breakthrough would end bitter struggles between neighbors, states and nations."

In the decades since, thousands of seawater and brackish water desalination plants have been constructed or planned all over the world, from drought-ridden California to sunbaked and water-starved Israel and Australia. Saudi Arabia has spent billions on desalination, and seawater is now the source for about half the potable water consumed in the kingdom.

In drought-prone Texas, however, desalination is still trying to find its sea legs. While there are more than one hundred brackish water desalination operations in Texas, most run by local water utilities, and more are in the works, the vast Gulf of Mexico remains largely untapped.

Without question, it would be a costly strategy. In fact, seawater desalination is among the costliest answers to dwindling water supplies. Saudi Arabia recently spent $7.9 billion on just one desalination plant. And then there is the cost of the pipelines that would need to be built to carry the freshened water, both in terms of money and in the disruption caused to people in their path. The state's most recent water plan estimates that desalted seawater could cost as much as $1,431 per acre-foot by 2070, twice what it is expected to cost to treat brackish water.

Those costs, in all likelihood, would be borne by consumers.

There are also environmental concerns. Desalination leaves behind brine, not all that different than the brine produced by oil and gas wells. And just like that brine, it would have to be disposed of, either by injection deep underground, raising the specter of earthquakes like those reported around disposal wells in Oklahoma and elsewhere, not to mention the risk, though slight, of groundwater contamination, or it could be dumped into the sea. That raises the risk of creating highly saline dead zones, environmentalists warn. In addition, there is the challenge of developing the kind of hardened desalination plants and the network of pipelines that would be strong enough to withstand the kind of beating that they would be subjected to in a future full of storms as furious as Hurricane Harvey. That kind of unrelenting natural fury not only can threaten the plants and pipelines themselves but can cut off the electrical power needed to operate the facilities, rendering them, at least temporarily, useless. Indeed, a few weeks after Hurricane Harvey barreled into

Texas, Hurricane Irma cut a swath through Florida, leaving some of that state's desalination plants largely intact but impotent until electrical service was restored.

Perhaps those challenges could be met. Dr. Robert Mace, a hydrologist by training who, as deputy assistant director for water science and conservation at the TWDB, has become the state government's go-to guy for all things water related, is confident that they can be. "That stuff can be engineered and dealt with," Mace said.

With the same perfect faith as Dyrenforth and the ancient Hebrews, Mace believes that, in the long run, salt and brackish water may be Texas's salvation. Indeed, El Paso currently treats twenty-seven million gallons a year of brackish water from its remote aquifers, and San Antonio is building an even larger plant. The state estimates that somewhere between 1 and 1.4 percent of its water—about 116,000 acre-feet of it—will come from the sea by 2070.[16]

Like everything else in water policy in Texas, it may take a prolonged drought to get people to support such a major engineering endeavor, but at least as far as Mace is concerned, the Gulf of Mexico is Texas' ace in the hole.

"Sometimes I think, what are we gonna do one hundred years out if we get hit with a drought far worse than the drought of record?" Mace says. "The Gulf of Mexico helps me sleep at night."

In a worst-case scenario he says, the Gulf "becomes a source of seawater desalination. If the state found itself in an unprecedented drought, I'm confident that we would be building seawater desalination plants and treating the water."

It would not be cheap. It would not be easy. But it could be done.

But is Mace's optimism realistic?

You can certainly lead a horse to treated water, or in this case, lead treated water to the horse. But as we will see in the next chapter, the real question is, can you make it drink?

In parts of Texas, that remains an open question.

CHAPTER 10

A TALE OF TWO COLONIAS

IT IS A TORPID LATE AFTERNOON in October, and at the Chili Pepper Café just outside Terlingua, the lunch rush, such as it is, is over. A rattletrap old Dodge pickup, the same color as the gravel in the parking lot, has just hissed its way onto the road north toward Alpine. The driver, a regular, left a decent tip. It is still sitting on the table as Dymphna De La Rosa, named to the consternation of her family's parish priest after the Irish patron saint of the mentally ill, sets down a glass of water in front of me, the café's sole remaining customer. The water is room temperature, is crystal clear, and tastes—well, it tastes like water.

And though it is free to customers—you only have to ask for it at the Chili Pepper Café—it is among the costliest water in the state of Texas. A thousand cubic feet of the stuff—roughly what the average Texas household uses in a month[1]—pumped out of the briny Santa Elena Aquifer and filtered through the stacked membranes in the state-of-the-art reverse osmosis desalination plant at the nearby Study Butte treatment facility costs $17. That is on top of the $40-per-month minimum customers must pay, authorities say, and the average household pays about $100 a month for service, more than three times the state average. That is especially dear in a place like Terlingua, where, according to the last US Census in 2010, the per capita income was $28,125 a year.

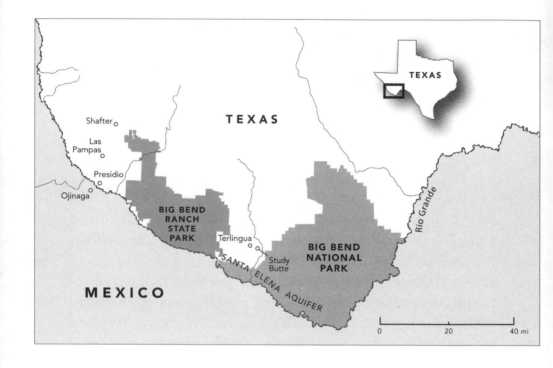

TEXAS

TEXAS

Shafter

Las
Pampas

Presidio

Ojinaga

BIG BEND
RANCH
STATE
PARK

Terlingua

Study
Butte

SANTA ELENA AQUIFER

BIG BEND
NATIONAL
PARK

Rio Grande

MEXICO

0   20   40 mi

The cost makes water among the most precious commodities in this odd and eclectic community at the edge of the vast Chihuahuan Desert. For some, it is a luxury they are willing to indulge even at the cost of other, less liquid pleasures.

"My brother-in-law works for the water company," De La Rosa tells me. "He says that you can tell whether somebody's Mexican or American by their water bills."

"How?" I ask.

"The Mexicans love to plant flowers around their houses—I love flowers," De La Rosa says. "And baths. The Mexicans love to takes baths. The hippies? Not so much."

You might be surprised to find what generally is regarded as one of the state's most modern and efficient desalination plants in a place like Terlingua, or that there is another, even more modern one that serves the guests at the nearby luxury resort of Lajitas. You might be equally surprised to learn that, despite the harsh desert conditions here, most of the fifty-eight residents of the ghost town of Terlingua or the roughly two thousand more who are scattered around the harsh countryside nearby turn their nose up at the extensively treated water. In fact, of those two thousand–odd residents who could hook up to the local water supply, only about twelve percent have done so. "I believe we have 228 customers," said Virgil Clark, the affable and hard-working manager of the Study Butte Water Supply Corporation in an interview shortly before his 2016 death at sixty-six of a heart attack. "We have what's been called . . . the most sophisticated water treatment system in West Texas."

And yet, for many in this odd, colorful community built around an abandoned cinnabar mining town at the edge of Big Bend National Park, it has become almost a badge of honor—a cultural touchstone every bit as telling as the Mexicans' long baths and floral displays—to remain proudly unshackled to the municipal water supply. Button-hole a Terlinguan and sooner or later they proudly will tell you how deep into the last drought they made it before they finally had to hook up the trailer and drive to Study Butte to fill up their tanks for a few dollars.

There are a number of reasons for that. One, Clark said, is the nature of the place itself and the people who are drawn there. If people outside Terlingua know of it at all, it is as the title of a Jerry Jeff Walker album (*Viva Terlingua!*) or as the site of an annual chili cook-off that draws upward of twenty thousand people each autumn to this strange little ghost town.

But to many residents, it is proudly hailed as the epicenter of weird in West Texas, a place that makes the goings on of the arts community in Marfa look like a dinner party for the Daughters of the American Revolution. It is a place that attracts New Agers and End Timers and tie-dyed, back-to-the-land refugees from every corner of the nation to a place where they can dig a hole, make adobe bricks out of the mud, and build a self-sustaining shelter against the world and the harsh desert sun. Among its most famous former residents was David Kaczynski, the less violent older brother of Unabomber Ted Kaczynski, who came here more than thirty years ago looking to live off the grid.

In fact, residents will proudly tell you they were led here to this secluded haven one hundred miles from the nearest Walmart by fate or luck or the unseen hand of the universe and decided to stay precisely because this was a place where you could make your own buckhorn-handled knife and cut the umbilical cord that previously bound you to the modern world of municipal water supplies and noncomposting toilets. If you are up to it.

"This is our island," says Zoey Sexton, a mature woman who refuses to say how "deep into her cronedom" she actually is, but who shares that she accidentally migrated here twenty-four years ago after retiring from a job in Minnesota. It is not a place suited to dilettantes, she says. "It's our unique island that attracts a certain kind of people. And you can almost tell when somebody's come here and says, 'Oh, I'm going to move here,' and you say to yourself, 'I'll give them two months.'"

To a great degree, though no one intended it to be, Terlingua and its environs, the most sparsely populated part of one of the state's most sparsely populated regions, have turned into a kind of laboratory and a battlefield, where two contending approaches to providing water have, for almost two decades now, been duking it out. On the one hand, you have the pump-it, treat-it, and sell-it model of the privately owned and federally subsidized Study Butte Water Supply Corporation and its cutting-edge desalination plant. On the other, you have a more small "d" democratic approach, one more aligned with the history of the place, where the denizens of the old abandoned mining town would, once upon a time, scoop up whatever rainwater they could, rely on the vagaries of the creek, and hope for the best. Walk the dusty trail from the water treatment plant to Terlingua and, as you come up behind most houses or the few businesses there, you will see large water catchment tanks, dozens of them. For many in this community, these large plastic tanks that catch the sporadic rains when they fall are their principal source of potable water. Yes, they hoard it—water conservation isn't just a virtue in a place like this, it is a survival strategy, they will tell you. And—except during the longest and deepest of droughts—the tanks are usually enough to sustain them.

State water planners have embraced both strategies. There are currently forty-six brackish water desalination plants in Texas, thirty-four of them treating brackish groundwater, among them the tiny facility in Terlingua and the 27.5-million-gallons-per-day Kay Bailey Hutchison Desalination plant 316 miles away in El Paso, the world's largest inland desalination facility. Together, these thirty-four plants had the capacity to provide 73 million gallons of treated water per day to customers in 2016.[2] But that is just a fraction of what briny aquifers could produce. According to the state comptroller's office, there are, within twenty-six of the state's thirty major aquifers, 880 trillion gallons of brackish water, 2.7 billion acre-feet of the stuff, enough to flood the entire state of Texas under fifteen feet of water. If it were all treated and pumped to consumers, it would be enough to meet the current demand for water for the entire state for 150 years,[3] officials say. As it is, state water planners have high hopes for this brackish deep water. By 2020, the state water plan recommends that the state be in a position to treat and deliver 111,000 acre-feet a year, and by all indications, they are well on their way. The San Antonio Water System, for example, located in one of the thirstiest metropolitan areas of the nation, expects the first phase of its new brackish water desalination plant to produce twelve million gallons of water per day from the salty depths of the Carrizo-Wilcox aquifer initially, rising, if all goes according to plan, to thirty million gallons a day by 2026.

But all that newfound water comes at a cost. When all is said and done, the San Antonio plant, for example, will cost $411 million. That isn't counting the costs of operating the facility. Or the debt service that goes along with such a massive undertaking. Indeed, for every gallon of water produced by a brackish water desalination plant in Texas, between $2.03 and $3.19 is sunk in capital costs. Depending on a variety of factors, including the saltiness of the water, it can cost up to $2.04 for every thousand gallons of brackish water treated.[4] And in most cases, those costs will be passed along to the consumer.

How the consumers might react to the added cost of water is, at this point, anybody's guess. But if the reaction in Terlingua is any indication of what the future holds, many will do what Texans have often done and simply declare their independence.

Ask Carolyn Burr, an entrepreneur who provides both bottled water and rain catchment systems to Terlinguans, about the water from the Study Butte treatment facility and, like one of those ancient Israelites at the Springs of Marah, she will wrinkle her nose and complain about the flavor. "I can't stand the taste of it," she said. "But evidently it passes muster to get those federal grants to keep those few people supplied with water."

That kind of slanderous allegation against the flavor of the water used to gall Virgil Clark. "I just had water at the Chili Pepper Café . . . and it was really good-tasting water," he told me, obviously wounded. Indeed, probe a little deeper, he said, and you will discover that it is not the water but the cost of it that leaves a bad taste in the mouth of many Terlinguans.

"Our water rates are probably the highest in the state," he said. It is not only that the facility—and ultimately the customer—has to deal with the cost of coaxing out water that averages 1,400 parts per million of total dissolved solids through twenty-eight membranes that cost $600 a piece. Nor is it just that those membranes have to suck out radionuclides as well as salt—there are small traces of uranium, radium 226, and radium 228 in the aquifer. But in Terlingua, which is technically classified as a "colonia"—essentially described by the state as an illegal subdivision lacking in at least some basic services—every new hookup requires a substantial and expensive investment in new infrastructure.

"You have service where the pipeline is, and where it isn't . . . it's cost prohibitive" to put it in, Clark said.

Add to that the fact that many Terlinguans, drawn to this place precisely because it is so remote, so off the grid, seem to be genetically predisposed to going their own way, and you can easily see why the state-of-the-art desalination plant at Study Butte is facing stiff competition from the new booming industry in town—rainwater catchment systems.

Rainwater harvesting, as many of its boosters call it, is, of course, an ancient technology, if the word *technology* can be stretched far enough to cover such a basic survival technique.

But it has been enjoying a kind of renaissance, becoming increasingly popular in Texas in recent years and wildly popular in Terlingua, in no small part because of the cost. The TWDB estimates that it can cost anywhere between $8,000 and $10,000 to get started—purchasing the tanks and setting up pipes to carry the rainwater once you catch it are the major expenses. In the twenty-four years since Zoey Sexton wandered down from the Land of Ten Thousand Lakes and, in her words, "lost my heart to this this place," she estimates that she has spent somewhere in the neighborhood of $13,000 to install twenty thousand gallons worth of rainwater storage. That is about the same amount that she and her husband have spent over the years rigging their remote home outside town with solar panels so that they can remain as self-sufficient as possible.

But once you get through with those expenses, she notes proudly, the rain, like the sunlight, is free. Try to drill a well in the coarse sands around Terlingua—it can cost up to $15,000 to sink one—and chances are you will come up dry, Sexton says. Even if you do hit water, it is often so hot and saline, "even my horse won't drink it." And yet, drilling one can add to a homeowner's property tax bill. "When you drill a well, your tax rate changes," she said.

Hoist a twelve-hundred-gallon tank up onto the roof, or throw it in the backyard, however, and the State of Texas will actually subsidize you. Recent changes to the state's tax code have made rainwater-harvesting equipment exempt from sales tax. What is more, the state "allows the exemption of part or all of the assessed value of the property on which approved water conservation initiatives, such as rainwater harvesting, are made,"[5] according to the state tax code.

The state has done that because it aggressively is trying to promote rainwater harvesting as a means of taking the pressure off its overtaxed water sources. In other words, as a means of conservation. Indeed, by 2070, state water planners conservatively hope to see seventeen thousand acre-feet of rainwater used to offset the demand on other supplies. In the City of Austin, where it rains thirty-two inches a year on average, and where a rain catchment system can expect to collect about one-tenth of an acre-foot a year annually, water planners are far more optimistic; they expect to harvest more than sixteen thousand acre-feet of rainwater in their city alone by 2070, according to the list of recommended strategies appended to the state water plan.[6]

In Terlingua, however, residents need no incentive to conserve water, at least not from the state, Sexton says. There is no surface water to speak of, the water from the treatment plant is costly, wells are expensive and unreliable, and so, every drop of the 12.15 inches of rain that falls each year—most of it coming down in buckets during brief but violent gully washers during the monsoon season from June to October—is precious, she says.

She does not dispute Dymphna De La Rosa's assertion that the "hippies" of Terlingua eschew long, luxurious baths. In fact, she embraces it. "I don't know a girl here who washes her hair every day," she says. To do so would be considered wasteful, almost profligate. "You have to learn to go with the flow of the desert . . . you learn to conserve and you must be willing to do that," she says.

Indeed, in a place like Terlingua, hair that has gone a little stringy or a pair of jeans that could use a wash are symbols of self-sufficiency and a fierce tie-dyed independence. Even during the depth of the drought that dried up most of Texas between 2010 and 2015, Terlinguans held out as long as they could before finally giving in to reality, carting their water tanks to the treatment plant and filling them up for a nickel a gallon.

Sexton takes pride in having made it almost to the end of the drought before she ran out of water. That experience has doubled her resolve to become even more independent, she says. "We learned from that experience," she says. "We expanded our water catchment system at home. We bought a couple more tanks . . . that will never happen again."

It may seem counterintuitive, but that countercultural instinct that seems to prod Sexton to individual action—that fierce independence that marks the entire odd collection of Jeremiahs who have settled here in Terlingua from all over the nation—may, in fact, be the glue that holds this community together.

You can see a hint of that on an overcast Saturday morning in October at the community garden. Under a corrugated aluminum awning, a young woman in a sari dances to imaginary music with a toddler. At a table a few feet away, over a plate of gluten-free muffins, an older man with a white, hand-stitched buckskin jacket, a turquoise ten-gallon hat the same color as a Chihuahuan sky, and a gray mustache you could comb with a pitchfork chats with his neighbors about the weather. "Not much rain," he says. It is hard to tell, but from the twinkle in his eye, he may be smiling under that mustache.

To a great degree, the community garden at Terlingua, a chicken-wire-enclosed quarter acre of reclaimed desert scree perched above the usually dry Terlingua Creek, has become a kind of local cultural touchstone for the folks who live in and around the ghost town. Artisans and bakers, some of whom grow most of their own ingredients, often in the community garden, come here once a week to set up tables and hawk their wares, mostly to each other. It is what economists like to refer to as a multiplier effect, one modest investment sparking others until a kind of economy begins to take root. "We've created a venue for people to have a reliable income, and there are people who rely on that, on the market, for a portion of their income. Selling their pots and their baked goods or whatever."

What started as a tiny little gesture by a handful of back-to-the-land pioneers, little by little, has grown into a regular event, a monthly market day. It is part country fair, part kaffee klatch.

Mostly, though, it is a chance to show off and celebrate what they consider to be their victory against the harsh desert conditions, and their dedication to the idea that they can win that victory on their own terms, using what little rain comes their way. In the summer, they plant melons and squash, even experimenting with ancient crops, beans and amaranth, for example, that are resistant to long dry spells. They brought in an archeologist to help them decide what to plant in the future. "The . . . archeologist has done a lot of studying about the indigenous peoples and how they grew and what they grew. And he was trying to create a similar situation," Sexton said.

So far, the community garden has thrived.

They have found that it usually rains just enough in summer to sustain the crops, Sexton says. And when the summer rains come up short, the water they catch in their tanks is generally enough to carry them through.

In the winter, "we plant out grains, chards, kale, mustard, spinach, broccoli, and cauliflower. Last year, after harvest, we weighed 550 pounds of greens," she said. "That's a lot of greens."

In fact, Sexton said, the gardeners of Terlingua are now considering plans to expand the operation, expanding the garden beyond its fifty-by-eighty-foot enclosure and maybe even bringing in interns to help tend it.

And in the increasingly likely event that one day the rains may not fall sufficiently to water the garden, in Terlingua, at least, there is always a safety net.

In a way, that is the lesson of Terlingua, where two seemingly contradictory approaches to water management—the industrial approach taken by the Study Butte Water Supply Corporation and the insurgent rainwater-harvesting movement—both supported in different ways by government—have developed a kind of synergy, Clark said. The independence, self-reliance, and frugality of the people that live there have a benefit, he said; it takes the pressure off the water authority in a place where water is precious. And for the hearty hippies of Terlingua, there is the comforting certainty that if the heavens don't provide enough water, the Study Butte Water Supply Corporation can.

There are, however, plenty of other communities, forgotten colonias along the Mexican–American border that are not as fortunate as Terlingua.

Las Pampas, a scattering of double-wide trailers and ramshackle houses on a desiccated spit of sand sixty miles to the west in Presidio County, is a case in point. A couple of decades ago, a pair of fast-talking real estate developers from the upper Midwest lured unsuspecting immigrants here with big promises of small down payments, easy terms, and a shot at the American Dream, says former Presidio County judge Monroe Elms. They also promised them water, he said. They didn't deliver. Instead, they pocketed their profits and vanished, leaving the residents of Las Pampas high and very, very dry.

That means that the fifty or so residents of this colonia—part of an overlooked subculture of an estimated 500,000 people,[7] most of them poor, more than one-third of them immigrants mostly from Mexico who often live in conditions like these in 2,294 such colonias within a few dozen miles of the 1,248-mile border between Texas and Mexico—are on their own.

Like many colonias, there are only the most rudimentary amenities. There is no surface water to speak of. Cipelo Creek, which snakes alongside the community, is dry most of the time—water rights owners upstream siphon off what little water does flow long before it reaches Las Pampas. When the rains do fall, the creek floods the village in a flash and disappears again just as quickly. As one resident wryly put it, "I had plenty of water three times in two months."

It is far too costly to pipe water five miles uphill from Presidio to service a handful of poor people. Forty percent of those who live in the state's colonias live below the poverty line, and almost twenty percent more of them are close to it, according to a 2015 report by the Federal Reserve Bank of Dallas.

And since the water won't come to them, most of the thirty or so remaining residents of Las Pampas go to the water, driving large tanks on the beds of their pickups down to Presidio a couple of times a month to fill up, says Charlotte Ishakawa, a resident who now splits her time between Presidio, where she has access to both clean water and a doctor to help her through her battle with cancer, and Las Pampas, where she has neither of those things.

It is enough of a hardship that little by little, Ishakawa says, many of the residents have just given up and moved on. The challenges the people of Las Pampas face are not uncommon. In fact, they are replicated in similar communities all across south Texas, says Dr. William Hargrove, a researcher for the University of Texas at El Paso who has spent decades studying colonias. "Las Pampas is not unique. Their story is multiplied all up and down the border, unfortunately."

It is not just that they were swindled by unscrupulous developers, says Monroe Elms, the former Presidio County judge who spent years futilely trying to rally the residents of Las Pampas to take legal action against the developers. The powers that be in Presidio County also turned a blind eye to their plight, he said.

Elms pushes back on a hardwood chair under a lush canopy of grapevines on his well-watered piece of land in the ghost town of Shafter, a few miles north of Las Pampas, a place that one could easily mistake for a villa in Tuscany if it weren't for the loaded nine-millimeter handgun on the wooden table next to a carafe of water. Elms measures his words carefully. Up here, Elms has plenty of water. (Though, as we will see later, there were concerns about potential contamination from the old copper mine across the road from his place; those worries for the most part have been addressed.) His wells produce enough for his needs, and though there are occasional disputes among neighbors over whether or not someone periodically takes more than their fair share from Cipelo Creek, there is usually enough left over to maintain at least a trickle in the creek bed. He sees that trickle as a mark of his prosperity and a sign of his standing in the community.

To be sure, he says, part of the reason Las Pampas largely has been ignored can be chalked up to racial animus. Like Brewster County, where the thriving, eccentric town of Terlingua is located, Presidio County is split north to south, he says. "People in the north of Brewster County don't care about the people in the south county. They got a big split. And we've got a split here. Theirs is more politically based," with "ultraconservatives" calling the shots in the northern part of the county while the hippies do their own thing in Terlingua. "Ours is more racially motivated," Elms says.

But there might be an even darker reason that Las Pampas has been ignored, one steeped in a particularly ignominious chapter of Presidio County's not-so-distant history, he says.

He recalls an incident a quarter century ago, at a time when he actively was trying to persuade the residents of Las Pampas to organize themselves, to sue the developers in an effort to force them to provide the water they had promised. That was, at the time, their best chance to wring water—or at least some satisfaction—out of the land they had purchased, Elms said. Because, like most colonias, it was an illegal development, the state was limited as to the kind of action it could take on the residents' behalf. "I called the State of Texas, and they said, 'We can't give 'em water because it is an illegal subdivision, but we will send the Attorney General's Office people out to work with you to sue these gentlemen. We can't sue them. The individuals who bought the land have to sue them. But we will help them for free and get them organized,'" Elms said. "So I had a meeting, and none of them wanted to sue."

Perhaps, he says, it was a cultural problem, a natural mistrust among immigrants of government and the courts. As it turned out, he said, their mistrust was not entirely unfounded. It was just about that time, Elms recalled, that the popular, straight-arrow local sheriff, a man named Rick Thompson, pulled Elms aside and whispered in his ear, "You leave those people alone."

Elms finally figured out why Thompson had buttonholed him

about blocking efforts to water Las Pampas. Sometime before dawn on December 3, 1991, smugglers had trudged through the badlands near the community, toting twenty-four hundred pounds of cocaine, some $48 million worth of it. In what was at the time the largest drug bust in Texas history, the cocaine was later found stashed in a horse trailer outside of Marfa that Thompson had placed there. The sheriff was among those convicted in federal court of conspiracy to smuggle drugs and was sentenced to life in prison. In 2015 his sentence was reduced, and he is expected to be released from prison as early as April of 2018.[8]

The way Elms sees it, the disgraced sheriff's opposition to his efforts to bring water to Las Pampas made perfect (if perverse) sense. The desperate isolation of the impoverished, sparsely populated badlands along the Mexican border always has lured drug traffickers and coyotes to this place, he says. On a frontier like this, a thriving community can be every bit as effective as a chunk of a multibillion-dollar border wall or a platoon of government agents. But to grow, to thrive, those communities need water. Turn on the water, he says, and you might well be opening the floodgates. Leave it off, and eventually places like this will just shrivel up and die.

To their credit, state and federal agencies seemed for a time to have recognized the importance of providing basic services to the colonias. Between 2006 and 2014, the state invested tens of millions of dollars to help upgrade all infrastructure in colonias in six counties—El Paso, Maverick, Webb, Hidalgo, Starr, and Cameron. In those six counties, thousands of residents of colonias have gained access to clean water. But that funding has started to dwindle.

And as anyone still left in Las Pampas can tell you, even when the tide was rising, it did not lift all the boats. After years of trying, in 2004 Ishakawa and the residents of Las Pampas managed to secure a federal grant to drill a community well. "They went down eleven hundred feet and did not hit anything," she said. They drilled a couple of more test wells. Still nothing.

Now, she said, the community is down to about fifteen people and is holding on by a thread.

Why is it that two communities, separated by what in Texas is a comparatively short distance, located in the same arid region, facing the same harsh conditions both above- and belowground, are facing such different fates? Terlingua doesn't see a drop more water in an average year than does Las Pampas—indeed it sees about an inch less. And yet it is—at least by the standards of its residents—thriving. The residents of Las Pampas have as much right to the rain as the residents of Terlingua do and as much access to it. And yet, in time, it will probably be a ghost town.

The answer may lie in something other than water. It is not the kind of thing you can measure out in acre-feet or gallons, or even in dollars. It is something more esoteric than that. It has been said that water is life. It is also culture.

The "hippies" of Terlingua, as Dymphna De La Rosa calls them, are in many cases refugees from the American Dream. Like Zoey, they grew up steeped in it, in big-box stores and tract homes, and they were weaned on the endless pursuit of *more*. They didn't come to Terlingua looking for more. They came looking for less. Precious less. And in Terlingua, they found it in abundance.

The residents of Las Pampas, like the residents of many of the colonias that dot the landscape in south and far West Texas, are different. In many cases they were fleeing poverty, sometimes violence, in search of that same American Dream the hippies of Terlingua had rejected. In Las Pampas, the way Judge Elms, sipping water and holding forth under the canopy of his grape arbor put it, they encountered the darkest side of the American Dream. They encountered unscrupulous developers, seizing on the age-old American maxim "Never give a sucker an even break," especially if he or she speaks broken English. There were corrupt officials, like the former Presidio County sheriff who wanted that desolate stretch of desert as desolate as possible so his drug-running friends could slip through undetected. As Hargrove, the University of Texas researcher, put it, "Many of the residents of Las Pampas worked their careers in Mexico; they were Mexican citizens and they emigrated to the United States to retire, thinking they would have a better life. It hasn't turned out."

Those who could press on did. Those who couldn't, remained behind, dying off or giving up one by one until eventually, the whole place almost certainly will just dry up and blow away like the Russian thistle on the roadside.

CHAPTER 11

UP AGAINST THE WALL

Luis Amendariz falls silent as he steers his pickup truck past the equipment shed where seven of his old tractors sit rusting under a corrugated steel awning. A distant cousin of his, a guy from Virginia who has been staying with him, has promised that he will get at least one of them running. One of these days.

There is no rush, Amendariz knows. There is nothing for the tractors to do.

Sure, maybe he could press one of them into service dragging out the unwanted immigrants that have invaded his five hundred acres of Rio Grande river bottom just within the city limits of Presidio. He thinks it would be nice to get rid of the Russian thistle and the mesquite that have taken over and sucked up every drop of available water, leaving the once-rich soil parched, cracked, and tawny. There is nothing the seventy-one-year-old would love more than to see his land just one more time the way it used to be years ago in early spring and fall: scraped clean and plowed, then, in the fullness of time and sun and water, blooming, lush and green, in a meticulously tended sea of onions here, a clutch of cantaloupes there, and a carpet of alfalfa over there a little ways farther.

And maybe someday his cousin will finish working on the tractor, and Amendariz will once again climb up onto the seat, toss it into low gear, and torque this rebellious land back into submission.

But for what?

It has been years now since the farming economy around Presidio started to falter and finally collapsed. The old loading docks at the edge of town that until a decade or so ago used to groan under the weight of tons upon tons of the sweetest onions this side of Vidalia, and cantaloupes that were twice as sweet, are in ruins now. So are the warehouses. The mighty cranes that used to hoist all that produce onto railcars are rusting skeletons the color of dried blood. The railroad siding that served them is just as overgrown as Amendariz's fields. Presidio is abandoned now, hit by the double curse of the failing farm economy and a fire in 2008 that knocked out the rail bridge that links it with Chihuahua, effectively ending rail traffic through the city. There is talk the rails will come back, at least if the Mexican government and the Texas Department of Transportation follow through on their plans. There is less optimism about the farms, though.

Amendariz muscles his truck onto a dirt track that leads to the top of the levee separating his land from the Rio Grande. The river—which the Mexicans call the Rio Bravo del Norte—is less than one hundred yards wide here. Most of the time it is no more than shoulder deep, but it moves with a grace and purpose, and at least for now there would be water enough to irrigate those fallow fields of his. Amendariz knows that there is no guarantee that will continue. Drought is a constant threat here. And most of the water that passes by here comes not from the Rio Grande itself but from the Rio Concho on the Mexican side of the border. Under a seventy-five-year-old treaty, the Mexicans are supposed to release about 1.75 million acre-feet of water in every five-year period into the Rio Grande, much of it from the Rio Concho. In exchange, the United States is required to release 1.5 million acre-feet of water from the Colorado River basin in Colorado, Utah, Arizona, Nevada, and California to Sonora and Baja California in Mexico. By and large the United States has kept up with its obligations under the treaty. By contrast, some years—maybe even most years—the Mexican government comes up short. Mexico was more than one-quarter million acre-feet shy of its obligation during the drought years between 2010 and 2015, according to the US Section of the International Boundary and Water Commission, which oversees the treaty. Other years, the country releases a bit more, but there is often a water debt that Mexico owes to the United States. The way Amendariz sees it, that debt only is going to get bigger if, as he expects, those droughts keep getting drier and longer and the Mexicans feel the need to hold onto more of their water. And things will get worse still if, as he fears, escalating tensions between politicians in Washington and Austin and Mexico City and Chihuahua City get uglier, and the commingled waters of the Rio Grande and the Rio Concho become a bargaining chip, or worse, a weapon in an international battle of wills. Indeed, at least one Texas lawmaker has already called on the United States to effectively hold the waters of the Colorado hostage if necessary to guarantee that the Mexicans keep their end of the bargain.[1]

"Politicians," he sighs. "They don't know anything about farming."

What they don't understand, he knows, is that it wasn't only—or even largely—the Mexican water debt that choked off farming in this corner of the Rio Grande Valley. If all the water in the world flowed past his land right now, Amendariz's fields would still be untended. There would be no one to plow those fields with him, no one to plant the onions or weed them, no one to harvest the onions or the cantaloupes, box them, and load them onto trucks. In a city where the vast majority of those who have jobs are working for the local school district or the Border Patrol—the two largest employers in this fading town—there is no local labor pool available.

Thirty years ago, things were different. Back then, both the water to grow the crops and the labor to harvest them flowed freely from the Mexican side of the border.

Thirty years ago, Amendariz could sit in his truck on this levee six days a week and watch a small army of undocumented field hands wade or boat across the Rio Grande and pour onto his land like water. And on the seventh day, they would wade across the river again, this time to collect their paychecks, which he carefully had calculated and from which he had deducted income tax that the migrants used to call the "Lincoln tax" and which most of them would never reclaim.

Those days are gone. It is open to debate how much a series of actions by the federal government—beginning with Ronald Reagan's Immigration Reform and Control Act of 1986, which granted amnesty to some four million undocumented workers in the United States while trying to block others from entering the country—have protected American workers from competition from lower-paid migrants. It is an open question whether those actions that have escalated in a cascading torrent of enforcement initiatives in the years since the United States hunkered down after the attacks of September 11, 2001, have made America safer. There are compelling arguments on either side of those questions.

But there is no question in Amendariz's mind that he has paid a steep price for those policies. Fields that used to be tended by undocumented day laborers are now in thrall to Russian thistle and mesquite. The economic consequences of his farm falling fallow ripple out far from the boundary of his land. If he is not earning money from his farm then neither are the guys who used to sell him seed and fertilizer and fuel for those tractors sitting idle under a rusted old canopy.

Neither are the farmers to the left and right of his land.

From up on the levee, he can look out across his fence line and see his neighbor Terry Bishop's fields. Bishop hasn't given up farming. Not completely. He still plants a few acres of alfalfa and irrigates it from wells he has drilled on his land. But in a nod to what he believed to be the reality of life on this part of the Rio Grande in the post-9/11 world, Bishop sold off his rights to draw water from the Rio Grande to the distant city of San Angelo. In a corner of Texas where water policy and border control policies and politics often set off a chain reaction of unanticipated consequences, Bishop's decision made a kind of cold sense. Water was the most valuable crop he could still harvest and sell.

Maybe it is that Amendariz takes the long view of events in this neighborhood. That might come easier when, like Amendariz, you come from a family that can trace part of its lineage on the banks of the Rio Grande back to the days before there was a Texas, or a

Mexico, long before the first Europeans set foot in this place, back to the days when the river was just a river, not a commodity or a barrier that divided two nations. Maybe it is that he has lived long enough himself to understand that the way things are is not necessarily the way they will always be. Maybe it is just that he nurtures the hope that one day he will be able to farm again. Or maybe it is all of those things. But he is not ready to follow his neighbor's lead and sell off his rights to the Rio Grande. Not yet at least.

If the Rio Grande has a core, a soul, a center, this remote bend along its 1,885 miles is it. Rising in western Colorado and running south along the border of New Mexico and Texas before snaking along the roughly 1,000-mile border with Mexico, the river provides water for some six million people. Replenished by streams and smaller rivers, some of them fed by groundwater, and stored in reservoirs like Elephant Butte Dam near the Texas–New Mexico border, the water is ladled out to downstream users under the terms of a strict interstate compact that is often honored more in the breach. To the north and west of Presidio, major cities like Albuquerque and the sprawling cross-border cities of El Paso and Ciudad Juarez often do battle with each other over the scant water in the river. Indeed, the State of Texas is currently suing New Mexico, claiming that the state failed to meet its obligations under the terms of the 1938 compact. That case is scheduled to be heard by the US Supreme Court.[2] And then there are the farmers and ranchers. It is estimated that seven out of every ten gallons of water that flow down the Rio Grande go to agriculture.

It is so utterly overallocated that by the time the Rio Grande stumbles into that triangle of river bottom known as La Junta de los Rios around the fading city of Presidio, the river is exhausted. Most of the time it is reduced to a dirt-brown trickle, not even strong enough to dilute the pollutants from agriculture and industry or the contaminants that ooze from inadequate sewers in colonias that cling to its banks, residents will tell you. Other times, it is really little more than a dry ditch, so degraded and desolate that the stretch of the river between El Paso and Presidio has been dubbed the "Forgotten River."

But just south of Presidio, it catches a second wind where, thanks to the surging flows of the Rio Concho on the Mexican side of the border and the obligations—not always honored—of the Mexican government to make sure that the waters of the Rio Concho reach the Rio Grande, the river is revived.

For a while anyway. Between here and the Gulf of Mexico, the river flows down to fill the Amistad and Falcon Reservoirs, and countless straws are stuck into it along the way from both sides of the border. Farmers, industry, the thirsty cities of Del Rio and Eagle Pass and Los Dos Laredos—so many draw water from it that in 2001, for the first time, the once-mighty river failed to make it to the Gulf at all, and the boundary between the two nations was nothing more than a mud bog.

Stand on Amendariz's levee on the US side and turn your back to the river, and it is hard to imagine that this hardscrabble, dried out, out-of-the-way corner of the state was, until comparatively recently, a lush and productive farm region. But it was.

Indeed, historians believe that La Junta, or "the juncture," which straddles 312.5 square miles of fertile, naturally irrigated land on both sides of the border, may be the oldest continuously farmed land in Texas.

There is archeological evidence that as long as 8,000 years ago, this surprisingly well-watered oasis in the Chihuahuan Desert was already attracting Paleo-Indians. In the centuries that followed, successive waves of nomads drifted into the region, finally settling down sometime around 800 CE.

By the time the shipwrecked Spanish explorer Cabeza de Vaca and his tiny band of survivors found their way here in 1535, midway along their six-year trek from the coast to Mexico City, La Junta had grown into a thriving agricultural community.

It was, to the explorer who had spent most of his trek either enslaved by less welcoming tribes or worshipped as a miraculous medicine man, a sanctuary surrounded by carefully tended fields of corn and squash and beans.

His heart soared when he saw it. After years of almost unfathomable hardship, the explorers' first glimpse of the settlements of

La Junta "gladdened us more than anything else in the world, and for this we gave infinite thanks to Our Lord,"[3] Cabeza de Vaca wrote in *La Relación*, his epic account of his sojourn across what would become the American Southwest. Anchored to and enriched by their connection to this fertile, watered land, the people there flourished, its residents proudly displaying "the most well formed bodies . . . of the greatest vitality." The wealth of the land, crowned by the water that flowed through it, gave the place and its inhabitants a stature and sense of permanence. Their homes, he wrote, were "the first dwellings we saw that had the semblance and appearance of houses."

For the next four centuries, the people of La Junta on both sides of what, after the Mexican–American War, became the indisputable border continued to thrive. Newcomers, lured there by the rich lands and ample water, rubbed shoulders and ultimately mixed their bloodlines with the descendants of Cabeza de Vaca's hosts. Indeed, to this day, many residents of Presidio, like Amendariz, trace their lineage back hundreds if not a thousand years to those Native Americans.

As for the newcomers, well, if the truth was told, some were more welcome than others. In January of 1914, for example, the charismatic, publicity-hungry bandit-cum-revolutionary Pancho Villa holed up at a remuda just across the river in Mexico in advance of his attack on Presidio's sister city on the Chihuahuan side, Ojinaga. Refugees loyal to the Mexican government flooded across the border to escape him, some of them later building charming cottages at the edge of Presidio, a neighborhood now known as the Puerto Rico section of town.

As it turned out, Villa wasn't in any real hurry to assault Ojinaga. According to the *New York Times* on January 8 of that year, a few days before his assault was expected to begin, Villa had signed a contract with moviemaker Frank M. Thayer of the Mutual Film Corporation of New York for a film, augmented by later studio re-creations, that would be released under the title *The Life of General Villa*. The media-savvy Villa had decided to hold off the attack—it would be a decisive battle in his war against Mexican federal forces in northern Mexico—while waiting for Thayer's camera crews to arrive. He had, after all, given his word that the filmmaker would capture stirring images of

Villa and his men in battle and had even agreed that Thayer would get his pictures regardless of the conditions on the battlefield. "If no good pictures are made during the present battle Villa has agree[d] to stage a battle for the benefit of the company,"[4] the *Times* reported.

And if he was going to linger, the lush banks of the Rio Grande below the confluence with the Rio Concho was a lovely place to do it.

By the 1920s, as the tensions along the Mexican border subsided, the little town of Presidio and its environs grew in tandem with their agricultural output. The town, which had a population of less than one hundred when Pancho Villa's rampages along the border came to an end, had grown steadily; by 1988 more than sixteen hundred people lived within the city limits. And many of them grew onions, a sweet onion, favorably compared to the Vidalia onion of Georgia, a winter crop that requires regular irrigation, and the famed Pecos cantaloupe, a spring crop that depends on getting just enough water to develop its sweetness.

Indeed, by the 1980s, while Ojinaga remained a crowded backwater, often blanketed in smoke from the wood fires people used there to heat their homes and cook their food, Presidio had become comparatively prosperous and proud enough of its produce that each year in May it pulled out all the stops and threw a festival to celebrate, even crowning an Onion Queen to oversee the festivities.

It didn't matter back then that Amendariz couldn't find people on the US side of the river to do the backbreaking work that farming required. Having grown up under the strict supervision of his very demanding father, he understood that his neighbors either were busy running their own farms or just didn't want to spend twelve-hour days bent under a blazing sun. Those few documented workers still willing and able to plant and pick were being lured up to Marfa, where a hydroponic farm gave them the opportunity to earn a paycheck year-round. Presidio just couldn't compete. It didn't matter. There were scores of willing workers who were ready to wade across the river every morning.

Some years, the good years, he had as many as fifty people working in his fields, each of them paid $0.60 a pound for the onions they harvested. They earned the equivalent of the minimum wage at the time, about $1.65 an hour. And they worked hard. One woman, in particular, stands out in his memory, a young woman with a couple of young kids in tow, who showed up every morning before the sun came up and insisted on staying in the fields clipping onions each day long after all the other workers crossed back to their homes on the Mexican side of the river. At first he and his twin brother, Carlos, had blanched at the idea of allowing her to work unsupervised after dark. But she was honest and sincere, and she had melted their hearts when she pleaded with them. "Please," she had said. "I'm not going to steal from you boys. I can do this." They relented. They were glad they did. The young woman was a powerhouse, bagging more than half a ton of onions every week and taking home as much as $800 a week at the height of the season.

Indeed there were workers enough that Amendariz could afford to split his time between his three jobs—farming, working as superintendent of wildlife at Big Bend State Park just outside town, and keeping an eye on the adobe-brick hardware store and lumberyard on the main drag that he and his brother had taken over from his father.

There were, of course, disruptions. Periodically, federal officers would show the stars and stripes. But they were local boys, many of them, and they understood the way things worked around Presidio, and so as often as not, they would let the farmers take turns getting raided and even give them a heads-up. The unwritten rules of the game were such that when the farmers knew a raid was coming, they would pick five or ten workers, send them up to the road and let them wait until the immigration officers arrived, loaded them in a van, let them sit around in an air-conditioned office with an ice-cold water fountain, and then turned them loose again.

He will never forget walking up to the road past his farm one hot summer afternoon after one such "raid" and seeing one of his workers, an older man, sitting dejectedly at the side of the road. The immigration officers had forgotten the poor man. He was brokenhearted. He really had been looking forward to the air conditioning and the water fountain.

By the beginning of the 1990s, though, the feds began to take their job more seriously. Farmers and ranchers who hired undocumented workers could find themselves facing fines of up to $5,000 per offense, and in the years that followed, the flood of undocumented workers across the river dried up. A drought at the end of the decade and a soft market for produce added to the farmers' misery. By the beginning of the twenty-first century, ruin was looming for the farm culture of Presidio. Old-timers recall seeing onions and cantaloupes rotting in the fields for want of water in the drought, for want of a buyer who would make it all worthwhile, but most of all for want of labor. It wasn't that some motivated migrants and refugees weren't still trying to reach the United States. It was just that when they did, they didn't stop in Presidio anymore, and they no longer went back home at night. Those who could obtain guest worker visas headed deeper into the interior, where more prosperous farms could afford to pay the $10-plus an hour the guest workers were guaranteed. Those who couldn't get the visas, or didn't, simply vanished into the parched south Texas landscape, turning up later in places hundreds or thousands of miles away. Many more simply have stayed on the Mexican side of the river. They still pick vegetables and fruit and tend alfalfa. They harvest pecans amply watered with Rio Concho water. But now, instead of dollars, they are paid in pesos.

And they are spending them on the Mexican side of the river as well.

Slowly but surely, the city of Ojinaga and its environs are developing the kind of confidence that comes with economic stability. There are signs that the prosperity once claimed by Presidio, along with the pecan trees in the groves along the river, has taken root here.

Sure, Federales still patrol the streets of Ojinaga in Humvees fitted with machine guns, but the fears of the kind of narco-gang violence that once paralyzed much of the Mexican border have ebbed in recent years. These days, the patrols roll almost casually past one of the modern new supermarkets in town. Those supermarkets would seem at home in a suburb of Dallas, and they tempt both longtime Ojinagans and more than a few Texans to spend their money in Mexico.

Infrastructure investment is up, Mexican officials proudly boast. You can see that as you head north out of Ojinaga past lush fields of alfalfa. A leathery man in a baseball cap sits on a remarkably well-fed horse lifting his cell phone to the heavens in the hopes of getting a better signal as the water of the Rio Concho races past him in an irrigation channel with the gates wide open. A hundred yards away, bulldozers slumber in the morning sun, waiting to resume work on a new highway, part of the Mexican interstate highway system that will link Ojinaga and its produce to markets on both sides of the border all the way to the Pacific coast and, from there, by ship to Asian markets that are also growing by leaps and bounds. Mexican President Enrique Peña Nieto announced the project with much fanfare early in his term and employed a small army of workers to build a lavish new bridge with a massive retaining wall along the Mexican side of the river as part of a model port of entry to the United States. The joke around Presidio is that "the Mexicans already built a wall, and they paid for it." A new natural gas pipeline—opposed by environmentalists on the US side of the border but fast-tracked by aspects of the North American Free Trade Agreement that view the United States and Mexico as a single market when it comes to oil and gas—will soon make its way to Ojinaga. When it does, it will provide the fuel for further economic development, Mexican officials say. It will also help reduce the choking smoke that still blankets this city in some places when the temperatures drop enough to warrant a fire for heat as well as cooking.

Prosperity, like water, follows the path of least resistance, and at the moment that path runs along the banks of the Rio Concho and the Rio Bravo. To be sure, the comparative prosperity on the Mexican side of the border also holds promise for the economy of Texas. The gas that flows through that forty-two-inch pipeline will come from the Permian basin, and a six-inch spur will come off that line to provide gas for a small plant planned just outside Presidio to process chili peppers. The chili peppers are grown in Mexico by Mennonite farmers in the village of Oasis, and the new plant will employ only six people full-time, but as Brad Newton, executive director of the Presidio Municipal Development District, puts it, "that's not nothing in a town of fifty-four hundred." The new bridge between Ojinaga and Presidio will be the only port of entry along the five-hundred-mile border between El Paso and Brownsville, and the trucks that traverse it carry goods in both directions.

The City of Presidio has established a port authority in the hopes of cashing in on some of that cross-border traffic and maybe "catching up with the Mexicans," as Newton puts it. It is just that, at least for now, there isn't much reason for those trucks to stop in Presidio. Here, on the American side of the river, the farms of Presidio have gone fallow. It is, Amendariz knows, just one of those unintended consequences. He would like to believe that perhaps someday, hopefully within his lifetime, things will change. But he is not optimistic. He hears that the president of the United States is planning on doubling down on border enforcement. "Mr. Trump says he wants to build a wall," he sighs, as he looks up toward that spot on the side of the road where the old man waited in vain for his turn at the water fountain. "There was a wall here. It was this road. When there was work . . . they came this far and no farther."

There is one last remaining commodity in Presidio that can still fetch a good price, says Terry Bishop, who owns a vast tract of land— still optimistically called Presidio Valley Farms—right alongside Amendariz's spread. Water. Specifically, Bishop's old water rights to the Rio Grande.

In a good year, when it rains enough and the Mexicans are feeling sufficiently generous to release their full quota of Rio Concho water, that commodity flows past Bishop's place strongly enough that, back in the old days, he had a permit that guaranteed him the right to siphon off 8,059 acre-feet a year of the stuff at a rate of 173.8 gallons a minute[5] to irrigate the roughly 3,000 acres of farmland he controlled. Once upon a time, those rights were more than enough to keep the farm he inherited from his father above water and awash in melons and onions. But by the end of the twentieth century, the enforced labor shortage, together with the recurring droughts and the bad market, had taken a devastating toll on Presidio Valley Farms. In fact, things got bad enough that in 2003, Presidio Valley Farms filed for bankruptcy protection.

It had been a few years coming. Indeed, by late summer of 2000, the writing was on the wall for Presidio and for Presidio Valley Farms. That year, B. J. Bishop, Terry's father, lamented that he had lost his onion crop altogether, and when he surveyed his fields, he saw nothing but acre after acre of rotting cantaloupes.

It was around that time that the farmers of Presidio first began considering the idea of selling off their water rights. It started with a modest proposal from a lawyer from up in Marfa. It struck him that there might be a way for the farmers to transfer their water rights upstream to El Paso. That fast-growing city, which had been severely affected by the drought of the late 1990s and was dependent on New Mexico releasing water from the Elephant Butte Reservoir, was already casting about for new sources of water. The idea was that since the farmers in Presidio weren't using the water that replenished the river from the Rio Concho anymore anyway, they might just as well sell their rights to 15,000 acre-feet of it to El Paso. It would, in effect, be a paper transfer. No pipelines would need to be built; no trucks would need to haul the water. El Paso would simply draw an extra 15,000 acre-feet of water when it could and pay the Presidio farmers for the privilege.

Most of the farmers were skeptical, and eventually the idea died a natural death. But the Bishops didn't give up. By 2003 they had struck a deal with the thirsty downstream cities of Eagle Pass and Laredo and with Maverick County to transfer their water rights, all 8,056 acre-feet a year of them, downriver.

It turned out to be a more complicated operation than anyone imagined at the time, said Glenn Jarvis, a lawyer who represented Presidio Valley Farms in what turned out to be a five-year legal battle to sell the water rights. That is because there are two completely different ways of allocating water rights along the Rio Grande in Texas. Above the two international reservoirs—the Amistad and the Falcon—water rights along the Rio Grande are allocated pretty much the same way they are in most river basins in the state: first in time, first in right. A permit holder can sell his or her water rights within the same basin, but those rights often lose their priority. A senior water right, such as the one held by the Bishop family, becomes a junior water right once it is transferred, which means that in dry times, those rights can and sometimes are suspended before older priority rights are. That, you will remember, was the issue at play in the case of *TCEQ v. Texas Farm Bureau*.

While that arrangement can and often does make water transferred from one part of a river basin to another less reliable and thus less valuable, it is not necessarily a deal breaker.

What made the Bishop plan so fraught, however, was that once the Rio Grande makes it to the international reservoirs, an entirely different allocation regime kicks in, Jarvis explained. Along that stretch of the river, known as the Middle Rio Grande Region, water is allocated to users based on the type of use rather than on the date of the permit. Thus a certain amount of water is allocated—and doled out by a watermaster—for municipal use, for industrial use, for irrigation, and so on.

In order to harmonize the two competing regulatory regimes, the then water master, Carlos Rubenstein, backed by the TCEQ, stepped in. The way Rubenstein saw it, Bishop had every right to sell his water, and the cities had every right to buy it. "It was his property right," Rubenstein recalled.

Unfortunately for Bishop, cities farther downstream along the lower Rio Grande—Brownsville, Bayville, and their water districts—didn't see it that way. Still reeling from a drought and overconsumption that by 2000 had turned the mouth of the Rio Grande into a mud flat, those entities would have much preferred that as long as Bishop wasn't using his water—and he wasn't—it just be allowed to flow south and keep the twin reservoirs fed. They sued.

In response, Rubenstein and the TCEQ developed an elaborate plan under which the amount of water—previously held by Bishop—was drastically reduced from 8,059 acre-feet a year to about 5,300, and it could be drawn at a far slower rate: rather than 173.8 cubic feet per second, it would have to be diverted at just 75 cubic feet per second. The flow would be carefully monitored at several locations on Bishop's property, and only the amount registered in Presidio County could be consumed downstream by Eagle Pass, Laredo, and

Maverick County. And its use would be changed from irrigation to municipal use, thus keeping its priority in its new home.

The cities of the lower Rio Grande Valley were not mollified, and a five-year legal battle ensued. In the end, Bishop was permitted to sell his now-diminished water rights. He was paid about $447,000 in a one-time deal and forever surrendered his rights to most of his Rio Grande water.

To a great degree, Rubenstein believes, the battle over what would become of Terry Bishop's water is a classic example of the way so many unrelated issues and competing interests intersect in unexpected ways in the state's piecemeal approach to water management. There are issues at play far beyond water itself. As Bishop himself notes, it wasn't just, or even principally, the unreliability of water in the Rio Grande that killed farming in Presidio. Issues of national security and border control also played a critical role in hastening the end of a farming tradition that stretched back thousands of years in that place. In a way, that is a sea change that is taking place all over Texas as agriculture, for a variety of reasons, becomes less a source of political power and more a fading culture.

In its place, thirsty urban areas are growing thirstier. Their needs will need to be met. In the Bishop case, Rubenstein believes, there may be a paradigm for how best to do that. It requires balancing the harsh reality of what is going on in places like Presidio with the needs of places like Laredo and Eagle Pass, he says. "You have to protect the area of origin. No argument there. You have to balance the economic impact on the place where you are taking the water versus where the water is going to go and the effect that it is going to have there," he says. To replicate the kind of transfer of water rights that the Bishop case represents on a statewide scale, the state also would have to break down some of the barriers that it has erected to such transfers, most importantly, the provision by which water rights lose their priority— and thus their value—when moved from one river basin to another.

So far, there has been little will to do that. And the deal Terry Bishop struck with the cities downriver from him remains the exception rather than the rule. Even in Presidio. To this day, Bishop remains the only one of his neighbors who has sold his water rights. "I'm still the only one that's ever done this," he says. He understands why his neighbors are holding on to their water rights. His five-year ordeal was costly enough to be a deterrent. And in those years when the water from the Rio Concho flows into La Junta the way it is supposed to, there isn't much incentive for the cities downstream to subject themselves to years of costly litigation. "There just aren't buyers now," he says.

But press him and he will tell you the real reason why his neighbors still cling to their water rights. It is because they are still clinging to hope. It is because when they look across the Rio Grande at the lush fields along the river on the Mexican side, they remember the glory days of Presidio and hope that someday, those lush times may return.

Bishop is not a particularly nostalgic man. He is a businessman. He knows that at least for the foreseeable future the present is all there is. Not long ago, he says, "I . . . sold my honeydew and my cantaloupe graders because I know that there's never gonna be enough people to harvest those things by hand, and in my lifetime, there won't be a machine that can harvest a ripe melon."

But even he is not willing to give up hope altogether. As proof, he cites the fact that he still holds on to his onion grader. "I haven't given up on this place," he says.

Using well water, "I keep experimenting with different things. A few rows of this, a few rows of that, trying to figure out what I can possibly grow. It's not just me. There's other people here who would like to grow something. I keep hoping. That's why I kept my onion machine. I keep hoping that someday I can use it on fresh onions because I can grow 'em. And if I can get 'em harvested and packed, I can get them sold. That's not the problem."

CHAPTER 12

FINDING A SOLUTION, COME HELL OR NO WATER

YOU PROBABLY COULDN'T PICK a worse place to plant one of the fastest-growing metropolitan areas in America than this arid patch of near desert that stretches roughly from Austin to San Antonio along the parched edges of Interstate 35.

This corner of South Central Texas gets roughly half the annual rainfall of Houston. The rain sometimes falls in buckets, other times not for months. This is a place where hundreds of years of experience have taught a hard lesson: reliance on fickle nature and on even more fickle human nature alone is not enough to slake the thirst of growing cities or keep the fields of farmers and ranchers lush.

But just beneath the ground there is an ace in the hole.

The sprawling eight-thousand-square-mile Edwards Aquifer, which snakes hundreds of miles underground from Brackettville in Kinney County in the southwest, through San Antonio and Austin to Mills County in the northeast, is one of the more unique and, for much of its run, one of the most permeable and productive carbonate aquifers in the United States. It currently provides water for upward of two million people.

What makes it especially unique, says Dr. Todd Votteler, an environmental geographer and a member of the Guadalupe–Blanco River Authority who has spent much of his career working on issues

NEW
MEXICO

OKLAHOMA

ARK.

Lubbock

18

El
Paso

10

10

14

10

26

Fort
Worth

Dallas

34

42

38

46

50

54

58

Austin

San
Antonio

30

22

Houston

MEXICO

Gulf of
Mexico

0   50   100 mi

—10— Isopleths of average annual precipitation (inches)

related to the Edwards, is that unlike many other aquifers, which are effectively sponges that collect water over thousands of years and dole it out reluctantly and parsimoniously, the Edwards is like a giant underground limestone flume through which water flows almost riverlike in real time. Whereas water that gets pumped out of the Ogallala Aquifer may have been trapped in it for eons, water bubbling up out of Comal Spring may have fallen as rain in the hills only weeks before.

In periods of normal or above-normal rainfall, the Edwards can be flush. But in droughts, like the drought of record in the 1950s that turned most of the state into a tinder-dry disaster area, or those droughts that followed in the '60s, the '80s, the '90s, and earlier in the 2010s, the water level in the Edwards can fall dangerously low, low enough to choke off flow to Comal Spring, with its lush yet vulnerable ecosystem, and to turn the San Marcos River into a muddy trickle. With more and more straws stuck into the aquifer to suck the water out, and with unrestricted pumping by municipalities and farmers and ranchers that grows ever more thirsty, as it has steadily from the 1950s on, the water supply for everyone who depends on the Edwards is endangered.

Overconsumption wasn't a problem back in the 1880s, when George W. Brackenridge drilled what generally is regarded as the first artesian well in the Edwards in San Antonio. Back then, the city leaders were far less concerned with rates of water consumption than they were with the periodic outbreaks of cholera that sometimes ravaged the city, once in 1849, another in the 1860s, and again in the 1870s (see chapter 2).

In fact, it wasn't until 1877, twelve years after the second deadly cholera outbreak in the city, that the city council did anything significant to address the water quality and supply issue in San Antonio. Even then, as was so often the case, there was a slight stench of putrefaction in the way it was done.

Years earlier, almost in secret in one of several moments of fiscal panic that the city has experienced before and since, the council had voted to sell off the land around San Antonio Springs, the poetically named "Blue Hole," the headwaters for the river and system of *acequias*, for a pittance—about $1,450. The council sold it to one of their own, an alderman named J. R. Sweet, who a few years later would sell it, together with other landholdings he had amassed, to Brackenridge's mother for a tidy profit.

Though he is often regarded in some quarters as a kind of paleo-monopolist and as a war profiteer who managed to exploit both the Union and the Confederacy to his advantage during the Civil War (allegations that are not entirely without merit), Brackenridge was, to some degree, also a visionary who recognized the pivotal role San Antonio could someday play in the history of the state and the nation. He also understood clearly the essential role a reliable source of "wholesome" water would play in that transformation.

So it probably wasn't entirely for venal reasons that Brackenridge tried repeatedly—and unsuccessfully—to sell the land his mother had bought from Sweet to the city, for a thirty percent profit, of course, so that San Antonio could at least control the source of its own water. And he probably still had at least a glimmer of that higher purpose in his mind when he ultimately leased that land to an entrepreneurial French émigré named Jean Baptiste LaCoste.

By 1877, LaCoste had formed the San Antonio Water Company—in which his landlord, Brackenridge, was a substantial shareholder—and had been awarded a contract to provide the city with that "wholesome water" the council had been talking about for at least a generation. He set about providing it, building a pump house and trace system that would carry the pristine waters of the spring around the fetid, outdated *acequias* and directly into people's backyards.

It was, it seemed, a foolproof business plan. After all, who in a city that twice had been ravaged by waterborne disease would turn down the opportunity to get crystal-clear, healthy water for what amounted to a few pennies?

No one. Except virtually the entire surviving population of San Antonio. Though LaCoste had expected to sign up subscribers in the growing city and its environs by the thousands, they, in fact, signed up by the tens. Part of the problem, almost certainly, was the problem that continues to bedevil ambitious start-ups even today, especially in the world of the internet. It is hard to get people to pay for things like water—or in the modern world, streaming music—when they are used to getting it for free.

There were also economic, class, and cultural issues at play. That was particularly true on the western bank of the river, where old Mexican families still lived much as they had for generations. Excluded from the pockets of prosperity that were enjoyed by at least some of the Anglo inhabitants of San Antonio, many still lived a subsistence lifestyle. Even if the water LaCoste wanted to provide cost only pennies, that was more than they could afford. In that part of town, water was still fetched daily from the rivers and *acequias* by *aquadores*, often just children who carried the pails and buckets hung from yokes on their necks, and paid for, or bartered for, with what little the consumer had. On that side of town, where if the householder wasn't directly related by blood to the *aquadore* he or she at least always had known them and probably knew their parents, economics, just like water, was governed by the concept of *derecho*. It would have seemed unjust to abandon the traditional *aquadores* and throw them into deeper poverty in exchange for a newfangled water delivery system that, in its most charitable interpretation, essentially turned what had always been a right into a commodity.

In the harsh light of hindsight, it is probably not surprising that LaCoste ultimately threw in the towel. What is a bit more surprising is that Brackenridge picked it up. And when he converted his minority interest in the water company to a majority interest in 1888, he doubled down on LaCoste's experiment, and with the same results. In the years that followed, he expanded the system as much as he could, before finally giving up and selling the company to a Belgian firm that would itself sell it off, sending it through various configurations until the city itself eventually bought it for $7 million in 1925, more than fifteen hundred times the price Brackenridge had offered the city half a century earlier and more than five thousand times what the city had pocketed when it sold the land to one of its own in the 1850s. And for that, they didn't even get the land itself or the "Blue Hole." Brackenridge sold that to the Sisters of Charity of the Incarnate Word, who continue to hold it to this day.

But before he finally did surrender his holdings in the water company and ended his twenty-three-year tenure as president of the San Antonio Water Works Company in 1906, Brackenridge did something that would not only vastly expand, for a while, the amount of water available to slake the thirst of the growing city of San Antonio, but profoundly transfigure the character of that water itself and the law and politics that surround it.

In 1888, Brackenridge drilled the first artesian well to pierce the Edwards, with mixed success. Three years later, in 1891, he tried again and hit the jackpot. According to reports from the time, the water that had been contained below erupted with enough force to send a plume of water five times taller a man into the air. It was to be the first of many. Within five years, there were more than forty wells drilled in the San Antonio area, and the city increasingly was relying on deep water to provide all its needs. Within ten years, the flow from San Antonio Springs, a once-copious flow that had sustained all those who passed by and those who lived there for hundreds of years, had slowed to a trickle.

But this was a different kind of water, at least as far as San Antonio and the region that surrounds it were concerned. It was not subject to the law of *derecho*. Because it was groundwater, it was subject to a different kind of law: the rule of capture, that legal doctrine first defined in the Texas Supreme Court's 1904 landmark case, *East v. Houston*, in which the court effectively made the concept of "whoever has the biggest pump wins" the law of the land.

As a practical matter, what the elevation of the rule of capture did was to substitute "a tort concept for regulation" said Robert Gulley, a lawyer, a scientist, and as we will see shortly, a savvy negotiator who would eventually play a critical role in the future of the Edwards Aquifer. Not only did it help turn the concept of property rights into an almost theological principle, it effectively ignored a crucial issue in a semi-arid region like South Central Texas, the inescapable fact that sometimes—often once or twice every couple of decades—there just wasn't going to be enough water in the Edwards to go around.

"In Texas," Gulley said, "we basically repealed the laws of hydrology."

It took a while for that crucial fact to become obvious in the areas served by the Edwards Aquifer. It wasn't until the 1950s that pumping of groundwater from the Edwards began in earnest, and it took even longer for that to expose a rift that would begin to fracture the various communities—urban, rural, those downstream on the Guadalupe–Blanco River who relied on the annual flows from the springs sustained by the Edwards, and, as we will see later, the environmental community.

By the middle of the twentieth century, all of those communities had become utterly dependent on the Edwards for their water supplies. San Antonio, though it paid lip service to the need to develop alternative sources of water, had to that point done little to secure them. Part of that might have been a twentieth-century version of the same factors that scuttled LaCoste's plans to provide water to the city. Until recently, San Antonio residents had among the lowest water bills in the country, and proposals to build dams and reservoirs that would have captured water in the flush years and carried them through the dry ones were greeted with little enthusiasm.

In the rural communities, in places like Uvalde and Medina Counties, the buried treasure of the Edwards, just there for the taking for any landowner, fueled an explosion of irrigated agriculture. As Todd Votteler put it in a 1998 article he wrote for the *Tulane Environmental Law Journal*, "One of the fastest-growing uses of Edwards Aquifer water over the last fifty years has been irrigated agriculture. Much of the irrigation relies on inefficient irrigation techniques. Because the cost of water to the farmer has been only the cost of the well and the energy to pump water from the Aquifer, few incentives have existed to encourage farmers to adopt more efficient irrigation methods."[1]

In years when ample rain fell and was sucked up by the aquifer, that approach to drawing from the Edwards didn't seem to be all that much of a problem. Farmers and ranchers could draw as much as their pumps would allow, confident that the rule of capture protected their right to do so. San Antonio, too, could take all it wanted.

After all, for the better part of the twentieth century, an average of 676,000 acre-feet of water flowed into Edwards, and even in the record year of 1989, only 542,400 were pumped out of it.

The problem with averages, of course, is that they are just that, and their comforting roundness often masks real-life jagged edges. They erase those flood years, like 1992 when more than 2.4 million acre-feet of water flowed into the Edwards. And they ignore those lean years, like those the region experienced in severe droughts through the twentieth century, including the devastating drought of record in the 1950s, when water levels in some place plunged nearly one hundred feet below their highest recorded levels. Several springs dried up altogether, and Barton Springs was reduced to coughing up an anemic average of about one hundred gallons a second, a little less than one-quarter of its usual discharge.[2]

That is not to say that those lean years didn't have an impact on the debate over how best to conserve and protect the flow of water out of the Edwards. In the years that followed, the state legislature would make a number of attempts if not to regulate consumption of water from the Edwards and other groundwater sources in the state, at least to keep an eye on it. In the late 1990s, following yet another significant drought, and after a series of attempts, with varying degrees of success, to monitor if not manage groundwater at the state, level, the legislature adopted Senate Bill 1, which in effect turned the system on its head, creating a bottom-up system that empowered local shareholders—farmers, urbanites, environmentalists—to take control of planning issues around water conservation. That, in due course, led to Senate Bill 2, which effectively enshrined in law for the first time the concept at which the Supreme Court in 1904 had hinted, that groundwater, perhaps, could be regulated. It established for the first time groundwater conservation districts, local entities that, at least on paper, had the authority to manage groundwater resources, an authority that, in several cases, would put those districts on a collision course with the overarching property rights articulated in the *East* decision. A few years later, the state legislature sidled up to the rule of capture yet again with Senate Bill 3, which for the first time established a process for guaranteeing flows to the state's rivers and streams, and in so doing effectively circumscribed the right of capture.

Taken together, says Gulley, the three bills were far from perfect. Much was murky in them. And even the groundwater conservation districts—there are now nearly one hundred of them because they were drawn on political boundaries rather than necessarily along the lines cut by the aquifers themselves—are less effective than they could have been. What is more, because they represent local interests, there has been a tendency for them to be parochial. In rural districts, agricultural interests tend to dominate, and the effects of that outsize influence ripple underground to affect other, more developed regions. "A hundred little fiefdoms" is the way Gulley describes them. And yet, for all their flaws, the package of bills represented a significant, maybe even revolutionary, change in the way that the state managed its water supplies and an equally significant setback for the once inviolate rule of capture.

But the path traveled to get to that point was every bit as "mysterious and occult" as the buried water sources themselves. It is one of those only-in-Texas stories, and it is where the fish—the catfish and the endangered fountain darter—rejoin the tale.

In 1991, a century after Brackenridge had rapped the Edwards with his staff and turned loose the flowing waters, and while San Antonio was still crawling out from underneath the effects of a two-year drought, the single largest water well in the world to that point was drilled in a sketchy spit of otherwise useless Medina River bottom just southwest of the city.

It was reported at the time that when the drill bit hit the sweet spot of the aquifer at sixteen hundred feet, "the ground rumbled like a freight train" and a geyser of water as wide as a church door and as high as its steeple burst out, blasting out rocks the size of pulpits as it soared into the air. It was a staggering amount of water—forty thousand gallons a minute, forty-three million gallons a day, forty-eight thousand acre-feet a year—the equivalent of one-fourth of all the water consumed by the city annually. If you imagine the Edwards to be an underground river, as officials would later try to do, all that water was being sucked out upstream of the city, in effect making the city vulnerable. And under the rule of capture, it all belonged to the guys who drilled the well, at least as long as they put it to "beneficial use."

They called the well the Ave Maria Number One, a suggestion that, at least in their minds, a whole decade of Ave Marias could someday follow.

The truth is, the owner of the land and his business partner didn't really know what to do with all that water, at first. Ron Pucek Jr., then a young entrepreneur from Alvin, Texas, and Louis Blumberg, a guy who had made his fortune building tract homes in New Jersey, originally had acquired the site with the idea that they might try to transplant a bit of the Garden State to Texas and subdivide the land for a housing development. And when that failed to pan out for a variety of reasons, they cast about for another option. Finally, they hit on one.

Catfish.

The water that rushed up out of the Edwards was pure and warm, between eighty-six and eighty-nine degrees Fahrenheit, the perfect temperature for raising fish. A few months after they tapped the Edwards, Pucek and Blumberg officially dubbed the eighty-five-acre tract the Living Waters Artesian Springs Catfish Farm and set about erecting a massive series of traces and ponds that they expected would provide a home for three-quarters of a million catfish.

The roughly one million San Antonians, many of them still under water restrictions from the drought of 1988–1990, were outraged. To them, Living Waters embodied everything that was wrong with the rule of capture. The idea that water enough for 250,000 people could be drawn for the benefit of 750,000 bottom-feeders was beyond absurd, and it pointed, in their minds, to the fatal flaw in the rule of capture, which for all intents and purposes had been the law of the land in Texas for nearly a century, and to the need for greater regulation.

Like a lightning bolt, Living Waters illuminated the fractured landscape between supporters and critics of the rule of capture as it had always been interpreted. While urban interests and downstream consumers and environmentalists angrily demanded that somebody—the state, local authorities, the federal government if need be—do something, rural interests took a decidedly different tack. They saw the issue as a stalking horse for efforts to wrest away their property rights, given by God, and if not by God, at least by the Texas Supreme Court. To the farmers and ranchers who depended on their right to pump as much water as they needed from the aquifer, the entrepreneur from Alvin and the developer from New Jersey were just like them, a couple of hard-working farmers trying to make their way in a harsh environment.

To most observers, the issue was not so cut and dried. Yes, the Living Waters project could be seen as a grotesque misapplication of a precious and limited resource; it could even be seen as a waste, though not in the narrow, technical, legal sense. But surely there could be a way through regulation and management to rein in such excesses and still protect the sacred right of private property.

As former San Antonio mayor and later Bexar County judge Nelson Wolff told a reporter for the *San Antonio Express-News*, "The catfish farm really gave more reason to have some regulation [of the Edwards Aquifer]."

As much as any event in recent memory, the battle over Living Waters, which would develop into a decade-long legal, political, and cultural war, focused the debate over the logical limits of the rule of capture. It helped prepare the ground for the legislative and legal actions that would follow, and it almost certainly gave added heft to the drive in the legislature in 1993 to create the EAA, the often-embattled body that would take up the struggle to protect and allocate the water from the Edwards.

In the end, however, it wasn't legislation that finally brought the great catfish war to an end. It was the US Clean Water Act and its implied abhorrence of catfish urine.

In constructing their million-dollar-plus catfish farm, Pucek and Blumberg had taken a number of precautions to make sure that their fish were fat and happy. They lined their ponds with concrete and aerated the water, and they were confident that because they were constantly replenishing the water, sending the used water tumbling into the Medina River, the risk of disease was small.

What they failed to consider, however, was how much catfish waste they were sending downstream with it. There was a certain "eww" factor in the idea that millions of gallons of catfish-urine-tainted water was flowing into the river from Living Waters, and while it may not have been as egregious as a bone-selling doctor dumping human soup into an *acequia* a century earlier, back then there was no federal Clean Water Act.

In 1991, less than a year after it opened, a judge ruled that Living Waters was in effect dumping untreated waste into the river without a permit in violation of the Clean Water Act and ordered the operation shut down. Three years later, the entrepreneurs reopened with a much smaller operation that used only about two percent of the water they had drawn in that first season, though some significant portion of the waste was still trickling into the Medina. Again, they found themselves in court, and again they lost. In 1996, Pucek and Blumberg decided that they had other fish to fry and gave up.

In the years that followed, the San Antonio Water System would spend more than $30 million to acquire the land and all of its water rights, eventually selling the land but keeping the water.

But more important, the saga of the catfish farm brought two key concepts into the battle. The first was that the rule of capture had its limits, and the second was that if the state legislature and local policy makers weren't up to the challenge, there was plenty of environmental legislation—state and especially federal, "the heavy axe of federal intervention" as it would come to be called—that would force their hands.

Which is precisely what happened next, when the battle of the endangered fountain darter began in earnest.

As fish go, fountain darters are not particularly impressive; most are small enough to make a K-turn within the circumference of a half dollar, and a freakishly robust specimen might grow to the size of a man's middle finger. Nor are they especially attractive, with a color scheme that ranges from mucous beige to tobacco juice brown.

What gives these tiny fish an outsize significance, however, is that they exist in only two places in the world: in the pristine springs of San Marcos and Comal, where the Edwards bubbles up to the surface. And as has happened at least once in the past, in 1956 during the drought of record when the Comal dried up for 144 consecutive days, their range is always at risk of being cut in half or eliminated entirely when the waters stop flowing. The drought of record, for example, wiped out the entire Comal Spring population of fountain darters, and they only returned to the spring with the help of volunteers who hand-carried a few hardy colonists in buckets from the San Marcos Spring when the waters began to flow again.

It is, in fact, their very vulnerability, or more precisely their vulnerability coupled with the grandma's-Sunday-china fragility of their unique environment (the two springs also host seven other endangered and threatened species, including the Texas blind salamander, Texas wild rice, and the Comal Springs riffle beetle), that gave the lowly fountain darter the power to do what no one had been able to do before and set in motion a process by which, for the first time in its century-long history, the rule of capture was itself threatened and endangered.

Over the next decade a series of courtroom dramas, and the occasional farce, would play out, pitting the comparatively modest water needs of the unassuming fountain darter and its friends against the loose and often fractious confederacy of consumers of that same water: farmers, ranchers, cities, those who held riparian rights to the water that flowed to the surface from the Edwards, and just about anybody who wanted to drill a well capable of producing enough water to do more than launder their jeans and wash their cars.

Hanging over it all was the threat that this time, things had better be different, that this time, the state legislature and the various state, regional, and local agencies deputized to carry out its will had better get it right, or "the heavy axe" of federal intervention would fall and do for Texas what the state had thus far failed to do on its own: develop a comprehensive, workable water policy that recognized and respected all of the needs of all of the users of Edwards water. Underlying it all, though hardly ever stated out loud, was the sense that whatever came of this, it almost certainly would have to be tinged with that ambiguous, almost forgotten concept that had governed the earliest settlers on this land: *derecho*.

The Fort Sumter moment in this next phase of the story began on May 19, 1991, as the region was still recovering from the two-year drought, and the region's inhabitants were just beginning to vent their outrage over Pucek and Blumberg's catfish, when the Sierra Club filed a lawsuit on behalf of the endangered fountain darter. So did the Guadalupe–Blanco River Authority, though it is far from certain that the authority was as sympathetic to the plight of the tiny fish as was the Sierra Club. "With all due respect to the endangered species, what was really driving the Guadalupe–Blanco River Authority is that they wanted more spring flow . . . for their customers," said Robert Puentes, then the state representative from San Antonio who chaired the House Natural Resource Committee and now the president and chief executive officer of the San Antonio Water System.

Regardless of the purity of the motives of the litigants, it was clear from the start that this was not going to be some state case.

No, the Guadalupe–Blanco River Authority and the Sierra Club were so serious about the fountain darter and their other interests that they were willing to make a federal case out of it.

They filed the suit in the US District Court for West Texas and named then secretary of the interior Bruce Babbitt at the top of a list of respondents who they alleged had failed to protect the endangered species at the San Marcos and Comal Springs, specifically by failing to meet their obligation under the US Endangered Species Act to determine how much flow needed to be maintained in the springs to ensure the fountain darter's survival.

Even before the four-day trial began in the autumn of 1992 in the case of *Sierra Club v. Babbitt*, it was clear that this was not going to be your run-of-the-mill court case. The judge who was assigned to the case, Lucius Bunton, was one of the more colorful characters ever to don a robe in Texas.

A native of the often-parched ranching and farming town of Marfa in Presidio County, a place then known to outsiders for an odd phenomenon in which weird lights appear in the night and vanish and as the site of the annual Mystery Lights Festival (now it is a mecca for desert-loving hipsters), Bunton had been appointed to the court by President Jimmy Carter. And he quickly developed a reputation as a whip-smart jurist with a withering wit that could be as dry as his hometown in the dead of winter.

He was no-nonsense when it came to the law, but he wasn't above indulging in the occasional antic himself. He was known for carrying concealed water pistols under his robes, which he would draw and use to douse attorneys who he thought had gotten a little long-winded. As a native West Texan, he had an ingrained appreciation for just how deeply many Texans mistrust what they see as the sanctimonious overreaching of federal authorities, be it from the judicial branch, Congress, or, as in the case of Babbitt, the executive branch. But he also had a deep respect for the role of the federal government, and he was not above tweaking his fellow Texans over their mistrust when the opportunity presented itself. The *San Antonio Express-News* once famously photographed him barefoot but otherwise in full bench regalia, in a picture that had been staged to make it look as if the federal judge was walking on water.

Those conflicting aspects of the judge's character were on full display on November 19, 1992, when, on the fourth day of what had been a fast-moving and contentious trial, the judge stepped to the bench to issue his ruling. The Sierra Club had been right on the money, he ruled. The Department of the Interior and the other defendants had failed in their mission to protect the fountain darter and the other vulnerable denizens of the springs, he declared. Bunton ordered the Department of Interior, through the Fish and Wildlife Service, to establish firm standards for the amount of flow that needed to be maintained in the two springs to protect and maintain the critters in them, and he ordered the Texas Water Commission (TWC) to take whatever steps were needed to guarantee that the water from the Edwards made it to the springs in sufficient quantities.

In effect, the judge was ordering the federal government to do what Texas had been unable or unwilling, or both, to do itself. But in a nod to that peculiarly Texan streak of independence that the judge himself displayed from time to time, the judge built a kind of escape clause. He effectively postponed implementing the decision until

May 1993, when the next term of the legislature was set to expire. What he was doing, Robert Gulley would later recall, was "giving the legislature one last chance to resolve the issue on their own."

According to published reports from the time, when the judge stepped to the bench to issue his ruling, he donned a bright yellow hard hat, a wry acknowledgement of the explosive controversy his decision was likely to provoke.

Even still, Bunton may have underestimated the sweep and complexity of the battle to bring all the competing interests in the Edwards into something approximating balance. As it would turn out, a full set of conquistador body armor might have been a more apt choice.

What he had set in motion was a decade-and-a-half-long battle between fast-growing urban interests and old entrenched rural ones, in what Gulley, in his book *Heads Above Water*, detailing the history of the Edwards Aquifer Authority, aptly called a war.

It wasn't as if the parties hadn't known for a very long time that they had a problem. Beginning with the drought of record and through subsequent droughts, the competing interests had watched with as much alarm as the environmentalists when the water levels in the aquifer would dip precariously low.

Indeed, as early as 1983, San Antonio, then led by Mayor Henry Cisneros, who would later go on to serve as the secretary of the Department of Housing and Urban Development under President Bill Clinton, and the Edwards Underground Water District, which included elected representatives from five rural counties over the Edwards—Bexar, Medina, Uvalde, Comal, and Hays—and later included a representative from San Antonio as well as from the Guadalupe–Blanco and Nueces River Authorities, established a joint commission to study the regional water need.

The commission was unique for the time because it focused not just on the needs of San Antonio but on the rural communities as well. In 1988, the commission released a region-wide water plan that, among other things, encouraged all stakeholders to find some alternative source of water. More important, however, it was one of the first times in Texas that officials allowed that maybe, just maybe, the rule of capture had outlived its usefulness. As Robert Hasslocher, then chairman of the water district's board and co-chairman of the commission, put it at the time, the rule had contributed to a "winner-take-all" attitude,[3] and, in what could be considered an echo of the old Spanish concept of *derecho*, he argued that the time had come for all the competing stakeholders to "compromise."

"In arriving at these compromises, every possible consideration has been afforded to the public interest, individual property and business rights, the environment, and the projected needs of the region. Compromise obviously implies mutual concessions. It also suggests—and this plan has been developed in that spirit—mutual gains and benefits. It is the intent of this plan that its burdens and benefits be fairly and rationally distributed among all the parties involved."[4]

The representatives of Uvalde and Medina counties didn't see it that way, and in the months that followed, the regional water management scheme died a slow and lingering death. Realizing they essentially were without an agency to establish the plan and drive compliance with it, the proponents of the plan turned to Austin and asked the legislature to grant them that authority. The rural interests went to Austin, too. Despite all that vaunted talk from Hasslocher about "compromise," none could be found.

Nor could any compromise be reached in the years that followed. In 1992, John Hall, the burly, no-nonsense chairman of the TWC, got so fed up that he announced that his agency would henceforth consider the Edwards an "underground river" rather than a classic aquifer, and as such, the TWC would have the authority to regulate the Edwards's use itself. The TWC's plan called for the total water pumped from the aquifer when it fell below 666 feet above mean sea level to be capped at 450,000 acre-feet, about seventy-five percent of its annual recharge rate, with deeper cuts anticipated in the future. Predictably, the edict elicited anger from the rural interests and scathing condemnations from some in the political class. Billy Clayton, a former leading light in the state senate turned lobbyist, dubbed it both "un-American and un-Texan."[5]

It also elicited a lawsuit. And two days after the final rules were adopted, the Texas Farm Bureau and other agricultural interests won an injunction from the Texas Court of Appeals in Austin blocking the TWC's actions.

What had driven the attempts to resolve the crisis over the Edwards Aquifer to a bitter stalemate were the same deep divisions, the same jealous protection of parochial prerogatives that have stymied efforts to meet the state's water needs ever since the first Spanish settlers displaced the cave painters of the Pecos. It is the same thing that has pitted Clayton and Jeff Williams against the water district in Fort Stockton; it is the same issue that is playing out with different players in Presidio and Las Palmas, in the rice fields of Matagorda County, and in that stretch of land from Austin to the Highland Lakes. It underscores the battle between the old-timers along the Sulfur River and the sprawling Metroplex. It is essentially this: How do you manage a resource that everyone needs when everyone thinks their needs are paramount?

Academics have a clever paradigm to describe that conundrum. They call it "the tragedy of the commons." First described in 1833 by a British economist named William Forster Lloyd, the theory states that when individuals all have access to the same resource—be it water or grazing land—the natural inclination of each of those individuals will be to take as much as possible for themselves, even if that means that the resource will be depleted or destroyed. By the late 1960s, thanks to an article in the influential journal *Science* by Garrett Harden, the theory gained currency and became a rallying point for environmentalists everywhere except, it seems, in Texas.

Here, as in Lloyd's England of the nineteenth century, the culture, and to some degree the law, seemed to condemn the various stakeholders to permanent conflict.

That is where Judge Bunton came in.

There is little doubt that Bunton, as a native Texan, understood that nothing motivates Texans like water unless it is the threat that the federal government will step in and tell them how to use that water. A generation earlier, Governor John Connally had waved that particular red flag to drum up support for the grandiose 1968 State Water Plan to replumb the entire state of Texas from the east to the west. Indeed, if just 6,277 more Texans had been baited by that argument, that measure would have passed. Bunton no doubt figured that it would be an even stronger motivation this time.

At first, it seemed the judge was right. In 1993, the state legislature, albeit reluctantly, responded to the judge's spurs and this time did create an authority that, technically at least, had the power to regulate the waters of the Edwards Aquifer. It is indicative of just how sharp that cultural divide between urban and rural interests was that even with the threat of federal intervention looming over their heads, the legislators still had to engage in a little harmless subterfuge to get the enabling legislation passed. Though Robert Puentes had been instrumental in developing the legislation, when the time came to sponsor the bill, Puentes kept his name off it and instead buttonholed an East Texas lawmaker named Ron Lewis, who hailed from the sleepy little town of Mauriceville, population 2,743, to slap his name on it. "I had to make a political decision to get off the bill because it had too much of a San Antonio taste to it," Puentes recalled. "It was hard for me to get support because people immediately thought, 'Well, you're just going to do what's best for San Antonio.'"

A nine-member board was created, empowered to limit pumping to 450,000 acre-feet of water per year, about seventy-five percent of the Edwards's annual recharge rate, with the intention of bringing that down further to 400,000 acre-feet by 2008.

But that board didn't get seated until 1996, and by then it was already becoming clear that the EAA's authority was in trouble. Bowing to entrenched interests, rural and urban, the authority effectively had undermined its own pumping limits by guaranteeing that existing users would be able to draw a minimum amount of water based on their historical usage, meaning that users had dibs on water that would exceed the 450,000-acre-feet-a-year cap by more than 100,000 acre-feet. The response was to borrow a page from surface water rights and effectively establish a system of junior water rights and senior water rights, except that in this case, those rights that kept the withdrawal below 450,000 acre-feet a year were designated senior rights; those above were designated junior rights. Those junior rights, however, still had value; to reduce the pumping to meet the cap, those junior rights would have to be purchased, at a cost of about $1 billion.

But the classic divisions, San Antonio versus the rural interests, remained, and by 2007 the battle lines had become so hardened that it seemed to most observers that Bunton would have no choice but to let "the blunt axe" of federal intervention fall.

That, at last, got the legislature's attention.

In 2007, working from a recommendation by the Fish and Wildlife Service and with Judge Bunton's threat hovering just above their heads, the state legislature at last stuck its neck out and passed Senate Bill 3. The bill created the Edwards Aquifer Recovery Implementation Program and mandated that representatives of all the stakeholder groups, cities, agriculture, and environmentalists, develop a plan to manage the aquifer and protect the springs and the endangered species that called them home.

It was, Gulley recalls in his book, a Herculean task. Especially for a 62-year-old man who relied on a cane to help him navigate his way between the competing factions. But it was a task for which Gulley, a San Antonio–bred scientist with a doctorate in anatomy, an attorney who had spent nearly a decade with the Department of Justice, was uniquely suited.

There were hard-nosed negotiations and even, according to some who lived through it, some odd, peculiarly Texan horse-trading that came very close to bending the rules. In one instance, allegedly, one rural county judge called a meeting between two particularly fractious groups, keeping one in the courthouse and the other in a bank parking lot across the street and ferried notes between them until a compromise could be reached. In another instance, the whole endeavor almost fell apart when the participants realized that in order to keep the springs flowing during a drought comparable to the drought of record, they would be required to cut their consumption by a staggering eighty-seven percent, a provision that meant that the stakeholders either would go dry or would have to come up with billions of dollars to find alternative sources of water.

But little by little, a consensus emerged. And there were compromises. The final plan, in the worst of droughts, would require the stakeholders to cut consumption by about forty-four percent. It made those draconian cuts less likely by requiring stakeholders to enact conservation measures, by paying farmers to irrigate less and use water more wisely during the frequent droughts that plagued the region, and by creating a mechanism to store water underground during wet years for use in dry times. It carried a hefty price tag— $18 billion—but the stakeholders negotiated a mechanism to pay for it through a combination of higher pumping fees and fees paid by users downstream of the springs who now, at least theoretically, were assured of a steady flow.

It has been twenty years since the EAA was first established and half a decade since the Edwards Aquifer Recovery Implementation Program was consummated. In that time, a profound shift has taken place in the region. Though there has been some grumbling, the confederation of competing interests largely has remained in place.

The Edwards Aquifer Recovery Implementation Program has not been without consequences, of course. In San Antonio, which before the Edwards controversy was the largest American city that depended on a single source for its water, the continuing search for new sources of water has added to the price tag customers of the San Antonio Water Supply (SAWS) pay to make sure that their taps flow. It also has pitted the thirsty city against opponents in rural communities like Burleson, where the city plans to begin pumping water from the Carrizo-Wilcox Aquifer through the 142-mile-long Vista Ridge Pipeline. But it also has had benefits. Indeed, for one former opponent of the project who now sees the EAA as a model that the rest of the state could emulate, in an odd way the drawbacks actually may be benefits.

"I was on the city council in San Antonio when Judge Bunton made his ruling," said Representative Lyle Larson, the San Antonio

Republican who now has Puentes's old job at the helm of the Natural Resources Committee, "and like most of my colleagues on councils in the Edwards region, we were furious."

But it soon became clear that, whether he had intended to or not, Judge Bunton effectively had set in motion a process that transubstantiated water in the Edwards region, turning it from a birthright bequeathed by Spanish kings and English common law into an almost mundane commodity with a price set by the invisible hand of the free market. Because the laws of supply and demand now held sway, the price of water did increase. That, Larson said, spurred a couple of significant changes. First, as the water became dearer, people conserved more. Indeed, in the years after the creation and empowerment of the EAA, San Antonio launched a significant initiative to educate its residents in the virtues of water conservation that has become a model nationwide. Back in the days before the EAA was established, the average San Antonio resident used about 200 gallons of water per day—by 2010, that had dropped to a little less than 140 gallons a day, according to SAWS.

And it wasn't just the urban or industrial users who were reducing their consumption. By 2008, Larson said, farmers in Uvalde and Medina Counties had installed $40 million worth of water-saving pivot irrigation systems, and because they were using less of their allotment—and still growing the same crops in the same amount— many of them found that they had spare water left over. And now, because the price of water had risen dramatically as a result of the caps on pumping from the aquifer, those farmers could sell that water to cities and suburbs that desperately needed it.

"They were slipping one acre-foot off to sell to the city of San Antonio and they were still farming, and they were still making money, but they had a check coming in the mailbox," Larson said.

That market, artificially and perhaps accidentally created as an unforeseen consequence of a lawsuit over the fountain darter, has driven innovation and diversification of water supplies all over the region.

As a result of the establishment of the EAA, SAWS has built a state-of-the-art water recycling plant that not only treats used water in sufficient quantities to slake the thirst of industrial clients like Toyota and Microsoft as well as municipal consumers but also siphons off the biogenic natural gas created by the process and sells it as fuel, earning a tidy $250,000 a year for SAWS. San Antonio is also the site of the largest brackish water desalination plant in the state, a twelve-million-gallon-a-day facility that pumps water from the Carrizo-Wilcox Aquifer, and the city is now doing reservoirs one better by developing a massive aquifer storage and recovery project that catches up to two hundred thousand acre-feet of the water that flows in wet times and pumps it into the sands around the Carrizo-Wilcox for use during dry times. Because the water is stored underground, evaporation, which plagues most reservoirs in Texas, is not a problem. However much water you put in it, Larson says, that is how much water you get out.

All of these developments, he says, and more, were unintended consequences of the creation of the EAA, or, more to the point, the unintended consequences of the accidental transfiguration of water from a birthright to a marketable commodity.

"We were furious when Judge Bunton made his ruling," Larson said. "But 20 years later . . . looking at the ruling and looking at the water market that has been created by it . . . it forced diversification . . . for the seventh largest city in America. . . . It created that water market, which has been good for people in the western part of the region. And the City of San Antonio has been able to continue to grow . . . because of that water market that materialized."

In that, he says, the Edwards could be a model for the rest of the state.

Right now, however, SAWS's authority to drive that market by effectively allocating groundwater rights in the Edwards has also been thrown into question by the courts, most dramatically in the *Day/McDaniel* case, which we explored earlier, in which the courts concluded that restrictions placed on pumping rights, under Texas law, could be considered a taking for which the landowner must be compensated, potentially bankrupting agencies like the EAA.

Still, the story of the Edwards Aquifer and the so-far successful effort to escape the tragedy of the commons remains a singular event in Texas's long and volatile struggle to make sure that its waters keep flowing. It marked the most successful effort to date to bring competing interests into alignment, and most importantly, it marked the single most significant attempt to rein in the rule of capture.

That, of course, begs the question, Was it a one-off, an odd and unique alignment of interests and events, of politics, of forces on the local, state, and national level? Or could it be replicated elsewhere? Is it a glimpse of the way forward in a state that has always grappled with water shortages and the demands of a growing population, a state where scientists and demographers expect both of those challenges to increase in coming years? Or is it, in a state where the notion that "whoever has the biggest pump wins" remains a cultural cornerstone, and at a time when the federal government under a new administration has given every indication that it will strip future judges of the blunt axe that Bunton wielded, simply a footnote?

As we will see later in this volume, these remain very much open questions.

CHAPTER 13

MUST BE SOMETHING IN THE WATER

TURN ON YOUR TAP IN HOUSTON, the saying goes, and chances are you are filling your glass with water that not too very long ago swirled clockwise down the drain of a porcelain bowl in Dallas. Houston, to a very great degree, is indeed drinking Dallas's flush. That is because a substantial part of the water that Houstonians consume first ran two hundred miles along the Trinity River before it settled in Lake Livingston, one of three major reservoirs serving the city.

By current state and federal standards, the water that ends up in Houston's homes is clean. The city, on its drinking water operations web page, proudly notes that Houston produces "some of the best quality drinking water in the nation" that "meets or exceeds state and federal drinking water regulations." The site goes on to say that the TCEQ has rated the system a "Superior Water Supply System," which is the highest water quality rating awarded to a water utility.

But it takes some aggressive treatment to get it there. Indeed, the Trinity River, which together with the San Jacinto River contributes eighty-seven percent of Houston's water supplies, long has been considered one of the most impaired rivers in the nation.

It is far cleaner than it once was. If you were to stroll upstream today along the banks of the Trinity River, you certainly would notice the detritus of modern life, the trash, the carefully regulated outflows from scores of industrial facilities that pour into the river and its tributaries. But it is nothing like the flow of waste and putrefaction that the river used to carry.

When a pioneer named A. W. Moore first set eyes on the river during a sojourn near Dallas in 1846, he described it as a "narrow, deep stinking affair."[1] Flush with decaying detritus from far upstream, by the turn of the twentieth century the river had become so putrid that Dallas ignored it altogether as a water source for its people, though city leaders still held out hope—finally dashed by the Army Corps of Engineers in 1981—that someday the barely navigable stream could host heavy barge traffic. That was not to be.

As the years passed in the first decades of the twentieth century, the quality of the water in the Trinity deteriorated even further. Large slaughterhouses around Fort Worth treated the river as a sewer, and there were times, according to local lore, when the river would run red with blood and offal. Indeed, in 1925 the state Health Department, in an unusually poetic and apocalyptic turn of phrase for a state bureaucracy, dubbed the Trinity a "mythical river of death."

And while the Trinity River remains one of the state's most impaired waterways—a 2010 report from the TCEQ ranked it in the top third of the state's most polluted waterways—it is far cleaner than it was in the bad old days.

To a great degree, that is thanks to a comparatively aggressive regimen of monitoring and regulation that has been in place in Texas since the early 1950s, efforts that expanded more than forty years ago with the advent of the US Clean Water Act.

Indeed, across the state, says David Eaton, the Bess Harris Jones Centennial Professor in Natural Resource Policy Studies at the University of Texas's LBJ School of Public Affairs, and a noted expert on river basin quality, Texas has made some progress in monitoring and in some cases mitigating the flow of contaminants into both groundwater and surface water supplies. But while the dumping of toxic or otherwise harmful contaminants has been reduced, illegal dumping and accidental discharges remain a critical challenge. Take, for example, the December 2016 incident that plunged the city of Corpus Christi into a near panic when a small amount of an asphalt emulsifier–perhaps no more than twenty-four gallons—seeped into the drinking water supplies of 320,000 people. The state, the city, and the federal government responded quickly, warning residents to use bottled water for their household needs, and within four days, the crisis abated. Assessing the threat was the easy part. Assigning blame—and holding someone fiscally and perhaps even criminally responsible for the spill—has proved to be far more challenging. As late as June 2017, the spill was still officially under investigation. As it turns out, the quip that water in Texas is "yours, mine, and ours"— mine when I am pumping it, ours when you are pumping, and yours when it is polluted—turns out to be a lot more complicated when it comes to actually holding someone accountable for the pollution. That is not just true when it comes to cases in which the pollution can be traced to a single, still-existing business or individual. Across the state, there are scores of polluted waterways languishing on the federal Superfund list because it is not clear who polluted them or when, or because the polluters have pulled up stakes or gone out of business

While the Corpus Christi incident cast into stark relief the continuing risks of contamination at a time when the state was struggling to find sufficient water to meet the needs of a fast-growing population and the needs of an expanding industrial base to support that population, it was far from an isolated case.

In fact, according to a 2012 report by the advocacy group Environment Texas, one trade-off for the state's robust development was that the state's surface waterways were ranked second worst in the nation just in terms of the number pounds of contaminants released into its waterways that year. Overall, more than sixteen million gallons of often toxic waste found its way into Texas's waterways, said Luke Metzgar of Environment Texas.[2]

Among the most compromised waterways, according to a 2010 study by the same group, were the Houston Ship Channel, the Brazos River, and both the Corpus Christi Bay and Inner Harbor.

Monitoring all the surface water sources in the state for industrial, agricultural, and other forms of straight-from-the-pipe pollution is a staggering task, says Eaton, the University of Texas professor. There are over two hundred thousand miles of streams and rivers in Texas, about one-fifth of them running year-round. There are more than eight million acres of inland and coastal wetlands in Texas that can absorb contamination, and nearly four thousand square miles of the Gulf of Mexico is under the state's jurisdiction. Monitoring them all would be a monumental undertaking. As a result, areas are targeted and evaluated, and, where possible, remediation steps are undertaken. Despite those efforts, levels of contamination remain high in many Texas waterways. In May 2017, for example, the US Fish and Wildlife Service tested sediment, fish (crappies, catfish, bass), and crabs taken from Champion Lake in Liberty County, a seven-hundred-acre lake inside a national wildlife refuge. The lake is fed almost entirely by the Trinity River as it winds it ways through the urban and industrial corridor of the Metroplex. The Fish and Wildlife Service found alarmingly high levels of PCBs and significant traces of mercury, high enough to threaten anyone who would rely on those fish for a regular meal.[3]

It is not an isolated case. In Donna, Texas, in the Rio Grande Valley, state officials for decades have been trying—unsuccessfully—to dissuade poor, largely Hispanic anglers from feeding their families with their catches from the reservoir there, a designated Superfund site laden with PBCs that, so far, has remained perilously contaminated. Similar scenarios play out to a lesser degree at scores of surface-water sources across the state, waters contaminated by industrial waste and agricultural runoff, as is the case along the Bosque River Basin, where state officials have been working with mixed success to reduce pollutants churned into the river basin from some 180 concentrated animal feeding operations. Then there is the witches' brew of chemicals and compounds that run downhill each day from the manicured lawns and driveways of tens of millions of Texans.

There are challenges with groundwater as well. In 2015, the TCEQ reported that it was investigating 276 new cases of groundwater contamination, a slight increase over the year before, bringing the total number of cases under investigation or remediation to just over 3,400 statewide.[4] That is a fraction of what it has been in previous years. In 1998, the state had some 8,000 cases in its sights. By far, oil and gas and related petroleum products made up the bulk of the contaminants detected, leaked either at the surface or belowground at various stages of the development and production process, from drilling to refining and shipping.

And while oil drilling per se accounts for a comparatively small fraction of the incidents reported, it is not a stretch to say that water pollution from extractive industries like mining and oil and gas exploration does indeed remove some otherwise developable water.

Take the now-abandoned Shafter Silver mine just a few yards from Monroe Elms's Tuscanesque villa and a few miles uphill from the water-starved colonia of La Pampas. A few yards beneath that parched landscape is a pool of water that, if tapped, would be the largest well ever drilled in Presidio, with enough water to serve the needs of Presidio for eight years and maybe even provide water for the hard-pressed residents of La Pampa. Unfortunately, it is sitting inside the honeycombed rock of the silver mine, and there are fears that mining chemicals and natural compounds have left the water too contaminated for human consumption, though that remains a subject of debate. Even if the water were accessed, and even if it were ultimately deemed clean enough to use, it would be far too costly to transport it the thirteen miles to La Pampas and the seven more miles to Presidio. According to a plan filed with the TCEQ, in the event that the mine ever is reopened, and the water needs to be drained, the water would instead be pumped into a holding pond that would be constructed in a nearby dry gulch, poetically named "Arroyo del Muerto," where it would be allowed to evaporate. It is not that the water would technically go to waste. It is just that, thanks to the laws of hydrology, it wouldn't do the residents of Presidio County much good. Instead, the beneficiaries of that water would be selected by the impassive rules of the natural cycle and the prevailing winds.

In recent years, the state aggressively has made progress tackling at least one energy-related source of contamination, says Texas Tech's noted water expert, the serendipitously named Dr. Ken Rainwater. "We had a big situation, starting in the late '80s, with leaking underground [gasoline] storage tanks," he said. The EPA estimated that "somewhere between a third to a half" of the gas stations in the state had leaking tanks, and service station owners were required to prove that their operations were leak-free or spend the money to replace them. While contaminants leaking from underground storage tanks still plague areas of the state—as of September 2016 there were, according to the TCEQ, some 1,554 substandard tanks still awaiting cleanup—Texas, with the help of federal funds, has cleaned up many of them. And those that have been installed since—mostly beneath mega–gas stations like Buc-ee's with the deep pockets to afford them—"were built properly," Rainwater says. "They dug holes, they put in liners, they have monitoring systems, and so the potential for the newer systems that have been built . . . to cause contamination, that's gone," or at least dramatically reduced.

The way Rainwater and other experts see it, the state has done an adequate and at times excellent job of addressing the big, obvious problems, the kinds of things that prompted the state's first tentative steps toward pollution control, the kinds of blood-and-oil-in-the-rivers events that outraged even the most casual observer in the 1960s and 1970s and led to the birth of the environmental movement.

The University of Texas's David Eaton agrees. It is not that the problems of groundwater and surface water pollution are markedly worse in Texas than they are elsewhere in the United States, Eaton says. Nor, he says, has the state been unusually lax in addressing them. For nearly sixty-five years, "we've had a program in the state that supports units of the state that are concerned with improving water quality. So we've had one of the longest—if not the longest and strongest—of the state revolving funds programs" to monitor and address pollution.

To be sure, those efforts are far from perfect.

"I would not say that we have no problems," Eaton says. "We have a very large number of stream segments that do not meet Texas's own standards."

But they are far better than they used to be, he says. It is rare these days for a dramatic incident like the Corpus Christi event to occur and rarer still for a body of water like the Trinity River to run red with blood. And when a segment of it does, like in 2012 when a local meatpacker allegedly dumped pig blood into a tributary of the river, the state is usually quick to find the source and stop it (though in that case, criminal charges against the meatpacker were eventually dropped).

The challenges take on a different hue in Texas, a place where an ever-increasing population is placing ever-increasing demands on water supplies, where a changing climate is likely to mean more of the same challenge that Texas has always faced, crippling droughts that can at once reduce water levels while in effect raising the concentrations of natural and human-introduced contaminants, punctuated in places by deluges, like those that arrived with Hurricane Harvey, that can wash all manner of toxins into the water supply. Indeed, while authorities continue to assess the environmental hazard that Harvey unleashed across much of East Texas, at least 560,0000 gallons of contaminants, including crude oil, gasoline, and saltwater, spilled into coastal waterways in the aftermath of the storm. Some of the state's most contaminated Superfund sites, including US Oil Recovery, a former petroleum industry waste-processing plant, suffered significant leaks. In some cases, weeks passed before the leaks were reported to authorities or the public. Sewage plants were overwhelmed, and in some cases destroyed, meaning water with high levels of fecal coliform bacteria and other pathogens and toxins flowed out unchecked. One group of researchers studying the silt and sand left behind after the floodwaters receded found traces of arsenic, chromium, cadmium, and lead, according to a report in the *Houston Chronicle*.[5] Customers of several major water suppliers had to boil their water before using it long after the storm had passed.[6]

That alone would make the challenge Texas faces daunting enough. But what makes the challenge even more acute is that state and federal agencies tend to apply a one-size-fits-all approach when it comes to safe water standards—protecting potable water when very little of the water we actually use ever crosses our lips.

That strikes Dr. David Klein, a former professional motorcycle racer and self-described foosball hustler who, as it happens, now spends most of his time studying and teaching about water quality at Texas Tech University in Lubbock, as a bit odd and perhaps a bit counterproductive.

"The average home in Texas uses about ten thousand gallons of water a month. Out of that ten thousand gallons, less than five hundred goes in your mouth," he says. "And therein lies the problem." All of those ten thousand gallons must be treated to potable standards, he says. And the standards have in recent years, gotten tougher. Beginning in 2006, for example, in a move that was decried by environmentalists as too lenient and by small government types as an unconscionable exercise in federal muscle flexing, the EPA lowered the acceptable standard for arsenic in water from fifty parts per billion to ten. The idea was that the move would reduce the risk of cancers or other health issues arising from long-term exposure to the often naturally occurring carcinogen. But not every community was prepared to meet the new standard. In fact, according to a March 2016 report by the Environmental Integrity Project, based on two years of data collected by the TCEQ, the average arsenic concentration in "65 Texas community water systems serving more than 82,000 people has exceeded that health based standard over the last two years. About 51,000 of these people in 34 communities have been exposed to contaminated drinking water for at least a decade, many at levels several times higher than the arsenic limit."[7]

While there can be a robust debate over the relative merits of the reduced arsenic in the water, Klein says, the upshot is that local water purveyors ultimately are going to pass along the hefty price tag for treating the water to their customers, who, for the most part, are using it for purposes for which a far less pristine water source would suffice. "At the end of the day, you're flushing your toilet with water that anybody in the world would drink right out of the bowl and pay to do so," he says. "We use water that's way, way, way too clean for washing our dogs, our houses, our cars, and watering the lawn, which is where most people's water goes."

In some cases utilities have sometimes found that it is more cost-effective not to treat the bulk of the water. Instead, they simply have given away cartons of potable water to their customers. Klein cites Lubbock as an example where the city in 2015 began handing out five-gallon jugs of drinking water to some eighty-six businesses and scores of residents whose water supply had been tainted by nitrates,[8] the lingering result of a decades-old incident in which effluent was allowed to seep into the aquifer. If, as expected, water continues to become more scarce, more precious, and, as a result, more costly, such, an approach may seem increasingly attractive from the standpoint of simple economics. Yes, bottled water is far more expensive than water that simply is pumped out of the ground or siphoned out of a reservoir and subjected to nominal treatment—water that has an estimated value of about $75 an acre-foot to a farmer can be worth more than a million dollars an acre-foot when it is squirted into a plastic bottle with a brand-name label slapped on its side, analysts say.

Considering the host of contaminants, from naturally occurring toxins like arsenic to pharmaceuticals and fertilizers, one potential solution, Klein says, would be to encourage individual consumers to install in-house treatment systems. That would scrub drinking water at the end of the faucet. The EPA, he notes, is generally skeptical of relying on end users to take on such responsibilities; the agency believes such tasks are better handled by larger, more easily monitored entities like utilities. "We're at that point where at end of use, it's cheaper to do this at your faucet than it is to treat every drop of water that comes through the world," he said.

But that kind of every-person-for-himself approach runs the risk of creating an almost class-based hierarchy of water purity, a system in which those who can afford often expensive home treatment systems have access to all the clean freshwater they want while less affluent Texans would be left behind, he says. Under that brand of damp Darwinism, "rich people go, 'I got mine and I really don't give a flying frick who drinks what outside my house,'" he said.

The ideal solution, Klein and others argue, would be to stop pretending that all water is created equal—that the water a farmer uses to irrigate his high-country cotton is the same stuff you use to wash your car and that it all needs to be at the same level of purity as the water you use to boil your rice—and develop a system that would classify the various qualities of water, price them differently, and deliver them through a separate water hookup.

This concept involves using so-called purple pipes, an approach that has been tried elsewhere in the United States and is even used by some industries in Texas.

The problem with that, of course, is that in a state that has been as heavily developed for as long as Texas has, the cost of rehabilitating that much infrastructure would be staggering, says Laura Huffman, state director for the Nature Conservancy. "In terms of purple pipes and things like that for flushing toilets and washing clothes, I think probably we will get there," she says, particularly as water supplies dwindle and the need to draw distinctions between different grades of water becomes more acute. "I think the holdup probably is that the infrastructure that you'd have to create in order to make that doable, that's a lot of pipe, right? You see it with some industrial uses, like cooling water and things like that, but [to plumb the whole new separate lines] for residential subdivisions and things like that, it's probably more a question of cost. As an idea it would probably be cost-prohibitive at the residential level at this point."

What Huffman recommends is a more—for lack of a better word—holistic approach to the challenge of making our water supplies cleaner and making sure that they remain that way. As she notes, the bulk of the water that most Texans use tends to be groundwater, though once it is used, it often ends up being treated and discharged into surface water systems. Thus the arbitrary distinction between groundwater and surface water is blurred. The trick is to make sure that on both ends of that stretch of the hydrological cycle, the water is kept as pristine as possible. In San Antonio and in Austin and elsewhere, part of the strategy for accomplishing that has been to protect the water BEFORE it enters the aquifer in the first place.

"When you're drinking groundwater, your interest is in making sure that water is safe and clean. So in San Antonio, starting in the late 1990s, they began with ballot initiatives that [earmarked] portions of the unutilized sales tax in San Antonio to purchase land or conservation easements up over the recharge features of the Edwards Aquifer," Huffman said. A so-called karst aquifer, "the Edwards is like a block of Swiss cheese, so when it rains, all of the runoff from developments, from roads, from parking lots, is shooting through these Swiss cheese holes as fast as fast can go, into the Edwards Aquifer, which is a drinking water supply. So the philosophy or the theory behind the Edwards Aquifer Protection Program in San Antonio was to buy to protect the recharge features so that when it rained, that rain is going into fully restored land that has all of its hydrological functions intact."

By protecting the recharge zone, she argues, the residents and ratepayers of places like San Antonio, who overwhelmingly have supported ballot measures to establish such protection zones, have placed a bet not only that can they capitalize on the natural cleansing that takes place when water percolates through the surface soil into the aquifer, but that they can do it in a way that is cost-effective.

That bet has paid off, she says. "We've protected nearly twenty-one percent of the recharge [zone] for the San Antonio drinking water supply. We've got a return-on-investment analysis that demonstrates that protecting the aquifer, protecting those recharge features, has actually saved the City of San Antonio treatment costs. So I count that as a water quality answer, but I also count that as an affordability measure for these Texas cities that are worried about cost of living."

And it is not just the blow of the cost of living that could be softened by such an approach, says Sam Brody, a flood impact expert and a professor of urban planning at Texas A&M University. So could the ravages of future storms like Hurricane Harvey, the 2017 storm that wreaked havoc on the vast sprawling metropolitan area around Houston in part because largely unchecked development in the region meant that there was so much more there to destroy. For years, Brody has been a kind of Cassandra warning about the risks of rampant, virtually unregulated development in the flood plains along the Texas coast. In fact, just two months before Harvey developed in the Gulf, at the start of 2017's unusually brutal hurricane season, Brody warned in an interview with *The Guardian* newspaper that the region was at risk of a massive disaster and had made itself even more vulnerable to that risk. "It's not if, it's when,"[9] Brody told the newspaper. "If you're going to put four million people in this flood-vulnerable area in a way which involves ubiquitous application of impervious surfaces, you're going to get flooding."

At the time, Brody's dire warning went unheeded. Now, as a member of the Governor's Commission to Rebuild Texas, established as the flood-ravaged regions of the state were still digging out and tallying up the cost of the disaster, Brody says he's hoping that his warnings may carry a bit more weight and that either through regulation or through warning home buyers and builders about the dangers of building in low-lying, flood-prone areas, and thus harnessing the power of the market, the region can better plan for the next flood.

Certainly, leaving land unmolested where possible would reduce the exposure to financial and human losses in the event of future Harvey-caliber floods. And it would preserve recharge areas for watersheds and aquifers. Just as importantly, it would address what has emerged in recent decades as one of the most significant threats to water quality above- and belowground, not just in Texas but also across the nation and the developed world. That would be the rising challenge of what is usually called "nonpoint-source" pollution, contaminants that seep into the water supply, not from a single, regulated, and monitored source, like a chemical plant's permitted outflow pipe, but from hundreds of thousands of small, largely unregulated points like lawns and driveways and golf courses and farms.

Indeed, if, as Eaton says, the state has made respectable if imperfect progress in the past forty years in addressing the challenges posed by traditional contaminants entering the state's water supply from large and largely regulated sources, that was the easy part. The biggest problem that Texas, like the rest of the country, now faces is nonpoint-source pollution. And the state is only just beginning to grapple with it.

From his modest office in Iowa City, Iowa, almost one thousand miles north of the Texas state line, the US Geological Survey's Dana Kolpin, head of the Emerging Contaminants Project, has been studying the potential impacts of nonpoint-source pollution for two decades, not just on the water supply in Texas but across the nation.

It is, he says, a daunting challenge. It is not just that the handful of researchers who make up his team need to sample thousands of water sources. It is that they are looking for whole new arrays of potentially disruptive chemicals and compounds, things that on the surface may seem far less toxic than traditional industrial waste products or the random oil spill, things like hormones and newly minted pesticides that find their way into surface and groundwater from farmers' fields, things like lawn care products and antidepressants, which can trickle into the water cycle even after they are consumed by the 16.7 percent of American adults—some forty million of them—who take them each day, according to a 2016 report by the *Journal of the American Medical Association*.[10]

And if that task wasn't tough enough already, add to it that as many as one thousand new chemicals and compounds are injected into the market—thus mainlined into the water—each and every year, he says. They are pulsing into our waterways from sewage treatment plants, they are in the runoff that escapes the state's farms, and they are being hosed down from front yards all over the state. There is virtually no regulation of them—water from treatment plants could and often does contain trace elements of all sorts of pharmaceuticals, he says, without violating any of the standards set by the state or the federal government for drinking water quality. "They're doing exactly what they're supposed to be doing," he says.

The question is, he says, are we doing enough?

For now, he says, our nation's understanding of the potential impact of those chemicals in our water is at best rudimentary. "We just don't have an understanding of the full ramifications of the presence of these compounds in the environment," he said. "We certainly have a growing body of knowledge that these compounds in general—these things we use in our everyday life—have a potential to become environmental contaminants."

But with limited resources to measure the levels in tens of thousands of places and even fewer resources to analyze how all of these chemicals and compounds interact with each other in the environment, Kolpin and his researchers, working side by side with independent researchers, admit that they have no clear idea at this point how the chemicals might interact with each other, how they might affect the environment, the flora or the fauna, let alone what health concerns might arise in human beings who consume them. But there have been troubling signs that over the long term, persistent exposure to ingredients from prescription medications like Zoloft and Prozac together with pesticides and other common household chemicals may be taking its toll. Researchers studying fish taken from Pecan Creek, a small stream that runs through Denton that receives treated effluent from the city's waste treatment plant before depositing it in Lake Lewisville, a reservoir that provides drinking water for millions in the Metroplex, have documented odd phenomena in some of the fish—males turning into females, for example.

While most researchers suspect that the concentrations remain low enough not to be an immediate threat to human health, they remain vigilant, and their research has taken on a growing sense of urgency, particularly as more and more communities consider "toilet to tap" technology—recycling wastewater to meet their ever-growing demand for "new water" to slake the thirst of fast-growing communities. To its credit, Texas has at least begun to grapple with the question. Since 2009, a task force created by the legislature has been searching for ways to keep these compounds out of the waterways, with mixed results. But communities by and large have been slow to take up the challenge, and few even test for several of the chemicals and compounds. That means it is up to guys like Kolpin, and a comparative handful of researchers across Texas and America, to take up the slack and ask the $64,000 question: "What *are* the consequences from these kinds of low-level exposures to meds on aquatic organisms or terrestrial organisms?" Kolpin says. "Is there any impact to human health to having trace levels in our drinking water, for example?"

Studies indicate that the intricate interplay between various elements for various creatures could, over time, trigger chain reactions that, for the moment, are beyond our ken, Kolpin says. In one study, for example, Kolpin's researchers found unusually high levels of antidepressants in water about eight kilometers downstream from the outfall pipe for a wastewater treatment facility. Fathead minnows culled from the area were found to have significant levels of the stuff in their tissue, he said. The consequences were not immediately obvious—no two-headed minnows or anything like that. "These things weren't killing them," he said. But further experiments—in which live minnows exposed to antidepressants were dosed with a stimulant to mimic their systems' natural response to predators— showed that the levels were high enough to alter the minnows' behavior. Kolpin noted, "They were slower in their response to predators and their escape velocity was slower." It would be easy to assume that such a change in behavior at one level of the food chain could ripple upward—slower minnows could mean short-term feast and long-term famine for the next predator up the food chain, and that, in turn, would likely have an effect on the next predator up the line, all the way, perhaps, to humans. "You just make the assumption that if you're in the food chain, you don't want to react slower to predators. So those kinds of things, where it could have impacts where the concentrations themselves might not have acute effects," said Kolpin.

For now, the research remains far from conclusive. "I'm not saying the sky is falling . . . but there's enough evidence in my mind that we need more research to find out is this an acceptable risk," Kolpin said. "Obviously we'd all prefer . . . to drink things that don't have pharmaceuticals in them. But we need more research. Obviously, pharmaceuticals have a definite benefit, so if trace levels are getting into our water, is that acceptable? Or is there something else—maybe—that goes on with other organisms that sometimes it takes two or three generations for something to crop up with those organisms. So we may be drinking something that's not observable, and our next generation may drink a little bit more and at some point will it tip the bucket?"

The only reasonable path forward, he says, is more research. But at a time when budget concerns and the politics that surround government research that could lead to tighter regulations down the road have become a battlefield, at a time when the federal government has signaled that it wants to step back from aggressive research and action on a host of environmental issues, the future of that kind of research remains, just the like the rivers and reservoirs themselves, uncertain.

CANADIAN

Canadian

OKLAHOMA

NEW
MEXICO

ARK.

RED

○ Lubbock

Red

SULPHUR

CYPRESS

BRAZOS

Fort Worth ⊙ ○ Dallas

SABINE

○ El Paso

Pecos

Colorado

TRINITY

NECHES

COLORADO

Brazos

RIO GRANDE

Rio Grande

Austin ⊙

SAN
JACINTO

NECHES-
TRINITY

GUADALUPE

LAVACA

Houston ⊙

TRINITY-
SAN JACINTO

SAN
ANTONIO

San
Antonio

SAN JACINTO-
BRAZOS

BRAZOS-COLORADO

COLORADO-LAVACA

NUECES

SAN ANTONIO

LAVACA-GUADALUPE

SAN ANTONIO-NUECES

MEXICO

NUECES-
RIO
GRANDE

Gulf of
Mexico

0   50   100 mi

Major river basin boundary

CHAPTER 14

HANGED IN A FORTNIGHT

A DRILL RIG BORES straight through the sandy loam and down more than a mile deep into the shale of the Permian Basin not far from the dry West Texas town of Midland. It is hot and dusty, thirsty work for the crew that mans the rig, as you can tell by the discarded water and soft drink bottles that pile up like cordwood at the edge of the pad. The din of the diesels that power it all is deafening. It will take a few days to hit the sweet spot of the shale. And when it is done, the crew will go home, take a shower, maybe throw a pot of water on the gas burner and boil up some dinner. A new crew will come in and blast the borehole with a million and a half gallons of water laced with sand and a blend of chemicals to shatter the buried shale and release a few million years' worth of oil and natural gas, just as another crew somewhere else did, to free the oil that drives that drill bit into the earth.

That million and a half gallons of water per well, though far less than the amount used by agriculture or by municipalities, is still a lot anywhere in Texas. That is particularly true in a place like Midland, a place where sometimes the rain doesn't fall at all; its average annual rainfall is less than fifteen inches, about one-quarter of what Houston gets in a year. There is water, of course, around Midland. The Colorado River Municipal Water District does its best to keep three nearby reservoirs—Lake Ivie, the E. V. Spence Reservoir just out-side Robert Lee, and the J. B. Thomas Reservoir south of Snyder—in operation. But in a place as prone to drought as Midland, that is not always easy. Indeed, in 2011, the Spence and Thomas reservoirs dropped to two percent of capacity, and Lake Ivie was a third drained when local authorities ordered strict conservation measures.

There is groundwater, too. Midland draws some of its ground-water from a series of wells west of Odessa, and since 2012, the city has been using some water from a well field it drilled on the T-Bar ranch outside town. Taken together, those combined sources are good enough for wet times, but the groundwater is not the best. It is alkaline and high in chlorides. There are traces of arsenic in it, and if the city really wanted to expand its use of groundwater, local authorities say, it would probably need to build a costly desalination plant.

The drillers could perhaps use less water. It is difficult to assess the precise amount of groundwater consumed by fracking because in Texas the oil and gas industry largely is exempt from reporting it, unless local groundwater districts require them to. It is estimated that, statewide, hydraulic fracturing used about twenty-five billion gallons of water a year at the beginning of this decade, with the Permian Basin, together with the Barnett, the Haynesville, and the Eagle Ford, accounting for the lion's share of that, a number that is expected to grow to forty billion gallons by 2020.[1] Though individual wells in the Permian tend to use less water than wells in other places like the Eagle Ford, there are enough wells packed close enough together to have a serious impact on the region's water supply. Drill-ers could recycle more of the water that flows back from the wells they drill. That, of course, is far costlier than the preferred option for disposing of flowback—simply injecting it into wells deep in the ground, a practice that has been linked to causing earthquakes. Still, according to a 2014 study by Ceres, a Boston-based nonprofit that focuses on sustainable investments, drillers in the Permian, where almost ninety percent of the wells are drilled in water-stressed areas, increasingly are experimenting with recycling techniques.[2] They also are experimenting with using a different mix of water, relying on more brackish water and less freshwater. But that is hardly a silver bullet in a place like West Texas, where, increasingly, oil and gas drillers find themselves in competition for whatever water there is with the largest consumer, agriculture, and the second-largest, municipal water suppliers, and where each of them is casting covetous eyes toward those same brackish groundwater supplies. And some of those drillers are also buying wastewater from the local municipalities, the same sort of water that, elsewhere in Texas, other municipalities are eyeing as a treatable source of water for their own needs.

Indeed, in places like Midland and Odessa, at the far end of the Great Plains Aquifer, in an arid region of overtaxed aquifers and sporadically undependable reservoirs, the issue of finding enough water for all of those who demand it is a Gordian knot. And it is going to get even more complicated to untie. Just recently, the US Geological Survey announced new estimates for a mammoth oil field—long out of reach by conventional drilling techniques—in the Midland Basin section of the Permian. Known as the Wolfcamp Shale, it is a 20-billion-barrel deposit of oil, three times larger than the Bakken Shale that turned a remote stretch of prairie in North Dakota into a boomtown overnight, with another 16 trillion cubic feet of natural gas, equivalent to 1.6 billion barrels of natural gas, that stretches 119 miles from Midland to Lubbock, under some of the driest land in Texas. It is going to take a lot of water to develop that shale, in a place where disparate interests will compete for dwindling supplies.

To believe that this is a local challenge would be tempting. It certainly is, but it is not just local. The truth is, the ripple effect of that development will have a profound impact on regions all over the state. Yes, there almost inevitably will be an increased demand for water for fracking in Midland and Odessa. But that is only one small piece of the puzzle. The expanded operations in the Permian Basin will mean economic growth in the region, and that will mean more people, more industry, and more thirsty consumers for the municipal water supplies. But the wealth that flows out of those oil and gas wells won't just stay in Midland. It will go to San Antonio and Fort

Worth and Houston as well, supporting the long-term growth and increased demand for water in those places. It is not a stretch to say that the discovery of a new oil field outside Midland will, in the long run, be one of the factors that prods the Dallas–Fort Worth Metroplex to continue its efforts to build a reservoir that will flood Shirley Shumake's family farm in the Sulphur River Basin. The growth fueled by this and other oil fields in Texas will mean that a growing San Antonio will continue to have to find sources of water other than the Edwards Aquifer to support itself, and that will mean increased friction between the city and its rural neighbors. But the hidden connections go even further. That gas and oil will heat San Antonio homes and provide them with electricity, all of which demands vast amounts of water. The nitrogen that will be extracted from the natural gas flowing from those wells outside Midland may well be turned, in part, into fertilizer so that farmers in faraway places can feed and clothe the ten million more people who are expected to turn up on the census rolls in Texas in the next fifteen years. And to grow that food and the fiber, farmers above the Ogallala will have to pump the overburdened aquifer even harder, and guys like Haskell Simon in the rice fields of Bay City will be looking upriver on the Lower Colorado wondering how long it will be before the rice farmers find themselves having to fight Austin and the Highland Lakes for water. And they will wonder whether next time the cuts to their allotments will be deeper and longer, deep and long enough that out in Fort Stockton or someplace like it, another Clayton and Jeff Williams will decide that they might as well grow rice in the desert rather than plunge into a costly and perhaps unsuccessful campaign to sell their water—guaranteed to them by the rule of capture—to Midland and Odessa.

If there is any lesson to be drawn from the challenges facing Midland and Odessa and the rest of the state, it is that for decades, ever since the defeat of the 1968 State Water Plan, Texas has been relying on ground-up local management while facing a challenge that affects the whole state, a challenge that does not respect arbitrary political boundaries.

To be fair, that approach—collecting sixteen separate regional water plans, all detailing local conditions current and future, all assessing local responses, and all reflecting decidedly local interests, and then codifying them every five years into a document called the Texas State Water Plan—has so far proved at least modestly serviceable. It is worth noting, says Dr. Robert Mace, executive administrator of the TWDB, that during the drought of 2011 to 2015, "we did not have a single community run out of water," though one, Spicewood Beach, a community of eleven hundred on the shores of Lake Travis about forty miles outside Austin, came perilously close and had to have water trucked in by the LCRA. In general, he says, the state narrowly had escaped a catastrophic outcome as a result of that drought. "In my opinion, that's directly related to the state water planning process."

If a drought comes along that is a little longer, a little deeper, however, there is little question that, as Dr. Andrew Sansom, former executive director of both the Texas Parks and Wildlife Department and the Texas Nature Conservancy and who is now running the Meadows Center for Water and the Environment, put it, "we're gonna be in a world of hurt."

Actually, make that "when."

You don't have to be a tie-dye-clad tree-hugger or a climate change activist to recognize that as far back as the days of the Pecos cave painters, Texas has been grappling with regular, destructive cycles of drought and flood, and even before you factor in the hazards of what most scientists believe is our role in a worsening climate, there almost certainly will be more severe droughts, worse even than the so-called drought of record, and perhaps soon.

Indeed, last year, the Texas House Natural Resources Committee commissioned a study by the National Oceanic and Atmospheric Administration, the National Aeronautics and Space Administration, and climatologists at Texas A&M to look at tree ring data going back 500 years,[3] and they concluded that most of the state of Texas had experienced a five- to seven-year drought pretty much every century.

The next one, says committee chairman Representative Lyle Larson, is looming on the horizon. It could be next year. It might not happen for decades. But "sometime in the next eighty years we'll have that five- to seven-year drought.

"Is the state of Texas prepared? Absolutely not. We lost eighty-four million acre-feet of water in the drought of 2011," he says. By the end of that drought, "fifty-six communities had a 180-day or less of water supply," and scores of others, including some of the most populous regions in the state, would have run out of water had that drought lasted six years. "We had populations of over one hundred thousand that had less than eighteen months of water supply—Wichita Falls and San Angelo."

In a drought that lasted seven years, hardly an unprecedented occurrence in a state where there are still plenty of people alive who remember the seven-year drought of record, the consequences would be even more disastrous. "What you'll see," Larson says, "is 70 of the 117 reservoirs that we've got in our state . . . will be completely dry," leaving cities and rural communities from Abilene to Austin high and dry. Things would be just as bad if not worse along the I-35 corridor, the study showed, where continued "explosive growth" is taking place at the very same time that annual rainfall amounts in the area have been declining at a rate of about an inch per year for the past eighty years, Larson says. The region is undergoing what Larson describes as an inexorable "desertification" while to the east, across what is often referred to as the "Pine Curtain," East Texas remains awash in water and is likely to remain so.

There is no corner of the state that would not be affected in some significant way by such a drought, say water experts. If the citizens of Austin and the residents of the Highland Lakes would be affected, so too would the rice farmers of Matagorda County. If Dow Chemical got thirsty, every city and farmer along the Brazos from northwest Texas to the Gulf of Mexico would be smacking their parched lips. Such is the intricate interplay between water resources in a state where when it rains it pours and when it doesn't, everyone suffers.

And yet, almost stubbornly, Larson says, Texans continue to view water as first and foremost a local issue.

He is not alone. Indeed, most of the water experts interviewed agree that if the state truly expects to gird itself for the next great drought, if it truly expects to develop sufficient resources to support the population it already has, let alone the growth it can expect in the future, if it wants to both be water secure and enjoy the economic benefits that come along with that, a far more top-down approach is going to be necessary. That, says Larson, requires a kind of leadership from legislators and bureaucrats in Austin that at least thus far has been as rare as a Comal Springs blind salamander.

"I think the state has abdicated our role with regard to that," Larson said. The way he sees it, lawmakers in Austin have delegated their authority over water to sixteen parochial interest groups. And when conflicts arise, they have allowed the courts to settle those disputes, says Amy Hardberger, a geoscientist and attorney who worked for the Environmental Defense Fund before becoming associate dean of the law school at St. Mary's University in San Antonio in 2016. Because those courts are made up of elected judges who reflect, perhaps even more than legislators, the political tenor of the times, they have increasingly been ruling in favor of unfettered individual property rights when it comes to groundwater, as they seemed to have done in the *Day/McDaniel* case, or the inviolability of surface water rights as they did in the *Farm Bureau* case, over the greater interests of the state at large. In that, decisions that could have a profound impact on water policy in the state are being made on the basis of a political sentiment that really has nothing to do with water or with the crisis the state is likely to be facing. In recent years, Hardberger says, the Supreme Court has consistently sided with landowners resisting efforts to place limits on their property rights.

Indeed, conservative, liberal, Republican, Democrat, most of those who study water issues in the state of Texas agree on one thing, that the state's bottom-up paradigm for developing water policy exacerbates local problems, institutionalizes conflicts between regions of the state—the dry west versus the water-logged east—and, most importantly, risks leaving the state woefully unprepared to face a prolonged water crisis that sooner or later is all but guaranteed.

You need look no further than Clayton and Jeff Williams's battles with their local groundwater district to see how the state's current approach has muddied the water. Yes, as the Williams will tell you, the rule of capture does prevail, albeit with some limitations. As long as the water they pumped from the aquifer beneath their Fort Stockton farmland stays in that bowl of parched soil between Interstate 10 and the mountains to the south, they could claim it, in all confidence, as "my water." But if they try to move some of that water out of the district, all of a sudden, it becomes, as far as the local groundwater district is concerned, "our water." Their final success in convincing the local groundwater district to at last grant them a permit to export their water was long in coming, it was costly, and it in no way guarantees that the next time someone wants to try it, it will be any easier.

If the growing cities and suburbs along the Brazos find themselves running short of water, they will have to get in line behind Dow Chemical and farmers with older, more established surface water rights, and if cities and suburbs in dryer regions find themselves in the same predicament, they will find it hard to navigate the byzantine obstacles the state has erected to transferring water from one river basin to another.

It is, as the lawyer quoted at the beginning of chapter 11 put it, truly a case of "yours, mine, and ours" when it comes to water policy in Texas, but in the almost inevitable event of a prolonged drought, that would be a recipe for an economic disaster.

Indeed, as Larson puts it, "we have Balkanized our state into sixteen regions. We fight each other fiercely on these imaginary lines that we set up. We don't have any interconnectivity between the regions. It's almost like a Friday Night Football mentality—'you're not going to get our water.' You could literally be one hundred yards across the county line and they can't get access to water because it's not within their region."

As a result, "our state water plan is a compilation of sixteen different regions' plans," says Larson, "and we put 'em in a book and every five years we close the book and say this is the state water plan. It does a good job identifying the local need five or ten years out. But when it comes to long-term strategic needs for water, I think the state is failing us. I think we have to take a more aggressive posture."

And even that state water plan admits that when the next great drought parches the horizon there is a grave risk that Texas will be unprepared. By 2070, the plan concludes, the 29.5 million people who siphon up the water in Texas now will grow to 51 million, with about half that growth occurring in the areas surrounding the Dallas–Fort Worth Metroplex and around Houston. All those new Texans will be demanding another 3.2 million acre-feet of water above the 18.4 million acre-feet the state uses now. What is more, they will be demanding it, the plan concludes, at a time when water supplies in some places—above the Ogallala, for example—are running scarce. In fact, in that same fifty-year stretch in which the demand increases by seventeen percent, the readily available supplies statewide are expected to decline by eleven percent. The amount of surface water available is expected to decline by one percent, part of that a result of sedimentation, the same issue that proved lethal to the first reservoir built around Austin. Groundwater too is expected to become scarcer. The plan estimates that owing to depletion of the Ogallala and restrictions on other aquifers for a variety of reasons, the state, which will draw about 7.2 million acre-feet from underground sources by 2020, by 2070 will have only 5.4 million at its disposal, a twenty-four percent cut.

Overall, the plan finds that just to tread water by 2070, those sixteen different water planning groups and the state would have to come up with almost nine million acre-feet a year of additional water. And if they don't?

"If strategies are not implemented, approximately one-third of Texas's population would have less than half the municipal water supplies they will require during a drought of record in 2070," the plan solemnly concludes, adding "annual economic losses resulting from water shortages would range from approximately $73 billion in 2020 to $151 billion in 2070."

The authors of the state water plan insist the sixteen regional strategies included in the 2017 state water plan, if fully implemented, are sufficient to allow Texas to dodge that bullet. Larson is not convinced. He believes that a more top-down approach is required.

But wresting authority back from that balkanized collection of local groundwater districts and river authorities is a heavy lift in a place like Texas, which, since the days of the Old Three Hundred, has insisted on individual rights *über alles* and where the ethos has long been that if there was going to be any authority at all, it had better be local. That sentiment was reflected as far back as 1969—around the same time the last grand statewide effort at top-down water management in Texas suffered an ignoble defeat at the polls—in geographer R. W. Meinig's landmark essay *Imperial Texas*. In it, Meinig argued that Texas wasn't so much a state as it was a classic empire, a collection of culturally, economically, and politically diverse regions straining against a distant ruler.

What was true in Texas in 1968 is just as true today. The state remains as divided as ever. When it comes to water issues, say many of those who study the challenges, there is not one Texas. There are sixteen of them, divided along political boundaries rather than along the natural boundaries of aquifers and basins, and within those sixteen semi-independent political entities, there are nearly one hundred local power centers, the state's myriad groundwater districts.

That, says Larson, in the long run will prove to be counterproductive. Though they recognize that it is a politically toxic idea in Texas at the moment, what Larson and other experts, like Sansom, advocate is a greater role in top-down management for the state. As Larson put it, "Either we're all Texans or we're not.

"We're all Texans when we're benefiting from it," he says. "Whether it be our highways, or dealing with our education system, or dealing with the parks system, in all of the collective interests, we all seem to get along well. But when it comes to water, that's where the division starts. I think the state has enabled that prevailing mentality by allowing locals to control the long-term sustainability of our state."

What really needs to happen, according to Puentes of SAWS, is for the voters and ratepayers and regulators and legislators of the state to recognize, once and for all, that "we are all connected."

Sansom agrees that there is a model for that kind of centralized management that would also recognize the interests of local stakeholders. It is the Edwards Aquifer Authority.

Using that hard-fought model as a template, the state at last clearly could define the limits of the rule of capture, with the added benefit that the legislature would at last be heeding the repeated pleas of the courts to do so. That is not to say that the rule of capture need be abolished, nor that authority of local groundwater districts would be entirely curtailed. Instead, the rights of the landowner—and the responsibilities that those rights entail—would be measured against the needs of the state as a whole, rather than just as a local matter.

Such a model might indeed find support even from the landowners themselves.

One idea, says water rights lawyer Ed McCarthy, who represented Jeff and Clayton Williams in their bid to export their water, would be to impose a tax on guys like Jeff Williams, charging them a per-acre-foot fee to ship their water out of the district, similar to the kind of tax the state already imposes on the gas and oil that flow out of the Permian Basin. The way McCarthy sees it, it would be a way of telling the local water district, "Your water has value to the extent that you're losing population or you're losing business because we're moving the water out. I don't think that's a real threat, but to the extent that it is, charge us the export fee and then reinvest that export fee where it needs to go. Put it into your roads and bridges, put it into your school systems."

For guys like his client, "it'd be a cost of doing business," he says. And while there is no doubt that cost ultimately would be added to the price the consumers at the other end of the pipeline would have to pay, in a state that is undergoing such rapid growth, where water is scarce and getting scarcer, and where people are plentiful and getting more so, there is no escaping that harsh reality. The bottom line, he says, is that sooner or later "water's going to be more expensive. We all have to realize that, and we'll all have to pay for it."

In short, what McCarthy is talking about is both inescapable and exceedingly controversial. He is talking about recognizing that water, though it is the stuff of life, is also a commodity, a product, like oil or gas, or timber in the Sulphur River Basin, which can be bought and sold and with a value that can be set by the market, a market that can be prodded or restrained as need be by the judicious application of tax policy.

That is a hard sell in a place like Texas, says Marty Jones, another Texas attorney who has spent decades wrestling with the state's water laws, and not just because Texas is a red state with a long history of balking at taxes and resisting what a lot of people see as the strong arm of distant government. What makes it a doubly hard sell is that for all their talk about property rights, and their oft-stated devotion to the principle of letting market forces drive all decisions, there is still a strong cultural resistance among a lot of Texans when it comes to applying those principles to groundwater.

"Groundwater evokes a visceral response from people. It's a very emotional issue because people tend to believe that keeping water local will be beneficial long term." Thus, particularly in rural parts of Texas, while landowners and groundwater districts are perfectly willing to view groundwater as an unassailable property right as long as it is still in the ground, a bizarre metamorphosis starts taking place the minute you begin pumping. Or as soon as their neighbors do. Then, all of a sudden, your water magically transubstantiates into "our" water, he says, a precious local resource to be guarded at all costs.

"What other asset do we look at in the same way?" he says. "If I have uranium under my property, it belongs to me. I can mine it. I can sell it subject to certain restrictions by the federal government, anywhere. If I have oil and gas, it's the same result. If I have sand or gravel . . . it's generally recognized that I have the . . . right to access, exploit, and sell any of those products of the soil. But when we start talking about groundwater, it gets emotional."

What Jones would advocate, if he were advocating for himself, would be to treat water as—here is that dirty word again—a commodity, like oil and gas, owned in place with the right to sell it or buy it contingent upon a uniform set of regulations and laws. It is ironic that when oil and gas development first took off in Texas at the beginning of the last century, judges and lawmakers turned to the rule of capture to define the rights to those resources. Over the last century, the legislature and the courts allowed the rule of capture to evolve as it relates to oil and gas. But when it comes to water, no such evolution has taken place. The law today is not markedly different than it was in 1904. What he would envision is a system that would respect the water needs of the local region and, within limits, the rights of the landowner enshrined in the rule of capture but which also would view groundwater as a fungible commodity. Indeed, he argues, a system could be established to identify different grades of water with different regulations governing them—just as there are grades of oil and gas. Freshwater could be marketed and regulated with one set of standards targeted to specific markets and specific local uses, whereas brackish water, depending on the level of treatment that would be needed and the potential uses—for mining, for industry, for ultimate development as potable supplies—would be subject to another.

Right now, he argues, a critical impediment to that kind of approach is simple parochialism.

It would be one thing if you were dealing with one or two or even a dozen local groundwater districts. But there are nearly one hundred of them in Texas, many of them sharing a common aquifer but not common rules or guidelines. The one thing they do have in common, says Jones, is that virtually all of them erect some kind of barrier to exporting their water. "Until you understand that we've got to treat groundwater aquifers like we treat oil and gas fields so that the same rules apply across the aquifer instead of across each county in the aquifer, you're never going to get a cohesive policy put together."

Jones, too, envisions something akin to the EAA, a single entity poised above each of the state's nine major aquifers with the legal authority and regional credibility to manage those supplies, with the added benefit of being allowed to market their water. But it was a long and contentious journey to get to the point at which the state was willing to intervene to establish the EAA and to adopt the recovery implementation program that gave it its teeth. As we saw in chapter 12, some of its authority is already being eroded by court decisions, such as the *Day/McDaniel* case, that breathed new life into the rule of capture and thus threaten to undermine the authority of the EAA to limit pumping. Furthermore there is little doubt that had it not been for that "dull axe" of federal intervention, all those competing interests might never have been forced to seek the kind of accommodation the EAA offered in the first place. With a new administration in the White House that has vowed to roll back regulation, dismantle the "administrative state," and rein in the EPA, and with a Congress that is working to roll back the Endangered Species Act—the very law that sparked the lawsuit that was the EAA's genesis—it remains an open question whether the Edwards model is likely to be replicated any time soon anywhere in Texas.

Of course the challenges are not limited to groundwater alone. Surface water also remains a critical challenge to Texas.

It took the state decades to properly adjudicate all those surface water rights, and by the time it got done, most of the rivers in the state, in effect, had been overallocated. There were more people who had rights to the water than there was water. That is not usually a problem in wet periods. In fact, says Rick Lowerre, because water rights were based on historical usage, and because farmers have become more conservation minded while some have given up farming altogether in the years since, often those allocations are greater than the amount of water the rights holder actually uses. "Texas has . . . gone to the point where the law . . . says you get a paper right for let's say fifty thousand acre-feet. You're allowed to use up to that. And you use thirty thousand on an annual basis to actually have more for expansion. But you never use it. You've perfected thirty thousand acre-feet."

As the law stands, that landowner who has rights to fifty thousand acre-feet and uses thirty thousand can sell the remaining twenty thousand acre-feet. But there is a catch. The water effectively has to remain in the same basin. Sell it outside the basin, for example, sell your Guadalupe River water to a buyer in the Brazos River basin, and that water automatically loses its priority. Your senior—and thus uninterruptible—water right on the Guadalupe River becomes a junior water right. In effect that drives down the value of that water, making it less attractive to the buyer and less lucrative for the sellers, says Carlos Rubenstein, the former watermaster for the Rio Grande. If Larson's scientists are right and the dry times are going to get drier, "Texas is going to need a heck of a lot more water," Rubenstein says, and getting it from where it is to where it isn't is going to become a much more urgent priority. "Surface water is pretty much already fully allocated," he says, "but you still need to move the surface water from where it is to where it isn't. And Texas regrettably has done things in law to make that harder. Particularly with the junior provision for interbasin transfer.

"When you do things like establish a junior provision for interbasin transfers, you're actually devaluing water, not adding value to it," Rubenstein says. What is more, you are adding to the impetus for those local regions that get significant rainfall, East Texas for example, to hold on to their allocations come hell or low water.

Ideally, Rubenstein says, the state would step in and limit or eliminate the distinctions between junior rights and senior water rights. "My only answer is get rid of it," he says. Yes, he argues, local stakeholders need to be represented in the discussions and their very real interests need to be protected. "You have to protect the area of origin. No argument there. You have to balance the economic impact on where you're taking the water versus where the water's going to go and the effect that it's going to have there, and you have to talk about how you value whatever compensation needs to be made there."

In short, he said, a statewide market for water as a commodity needs to be developed. In that, he echoes the arguments of those who also advocate a statewide market for groundwater.

Indeed, such a market-driven approach would mean that the state would have to pick up the tab for some of the development. But there does seem be a willingness to shoulder at least some of that cost. As Laura Huffman, state director for the Nature Conservancy notes, the state has allocated $2 billion from its appropriately named Rainy Day Fund for water development projects in Texas, though that mostly is devoted to loans, which would go to those municipalities and authorities that could afford to pay them back. And there is no denying that in most cases, the cost of freeing up more water, from East Texas to the bone-dry environs of El Paso, in all probability would be passed along to the end user, be it the gas and oil driller in Midland or the guy who wants to water his lawn in Austin. The challenge to dealing with water as a commodity, she says, is that while it may be a marketable resource, water is different than oil or gas or pork bellies. It is not just a commodity, it is the stuff of life, she says. "I think when people react badly to the word commoditize it's because water isn't like stuffing at Thanksgiving—you can do it or you can not do it. Water's something that's essential and we want to be careful of anything—our rate structure, the governance model, the allocation model—anything that starts to make water a luxury item, that makes it unaffordable or hard to access. Those are problems that we want to think through at the front end.

"I find so many people saying very casually, 'Well, you know if we just priced water for its true value . . . then the laws of economics would solve the problem,' and I always think to myself, well, how on earth will affordability fit into that? And how will underserved populations benefit from that philosophy? And so I think when we talk about price of water and commodity, we ought to be really careful that we're not taking something that is so essential to all of life and making it inaccessible."

That is not to say that a more comprehensive approach to water management, one that calculates supply and demand on a statewide basis, couldn't be developed with the idea that water must remain available across economic divides as well as geographic ones. Indeed, Huffman says. "We can balance those concepts."

The challenge, she argues, is not that treating water as a commodity, buying and selling on an open market, is itself a hard sell. "Buying and selling water? We buy and sell water within cities all the time," she says. The hard part is making sure that in creating that market, the unseen hand isn't just given a free hand. The objective must not simply be to keep the costs of water down for those who can least afford it, as critical as that is, but also to make sure that that emerging market drives conservation.

That, too, is achievable, she says. "I think there are clever rate structures that have not been used yet. If you've got a rate structure where the more water you use the more the cost gets, well that's designed essentially to create a negative cost signal for people who use a ton of water. Well, who uses a ton of water? At least in Texas, the people who use a ton of water are people who have great big lawns. Well, what's usually behind a great big lawn? Usually a great big house. That makes sense enough. I think that that's just fine if it creates enough of a negative price signal that it were to curb that behavior. So what if we created a conservation rate structure where we said we're going to reward every family, every business that uses X amount of water or less. It would be a little bit like the electric utility structure that rewards someone who has a solar panel on their roof."

In essence, that kind of rate structure would be a way of tapping into the same parsimonious approach to water that defines the hippies' community garden in parched Terlingua and replicating it statewide. And the state water plan does indeed already stress conservation as a principal strategy. It is worth noting that conservation, which remains the principal strategy in most of the state's sixteen water plans, is, according to virtually every water expert, the single most effective way of preparing for a coming drought.

Ask Sansom, for example, to describe the most important thing that Texas can do to meet the challenge of the next drought, and he responds with three words: "Use less water."

As a principle and as a strategy, strict water conservation is, indeed, the single most cost-effective way of stretching water supplies in a geographically, economically, and culturally diverse state. In fact, as Dr. Robert Mace, the executive director of the TWDB acknowledges, to some degree conservation is becoming a strategy whether folks want it to or not, and that is simply a function of the competition for a diminishing water supply. And there are winners and losers. To be sure, state water planners expect that cities and the industries and utilities that power their growth will continue to play an increasingly outsize role in the state's water future. And some significant part of the water that they will consume will be coming from agricultural interests. Part of that water the cities use will come from farmers and ranchers who, by necessity, will become better at conserving water. Part of it will be the grim Darwinism of basic economics—money and water both flow in the same direction, and in the future, that is going to be toward the urban centers. And part of it will be simply that in some places farmers and ranchers will just give up, understanding at last that sometimes technology just can't overcome the limits of a resource. That lush, irrigated stretch of the Panhandle above the Ogallala that Dennis Holmberg eyes with a mixture of rage and envy when he looks across the New Mexico border is a case in point. "Out in the High Plains of Texas, the Ogallala, we're pumping that aquifer six times the rate that the water's coming back in and there's no obvious source of water to replace that," he says. "So what we're seeing slowly happening over time is a conversion to dry-land farming over irrigated agriculture."

That is a kind of enforced conservation. If you have less water, you will use less water.

But there are few who believe that conservation alone can accomplish what the state of Texas desperately needs: to provide more water for millions more people in a comparatively short period of time.

To achieve that, the state has to go beyond passive conservation into a more dynamic realm, where conservation and technology meld. There are already examples happening across the state. One partial example already in play, though for some it is a stomach-churning one, is the idea of treating and reusing at least some of the water that Texans flush down their toilets every year—it is a rough number, but estimates are that it accounts for twenty-seven percent of the roughly eighty-three gallons[4] of water the average Texan uses every day—to replenish drinking water supplies.

In fact, it is an idea that is gaining acceptance, albeit reluctantly, in other parts of the nation. In Virginia, which has been grappling with its own prolonged dry spell in recent years, one affluent Washington suburb has begun drawing about five percent of its drinking water from sources that at one point in their life cycle tarried for a time in porcelain bowls. And lest you think that is simply because living that close to the nation's political epicenter people have become inured to the idea of consuming effluent, consider this: California has been tinkering with the idea for a generation and within a decade and a half, the *New York Times* reported, up to one-third of the ice that San Diegans crush and put into their margaritas could have begun its journey swirling counterclockwise in the master bathroom. In most of those cases where it has been employed, the treated water is injected into an aquifer before it is reused, not because it needs to be—the treatment purifies the water sufficiently to exceed potable standards—but simply to preserve the delicate sense of decorum among some of the more skittish customers, to persuade them that they are not lapping up water directly out of the bowl, like their AKC-registered shih tzus. And it is not just in the United States that the technology is gaining ground. At the bottom of the globe, where the water swirls in the opposite direction, a three-year pilot program proved that the city of Perth in Australia could ease its perennial water woes through flush-to-faucet technology, and the city has recently brought it online.

But it is in Texas, Mace contends, that some of the most significant progress has been made. "It's going to be big," he says. "It's already becoming big. We have installed the second and third direct potable reuse plants in the world."

The first—a facility at Big Spring that can provide about two million gallons of water a day to customers in Odessa, Snyder, Big Spring, and Midland, the same neck of the woods that Jeff Williams had eyed as a target for his proposed exports from Fort Stockton—went online in May 2013, right in the middle of the recent drought. A year later, another facility opened in Wichita Falls, able to treat up to ten million gallons a day.

To be sure, the Big Spring facility required some engineering—reverse osmosis, microfiltration, ultraviolet disinfection—and then the treated water had to be mixed with water from a more socially acceptable source, in that case a nearby lake. But none of it required technology that didn't already exist and wasn't easily available.

In Wichita Falls, it took even less engineering. Officials there already had much of what they needed in place, since it was similar to what was required to treat some of the brackish groundwater they were already using.

Those early successes, Mace said, have helped overcome some of the resistance and have encouraged others to follow suit. "We've got El Paso looking to put one in," he said. "San Angelo is flirting with the idea right now."

To be sure, there remains a kind of queasiness about the whole idea. But it is unfounded. The fact of the matter is, for years, treated water from the states' cities and suburbs, and even from its rural areas, has been released into the wild, diluted by moving rivers or the reservoirs, only to be recaptured and reused downstream. It is a measure of how interconnected things are that it has become an axiom in the environmental community that "Houston drinks Dallas's flush and Dallas breathes Houston's air."

Acknowledging that, and building upon it, storing the water and using it locally could go a long way toward easing hardships in the cities in times of drought, Mace says. And that, in turn, could ease the demands those cities make on rural regions. "With potable reuse, there's like five hundred million gallons per day being put in the Trinity River out of the Dallas–Fort Worth area. That becomes a resource that could be tapped."

But like everything else in the giant game of Whac-A-Mole that is water policy in Texas, it has thus far been a piecemeal, localized solution. To replicate it on a statewide basis likely would require a more robust effort from Austin and a willingness to work with those areas that would be likely to implement it on an equally robust funding mechanism that has yet to emerge.

The same can be said for another potential water supply mechanism that has been used widely in the West and elsewhere, one that relies on the wild cycles peculiar to the climates in Texas, where killer droughts are often broken by raging storms that turn sunbaked arroyos into raging rivers and then vanish just as suddenly.

The technique, aquifer storage and recovery (ASR), is deceptively simple: you simply catch the rain as it falls and rather than store it in a reservoir, where evaporation can rob you of a significant amount of the water, you store it underground, effectively eliminating losses to evaporation. Some experts estimate that the state's reservoirs lose more than five million acre-feet a year of water to evaporation. Pump the water below ground, however, and "you get one hundred percent of that water" when you need it, says Larson, who has in recent years emerged as one of the state's leading advocates for ASR.

That is not to say that there are not drawbacks. Aquifers targeted for recharge would have to be selected carefully to make sure that they didn't contain salts or chemicals that could contaminate the water over time, and of course the water you pump into it also would have to meet rigid standards. But preliminary studies indicate that half the aquifers in the state could be pressed into service, Larson said, and while developing them would be costly, it would be less costly and less time-consuming than going through the expense and the bureaucratic nightmare of trying to build a new reservoir.

Indeed, as a strategy, ASR has been used to great effect in other states. There are at last count, according to a 2014 report by the Texas Water Resources Institute, 130 such ASRs nationwide. Even comparatively rainy Florida has nearly thirty of them.

And yet, Texas lags far behind. Only six of the state's sixteen regions have identified them as potential strategies to meet their region's water needs going forward, and even then they are expected to account for a scant eighty-one thousand acre-feet of water by 2060, roughly one-sixtieth of the amount of water the sun sucks up out of the state's reservoirs each year.

Driven by the top-down imperative to conserve the water in the Edwards, and focused by the market forces that the top-down approach unleashed, San Antonio recently completed a $250 million project to take excess rainwater and its allocation from the Edwards that it does not immediately need and store it in the Carrizo-Wilcox Aquifer. San Antonio can store up to 120,000 acre-feet of water and can provide the city with up to sixty million gallons of water a day, says Puentes of SAWS.

Larson contends that other parched cities easily could follow San Antonio's lead. "Look at the city of Dallas," he says. Between 1990 and 2010, groundwater withdrawals decimated the aquifer under the city, leaving behind "a thousand-foot cone depression under the city." That depleted aquifer, he argues, would be an ideal ASR, capable of holding more than the 775,000 gallons available from Lake Ray Roberts during the wettest of seasons. "You could take Ray Roberts and store it under the city of Dallas and have a strategic reserve where you lose zero to evaporation." Not only would a project like that go a long way toward addressing the long-term needs of Dallas and neighboring communities, Larson says, it would also make the notion of flooding Shirley Shumake's land seem a lot less attractive.

Last session, Larson shepherded a bill through the legislature that stripped away the authority of the local groundwater districts to stand in the way of ASRs and placed the permitting authority for them with the TCEQ, but he contends that even more muscular leadership is required from Austin if the potential of ASR is going to be realized statewide.

State leadership also would be required to tap the single largest potential source of new water in the state: Mace's ace in the hole, the one source big enough to stave off the potential calamity that Texas would likely face in the event of a drought worse than the drought of record—the Gulf of Mexico.

Already, in places like Terlingua, water suppliers are tapping into sources of so-called new water that, he contends, with the help of a $2 billion fund the state has allocated for loans and grants, can be leveraged into $27 billion in buying power. More can be brought online as the need arises. Though costly, sources are out there, he says. Desalination, already taking place in parts of the state where groundwater tends to be brackish, could be expanded, though not without cost and not without resistance from some of its anticipated consumers. Still, "we do have a lot of brackish groundwater, that could become a source of supply . . . something we planned for fifty years out," Mace says.

But to fully press the state's brackish water and its boundless seawater into service, indeed, to employ most of the strategies laid out in this chapter, it would take what has so far been an almost unprecedented centralization of authority. That authority would have the power to bring together wildly disparate competing interests—

cities, suburbs, farmers, and industry—and at last place real, state-wide limits on the rule of capture. It would have to be able to navigate the cross-currents of sixteen parochial interests to remove the obstacles to transferring surface water from one river basin to the next as the need arises. It would have to have the clout to forge the empire that is Texas into a single state. It would need to be an authority with the vision and the financial wherewithal to develop enough ASRs to see us through the next time it doesn't rain or, finally, more than half a century after President Kennedy flipped a switch to turn on the state's first seawater desalination plant, to turn saltwater fresh.

Unfortunately, there are few models for that kind of grand vision. To be sure, says Puentes, the EAA was one. But it took a unique set of circumstances for the Edwards to become a reality, for the factions that had been warring for decades finally to agree to pool their parochial interests and work within a common, aquifer-wide set of rules. Mostly, it took the threat of federal action in the form of Judge Bunton's ruling.

Right now, as the federal government under a new administration is retreating from the kinds of environmental engagement that led to the creation of the EAA, an administration that is more dedicated to the idea of building a wall to make sure that no stray Mexican laborers turn up on Luis Amendariz's farm in Presidio than it is to litigating water issues, that kind of federal pressure is unlikely to be repeated anytime soon.

There is, of course, another mechanism, even more despised by Texans than the federal government, that can prod the powers that be to assume authority over the state's bafflingly complex water issues and can encourage the various factions within the state to work with that authority. "Depend upon it, sir," the poet Samuel Johnson once said. "When a man knows that he is to be hanged in a fortnight, it concentrates the mind wonderfully."[5]

Puentes offers a more Texas version of the quote. "I don't think that this state can do anything meaningful regarding water policy unless some things happen, a huge, long-term severe drought. And a budget surplus."

It may be difficult to predict a budget surplus, but if Larson's scientists are right, that long-term severe drought, just like the ones before, is looming, and it should focus the minds of Texans because, as Sansom put it, "we're gonna be in a world of hurt unless we address it."

EPILOGUE

IT IS A FEW MINUTES UNTIL NOON on a still December day in the Trans Pecos, and the sky is so pale it is almost white. Beneath a rock overhang, far above a wounded and overdrawn river—a river parsed by permits and parceled out by the acre-foot all along its meandering way through the desert—the sunlight slithers like a snake into this chamber. Inch by inch, minute by minute, it climbs upward, exposing the ancient moon goddess of a vanished people.

There is no one here to see her now. There is only the occasional gust of wind and the hum of tourists' tires passing by on a distant highway bridge to disturb the silence.

The primitive, superstitious people who gave all they had to create this goddess are long gone. Was it famine? Was it flood? Were they overrun by hordes of warriors driven to this remote place when their own lands were ravaged by the cycles of nature? Or was it just the cycles of nature in this harsh landscape?

We don't know how their story ended, says Carolyn Boyd, the artist turned archeologist who has spent decades trying to tease out the riddle of these places. All they left us were a few of these enigmatic paintings that speak to their understanding of the ways in which forces of water and fire formed them and informed them. And even those are threatened by time, by nature, and by the works of modern men and women. Many of the paintings have already been lost, Boyd says, drowned beneath the water of the Amistad Reservoir back in the 1960s, when we still had unbounded faith in our ability to bend the desert to our will, and still had the will to try.

A few minutes more and the sun will reach its zenith, and in an act of self-sacrifice that has played out exactly this way at exactly this moment on precisely this day every year for some fifteen hundred years, the moon goddess will die, again, so that the balance between water and life can be sustained.

In Fort Stockton, 153 miles to the northwest, no one knows or cares about the ancient rituals of an unlettered and lost people. A more modern battle is being fought out there, one that recently pitted Jeff and Clayton Williams, twenty-first-century men, against local authorities over who has ultimate control over their groundwater rights. It is a battle over modern concerns, like economics and the laws of supply and demand, over the extent of something those primitive natives of the Trans Pecos couldn't even begin to comprehend: property rights.

Travel farther north and farther west, to the Panhandle and the unnaturally lush farmland along the New Mexico border, and there the ancient whispers are drowned out by the roar of countless pumps racing each other despite the certain knowledge that eventually they will suck the Ogallala Aquifer dry. Wander east to the thirsty cities of San Antonio and Austin and Dallas and Fort Worth, or to Houston, where its people guided into place the state-of-the-art satellites that, perhaps too late, will warn us when another drought or another flood is coming.

Each of those cities will take its own steps to address that coming hardship, be it through technology or conservation. These are modern people. Educated. Rational. And above all, independent, absolutely certain that in each of their local regions they have the wisdom and the wherewithal to meet the challenges of a dwindling water supply in some of the fastest-growing regions in the nation.

There is nothing they can learn from the primitive cave-scrawling of a lost and forgotten people who could not ultimately change their own fate.

Or is there?

The ancient painters who left us these riddles on the rocks did not believe that they were somehow independent of nature, or that they had authority over it, or could bend it to their will, says Boyd. They did not imagine that they were masters over the elements, she says. Instead they saw themselves as part of an ongoing act of creation, as much an element of it as the air or the water. The world they inhabited was not defined by arbitrary geographical borders but by the dictates of nature, by the rain and the wind, the cycles of drought and flood. Survival in that world demanded obedience to those immutable laws of nature. It required an appreciation, Boyd says, that everything, the water that falls and the water that flows, the water underground, all are linked and that only by working together, by making whatever sacrifices are required collectively, can survival in this harsh, unforgiving land be assured.

That alone, of course, was not enough to save them, any more than our technology alone can save us from an uncertain future. But maybe, just maybe, if we look deeply enough, the winter sun rising in a forgotten cave can give us just enough light to begin to see a path forward.

ACKNOWLEDGMENTS

AT THE TIME, IT STRUCK ME as comical and maybe even a little bit chauvinistic. A few years back, just after my last book had been released, I was invited to serve as one of the supernumeraries rounded up to fill out the background behind better-known—and frankly, better—writers at the annual Texas Book Festival in Austin. Since few of the organizers had any idea of who I was, they sent me a lengthy and by and large pro forma questionnaire to fill out with all the usual fill-in-the-blank, getting-to-know-you queries:

Do you identify as white, African American, Asian, Native American, Pacific Islander?

Do you identify as gay, straight, lesbian, bisexual, or transgender?

But then, somewhere around the middle of page two, I came across the oddest question I have ever been asked on this sort of thing.

Do you identify as Texan?

In ten years of hawking books on the road, not once had anyone in any other state ever asked me a question like that, not even in my home state of Pennsylvania, where they really don't care whether you think of yourself as a Pennsylvanian as long as you get your state income tax return in on time.

I answered no, of course.

Now, however, I am starting to realize that my answer was, if not technically wrong, at least incomplete.

If I have learned anything in the roughly two years that it took me to report and write this book, if I have learned anything from talking—more often than not for far more hours than I had planned—to Texans from every corner of the state, if I have gleaned anything from hustling through its cities and rocketing along back roads, it is that Texas isn't just a part of America, it is the heart of it. If New York and Los Angeles are the twin egos of America, Texas in all its spectacular contradictions is its id.

Every challenge that America faces—economically, environmentally, culturally, and politically—is cast against the varied and magnificent landscape of Texas in stark relief. And there is no single issue in which those challenges appear more crystal clear than on the issue of water. All of America, be it the harsh arid lands of the West or the drowning coastlines of the Southeast, can see its reflection somewhere in the waters of Texas.

And if America is ever going to be able to cope with the looming hydra-headed crisis spawned by a rising population, rising seas, and a changing climate that is certainly going to make the dry places drier and threaten to wash the already wet ones away, it would do well to watch Texas and draw lessons—both cautionary and visionary—from it.

There is a metaphor and a lesson in that as I write this, millions of people along the southeastern coastline of the United States and in the Caribbean are just beginning to crawl out from under the wreckage of a devastating storm, Hurricane Irma, that slammed into the coast with what would once have been unimaginable fury. It is no longer unimaginable. A week earlier, Harvey, a storm every bit as vicious, drowned much of east Texas.

If I have learned anything while writing this book, it is that the challenges that America has faced in the past have often been faced first in Texas, and the responses, however halting or incomplete, whether successful or disastrous, have often been tried in Texas first. Texas showed America the way west. She showed us the way to the moon. The good lord willing and the creeks don't rise, she will have a thing or two to teach us about water as well.

I personally owe a deep debt of gratitude to the many Texans who, with grace and generosity, have taken the time to help me begin to understand the magnitude of the challenge and the depth of understanding that Texans bring to it. I don't know the right words to properly thank people like author Charles Porter or Robert Gulley, who helped forge the EAA, or Todd Votteler or Robert Mace or a host of others for trying to school me.

I am not writer enough to tell you how much I really learned from the everyday Texans who spent hours with me, people like Haskell Simon, the rice farmer from Bay City whom I am proud now to call a friend, or Luis Amendariz, the farmer, rancher, and hardware store owner from Presidio who showed me that the debate about water is never really just about water. I am grateful to Charlie Angell, the river guide from around Big Bend who took me into Mexico and showed me what the world looked like from the other side. I am in debt to and in awe of Shirley Shumake and her neighbors for generously sharing with me a glimpse of the fault line between two competing cultures, a fracture that is as stressed across much of America as it is in the Sulphur River Basin.

There isn't enough ink or enough time for me to individually thank all the people who formed this book. Just know that whatever failures are in it are mine. Whatever truth is in it is theirs.

I am also incredibly grateful to the many people at University of Texas Press for giving me the opportunity to pursue this important story, especially my long-suffering editor, Casey Kittrell, and Lynne Ferguson Chapman, who is the driving force behind a team of the best copy editors I have ever worked with without subsequently marrying—among them, Eva Silverfine. Eva is a master who not only challenged my grammar but on a couple of occasions successfully challenged my unconscious biases. For that, I'm in her debt, just as I am in the debt of Erin Greb, whose maps make this book not only more comprehensible but also a bit more pleasant to look at. And of course, for the second time now, I find myself coming up short for ways to express my gratitude to Gianna LaMorte, who for reasons that utterly escape me, seems to have an unrealistically high opinion of my abilities, and who has, over the course of two books now, become a kind of muse for me.

I also need to express my undying gratitude to the copy editor I did marry, my wife, Kren, who, together with our children, has once again suffered through the rages and periods of despondency that punctuate our lives whenever I am working on a book.

To all of them and to those I didn't name, thank you.

I hope that with your help, we have put together a book that might help the rest of the nation grapple with a looming crisis. And who knows? Maybe it might also help wrangle us another invitation to the Texas Book Festival.

This time, however, I would urge them to modify their questionnaire. Instead of allowing a binary yes or no option for the question "*Do you identify as a Texan*?," there ought to be a third choice.

Shouldn't we all?

NOTES

PROLOGUE

1. Heather Pringle, "The First Americans," *Scientific American*, March 2011.

2. Justice Jones, April Saginor, and Brad Smith, "2011 Texas Wildfires, Common Denominators of Home Destruction," Texas A&M Forest Service.

3. Karen Jackson, "Case Study of the 2015 Hidden Pines Wildland–Urban Interface Fire in Bastrop Texas," Bastrop County Office of Emergency Management, 2015.

4. Eva Ruth Moravec, "Texas Officials: Hurricane Harvey Death Toll at 82, 'Mass Casualties Have Absolutely Not Happened,'" *Washington Post*, September 14, 2017.

5. David Hendricks, "Harvey, Irma Damages Approach $300 Billion," *San Antonio Express-News*, September 13, 2017.

CHAPTER 1

1. "City Population History for 1850–2000," *Texas Almanac*.

2. "The Canary Islanders," excerpt from Mary Ann Noonan Guerra, *San Fernando, Heart of San Antonio*, 1977, in *Journal of the Life and Culture of San Antonio*, University of the Incarnate Word.

3. David Roth, *Texas Hurricane History*, National Weather Service, Camp Springs, Maryland.

4. Floyd E. Dominy, oral history interview conducted by Brit Allan Storey, Senior Historian Bureau of Reclamation. See also, "Who's Going to Clean Up Nicaro?" *Fortune Magazine*, June 1953; and Simon W. Freese and D. L. Sizemore, *A*

Century in the Works: 100 Years of Progress in Civil and Environmental Engineering; Freese and Nichols Consulting Engineers 1894–1994, College Station: Texas A&M University Press, 1994.

5. As quoted in *The Texas Water Plan,* Texas Water Development Board, pp. 24–25, November 1968.

6. Freese and Sizemore, *A Century in the Works.*

7. Todd H. Votteler, "Water Boondoggles, The Biggest Little Water Plan," available from www.edwardsaquifer.net.

8. Stuart Long, "Texas, E.P. Water Plan Unveiled, Meets Needs of State for 50 Years," *El Paso Herald,* December 17, 1968.

9. "Texas Water Plan Needs Closer Study," *Gilmer Mirror,* July 24, 1969.

10. "County Voters Support Six of 9 Amendments," *The Fort Stockton Pioneer,* August 7, 1969.

11. United Press International, "Texans Give Big Okay to Welfare," *El Paso Herald Post,* August 6, 1969.

CHAPTER 2

1. See Barshop v. Medina County Underground Water Conservation Dist., 925 S.W.2d 618, 626 (Tex. 1996).

2. Sipriano v. Great Spring Waters of America, 1 S.W.3d 75 (Tex. 1999).

3. Jacob Beltran, "Cholera Epidemics Killed At Least 700 in the 1800s," *San Antonio Express-News,* February 14, 2015.

4. Ibid.

5. Gary K. Grice, *History of Weather Observations, San Antonio, Texas, 1846–1955,* prepared for the Midwestern Regional Climate Center under the auspices of the Climate Database Modernization Program, National Oceanic and Atmospheric Administration's National Climatic Data Center, Asheville, North Carolina, January 2007.

6. East v. Houston and Central Texas Railroad Company, 77 S.W. 647 (Civ. App. Dallas 1903, Plaintiff's Amended Original Petition).

CHAPTER 3

1. Freese and Nichols, Inc.; Alan Plummer Associates, Inc; CP&Y, Inc., and Cooksey Communications, Inc., *2016 Region C Water Plan,* Vol. 1, *Main Report,* Texas Water Development Board, December 2015.

2. Freese and Nichols; Alan Plummer Associates; Chiang, Patel and Yerby, Inc.; and Cooksey Communications, *2001 Region C Water Plan,* Texas Water Development Board, December 2001.

3. Raul I. Cabrera, Kevin L. Wagner, Benjamin Wherley, and Leslie Lee, "Urban Landscape Water Use in Texas, A Special Report by the Texas Water Resources Institute," Texas A&M AgriLife Research Extension, 2013.

4. Interview with Dr. Robert Mace, Assistant Executive Director of the Texas Water Development Board, conducted by the author.

CHAPTER 4

1. Kate Galbraith, "Farmers and Regulators Square Off in Battle Over Ogallala Aquifer Rules," *Texas Tribune*, March 18, 2012.

2. "Ballgame, Parade, Water Shows, Aquacade and Dances on Opening Day's Schedule," *Fort Stockton Pioneer*, June 20, 1947.

3. "Water District Offers Free Use of Water for Swimming; County Asked to Build Pool," *Fort Stockton Pioneer*, August 14, 1952.

4. Gunnar M. Brune, *Springs of Texas*, Vol. 1, College Station: Texas A&M University, 2002. First published 1981.

CHAPTER 5

1. Sipriano v. Great Spring Waters of America, 1 S.W.3d 75 (Tex. 1999).

2. Guitar Holding Company, L.P. v. Hudspeth County Underground Water Conservation District No. 1, et al.; from Hudspeth County; Eighth District (08-04-00296-CV and 08-05-00115-CV, 209 S.W.3d 172, August 31, 2006).

3. The Edwards Aquifer Authority, and Roland Ruiz in his official capacity as General Manager of the Edwards Aquifer Authority, Appellants/Cross Appellees v. Glenn and JoLynn Bragg, Appellees/Cross Appellants. No. 04–11–00018–CV. Decided November 13, 2013.

CHAPTER 6

1. Jimmy Banks and John E. Babcock, *Corralling the Colorado: The First Fifty Years of the Lower Colorado River Authority*, Woodway, Texas: Eakin Press, 1988.

2. Ibid.

3. Kate Galbraith, "A Grain of Doubt," *Texas Monthly* April 2012.

CHAPTER 7

1. US Geological Survey, National Water Information System 08116650, Brazos River near Rosharon, Texas.

2. Texas Commission on Environmental Quality, Appellant, v. Texas Farm

Bureau, Frank Volleman, Frank Destefano, David and Mary Ballew, Ron and Sherie Burnette, Sam Jones, Theodore and Mary Kallus, Glenn Marecek, John Gaulding, and Charles and Katherine Harless. No. 13–13–00415-CV Court of Appeals, Thirteenth District of Texas, Corpus Christi–Edinburg.

3. Neena Satija, "Appointment of Brazos Watermaster Hotly Contested in East Texas," *Texas Tribune*, April 20, 2014.

CHAPTER 8

1. Texas Water Development Board, Appellant v. Ward Timber, Ltd.; Ward Timber Holdings; Shirley Shumake; Gary Cheatwood; Richard LeTourneau; and Pat Donelson, Appellees. Texas Court of Appeals for the Eleventh District, Eastland Division, May 23, 2013.

2. Freese and Nichols, Inc., *Analysis and Quantification of the Impacts of the Marvin Nichols Reservoir Water Management Strategy on the Agricultural and Natural Resources of Region D and the State*, prepared for Region C Water Planning Group, 2014.

3. M. P. A. Jackson, *Fault Tectonics of the East Texas Basin*, assisted by B. D. Wilson, Bureau of Economic Geology, University of Texas at Austin, 1982.

4. *2012 Texas State Water Plan*, Texas Water Development Board.

5. John Burnett, "When the Sky Ran Dry," *Texas Monthly*, July 2012.

6. "Resourceful Citizens Tap City Water Well," *Dallas Morning News*, October 16, 1956.

7. Freese and Nichols, et al. *2016 Region C Water Plan*, Vol. 1.

8. Ibid.

CHAPTER 9

1. Robert M. Hutchins, ed., *Plutarch*. Vol. 14 of *Great Books of the Western World*, Chicago: Encyclopedia Britannica, 1952, p. 341.

2. Letters to the Editor, *Nature Magazine*, October 29, 1891.

3. "The Texas Rainmaking Experiments," *Scientific American*, Vol. 66, January 1892.

4. David G. McComb, *Texas, A Modern History*, Austin: University of Texas Press, 1989, p. 128.

5. Charles Dudley Eaves, "Colonization Activities of Charles William Post," *Southwestern Historical Quarterly* XL, July 1939: 82–141.

6. "Town Founded by Breakfast Food Magnate Marks Golden Jubilee," *Corsica Daily Sun*, September 13, 1957, p. 12.

7. Bruce Lambert, "Vincent J. Schaefer, 87, is Dead; Chemist Who First Seeded Clouds," *New York Times*, July 28, 1993.

8. Ibid.

9. David Fennig, *2013-2015 United States Hail Loss Claims*, National Insurance Crime Bureau Report ForeCAST Report, May 2, 2016.

10. United States Senate Subcommittee on Oceans and International Environment of the Committee on Foreign Relations, Hearing on Weather Modification, March 20, 1974. Declassified, May 19, 1974.

11. Gwinn Guilford, "China Creates 55 Billion Tons of Artificial Rain a Year—And It Plans to Quintuple That," *Quartz*, October 22, 2013.

12. Southwest Weather Research Inc. v. Duncan, 319 S.W.2d 940, Tex. App. 1958.

13. Texas Water Development Board, *Water Use of Texas Utilities*, Report to the 84th Texas Legislature, January 2015. Table 7, Average Per-Connection Daily Water Use (Gallons) by Utility Size (p. 22).

14. Exodus 15:23.

15. James D. Birkett, "The History of Desalination before Large-Scale Use," in *Desalination and Water Resources: History, Development and Management of Water Resources*, Vol. 1, ed. D. M. K. Al-Gobaisi, EOLSS/UNESCO, 2010.

16. Texas Water Development Board, *Water for Texas: 2017 State Water Plan*, table 8.3.

CHAPTER 10

1. Texas Water Development Board, *Water Use of Texas Water Utilities*, Report to the 84th Texas Legislature, January 2015.

2. Texas Water Development Board, "Innovative Water Technologies," *Water for Texas: 2017 State Water,* December 2016.

3. Susan Combs, "Texas Water Report, Going Deeper for the Solution," Office of Texas Comptroller of Public Accounts, 2014.

4. Jorge Arroyo and Saqib Shirazi, "Cost of Brackish Water Development in Texas," Innovative Water Technologies, Texas Water Development Board, September 2012.

5. Texas Tax Code §151.355.

6. Texas Water Development Board, "Recommended Water Management Strategies," *2017 State Water Plan*.

7. Jordana Barton, Emily Ryder Perlmeter, Elizabeth Sobel Blum, and Raquel R. Marquez. *La Colonias in the 21st Century, Progress Along the Texas-Mexico Border*, Federal Reserve Bank of Dallas, April 2015.

8. United States of America v. Richard Dee Thompson, District Court for the Western District of Texas, Case No. 4.92-CR-003 (01) filed November 18, 2015.

CHAPTER 11

1. Lyle Larson, "A Tale of Two Rivers and What Happens When Mexico Doesn't Pay Its Water Debt," *Monitor*, January 3, 2017.

2. Texas v. State of New Mexico and State of Colorado.

3. Cabeza de Vaca, *The Narrative of Cabeza de Vaca*, translation by Rolena Adorno and Charles Pautz, Lincoln: University of Nebraska Press, 2003.

4. "Villa Delays Ojinaga Attack for Operators' Arrival," *New York Times*, January 8, 1914.

5. Brownsville Irrigation District, Bayview Irrigation District, Cameron County Irrigation District No. 6, Hidalgo and Cameron Counties Irrigation District No. 9, and Valley Acres Irrigation District, Appellants v. Texas Commission on Environmental Quality; Presidio Valley Farms, Inc.; Maverick County; City of Laredo; and City of Eagle Pass Water Works System, Appellees. No. 03–06–00690-CV, Court of Appeals of Texas, Austin, Decided August 28, 2008.

CHAPTER 12

1. Todd. H. Votteler, "The Little Fish that Roared: The Endangered Species Act, State Ground Water Law, and Private Property Rights Collide over the Edwards Aquifer," *Tulane Environmental Law Review* 28(4), 1998.

2. Gregg Eckhardt, "The J-17 Index Well," *The Edwards Aquifer Website*.

3. Transmittal letter to the Citizens of the Edwards Region from Henry G. Cisneros, Mayor of the City of San Antonio, and Robert C. Hasslocher, Chairman of the Edwards Underground Water District, July 1988.

4. Ibid.

5. Robert L. Gulley, *Heads Above Water, the Inside Story of the Edwards Aquifer Recovery Implementation Program*, College Station: Texas A&M University Press, 2015, p. 38.

CHAPTER 13

1. Trinity River Authority of Texas, "History of Water Quality in the Trinity River Basin."

2. Gilad Edelman, "Texas among Nation's Worst Water Polluters," *Texas Tribune*, June 1, 2014.

3. US Fish and Wildlife Service, *Contamination in Aquatics and Sediment at Trinity River National Wildlife Refuge, Texas*, April 2014 (updated May 2017).

4. Texas Council on Environmental Quality, *Joint Groundwater Monitoring and Contamination Report—2015*, June 2016.

5. Allyn West, "What Lurks in the Sludge that Harvey Left Behind?", *Houston Chronicle*, September 20, 2017.

6. Ralph K. M. Haurwitz, "Hurricane Harvey's Toll on Air and Water Pollution Slowly Coming into Focus," *Austin American-Statesman*, September 15, 2017.

7. Courtney Bernhardt, Abel Russ, Eric Schaeffer, Tom Pelton, and Kira Burkhart, "Don't Drink the Water: Water in 65 Texas Communities Contains Toxic Levels of Arsenic, but State Fails to Advise Citizens to Use Alternate Water Supplies," Environmental Integrity Project, March 14, 2016.

8. "Lubbock's Bottled Water Program a Price for City's Past Pollution, *Lubbock Avalanche Journal*, April 2015.

9. Tom Dart, "Houston Fears Climate Change Will Cause Catastrophic Flooding: 'It's Not If, It's When,'" *The Guardian*, June 16, 2017.

10. Thomas J. Moore and Donald R. Mattison, "Adult Utilization of Psychiatric Drugs and Differences by Sex, Age, and Race," *JAMA Internal Medicine* 177, no. 2 (2017): 274–275.

CHAPTER 14

1. Nicot, Jean-Philippe, Robert C. Reedy, Ruth A. Costley, and Yun Huang, *Oil and Gas Water Uses in Texas: Update to the 2011 Mining Water Use Report*, Bureau of Economic Geology, University of Texas, Austin, September 2012.

2. Monica Freyman, "Hydraulic Fracturing and Water Stress, Water Demand by the Numbers," *Ceres*, February 2014.

3. Lyle Larson, "The Thirst of Texas Tomorrow Is Our Responsibility Today," *Texas Water Journal* 8, no. 1 (2017): 16–17.

4. Texas Water Development Board, *Water Use of Texas Water Utilities*, Report to the 84th Legislature, January 2015.

5. James Boswell, *The Life of Samuel Johnson, LL.D.*, Vol. 3, New York: Penguin Classics, 2008, original publication 1791.

SOURCES AND SUGGESTIONS
FOR FURTHER READING

While much that appears in this volume was developed out of hundreds of hours of interviews and culled from the four hundred–plus pages of transcripts that resulted, published sources also proved invaluable. The TWDB (http://www.twdb. texas.gov/waterplanning/swp/2017/), for example, maintains an archive of all the state's water plans dating back to 1961. Both the overall state plans and the sixteen distinct regional plans that contribute to it each cycle are an essential tool in understanding how various regions of the state have viewed the evolving challenge of providing water to Texas.

Those plans, of course, offer insight into only part of the story. The dry, official part. For the blood of the story, the human part of it, particularly for historical events for which no one was available who had a living memory of events, contemporaneous newspaper accounts culled from archives were used. These are footnoted as they appear throughout the manuscript, as are various academic studies and state and regional reports that shed light on individual aspects of the issue.

In addition, this manuscript could not have been written without the work of authors who came before. Any book about water policy, especially in the West, owes a debt to *Cadillac Desert: The American West and Its Disappearing Water*, by the late Marc Reisner, first published in 1986 and revised in 1993 by Penguin Books. His insights into the often-tense relationship between the US Bureau of Reclamation and state and local authorities were crucial. And any book about anything in Texas also owes a debt to the late T. R. Fehrenbach and his 1968 book, *Lone Star: A History of Texas and Texans* (Da Capo Press, revised in 2000). I was also fortunate enough to have been permitted to review portions of Stephen

Harrigan's forthcoming volume on the history of Texas, from University of Texas Press, which I expect will soon rival Fehrenbach's book as the indispensable history of Texas.

There are some aspects of the water issue in Texas that go beyond the data that can be captured in a nonfiction book. They are visceral, emotional, and yet crucial elements of the story; they go to the essence of what it meant and what it means to be a Texan facing hard times. No one has ever offered a more searing look at that than Elmer Kelton in his 1973 book, *The Time It Never Rained* (Forge Books, rereleased April 2008).

What follows is a chapter-by-chapter bibliography of other books that have informed this manuscript. If this book accomplishes nothing else, I hope it will help introduce readers to the works of these accomplished authors and scholars.

PROLOGUE

Boyd, Carolyn. *The White Shaman Mural: An Enduring Creation Narrative in the Rock Art of the Lower Pecos*. Austin: University of Texas Press, 2016.
Sansom, Andrew. *Water in Texas: An Introduction*. Austin: University of Texas Press, 2008.

CHAPTER 1

Kelton, Elmer. *The Time It Never Rained*. New York: Forge Books, 2008.
Freese, Simon W., and D. L. Sizemore. *A Century in the Works: 100 Years of Progress in Civil and Environmental Engineering; Freese and Nichols Consulting Engineers 1894–1994*. College Station: Texas A&M University Press, 1994.
Norwine, Jim, John R. Giardino, and Sushma Kristamurthy. *Water for Texas*. College Station: Texas A&M University Press, 2005.

CHAPTER 2

Porter, Charles R. *Spanish Water, Anglo Water: Early Development in San Antonio*. College Station: Texas A&M University Press, 2009.

CHAPTER 3

Freese and Nichols, Inc; Alan Plummer Associates, Inc; CP&Y, Inc.; and Cooksey Communications, Inc. 2016 *Region C Water Plan*, Vol. 1. *Main Report*. Texas Water Development Board, December 2015.

Freese and Nichols, Inc.; Alan Plummer Associates, Inc.; Chiang, Patel and Yerby, Inc.; and Cooksey Communications, Inc. *2001 Region C Water Plan*. Texas Water Development Board, December 2001.

CHAPTER 4

Ashworth, William. *Ogallala Blue: Water and Life on the High Plains*. Woodstock, Vermont: Countryman Press, 2006.

CHAPTER 5

Brune, Gunnar. *Springs of Texas*, Vol. 1. College Station: Texas A&M University Press, 2002. First published 1981.

CHAPTER 6

Banks, Jimmy, and John E. Babcock. *Corralling the Colorado: The First Fifty Years of the Lower Colorado River Authority*. Woodway, Texas: Eakin Press, 1988.
Williams, John. *The Untold Story of the Lower Colorado River Authority*. With a foreword by Andrew Sansom. College Station: Texas A&M University Press, 2016.

CHAPTER 7

Boyle, Robert H. *The Water Hustlers*. San Francisco: Sierra Club, 1971.

CHAPTER 8

Jackson, M. P. A. *Fault Tectonics of the East Texas Basin*. Assisted by B. D. Wilson. Bureau of Economic Geology, University of Texas at Austin, 1982.

CHAPTER 9

Egan, Timothy. *The Worst Hard Time: The Untold Story of Those Who Survived the Great American Dustbowl*. New York: Houghton Mifflin, 2006.
David G. McComb. *Texas, A Modern History*. Austin: University of Texas Press, 1989.
Al-Gobaisi, D. M. K., ed. *Desalinization and Water Resources: History, Development and Management of Water Resources*, Vol. 1. EOLSS/UNESCO, 2010.

CHAPTER 10

Barton, Jordana, Emily Ryder Perlmeter, Elizabeth Sobel Blum, and Raquel R. Marquez. *La Colonias in the 21st Century: Progress Along the Texas–Mexico Border*. Federal Reserve Bank of Dallas, April 2015.

Reid, Jan, ed. *Rio Grande*. Austin: University of Texas Press, 2004.

CHAPTER 11

Adorno, Rolena, and Patrick Charles Pautz, eds. *The Narrative of Cabeza de Vaca*. Translation and introduction by Rolena Adorno and Patrick Charles Pautz. Lincoln: University of Nebraska Press, 2003.

CHAPTER 12

Gulley, Robert L. *Heads Above Water: The Inside Story of the Edwards Aquifer Authority Recovery Implementation Program*. College Station: Texas A&M University Press, 2015.

Porter, Charles R. *Spanish Water, Anglo Water: Early Development in San Antonio*. College Station: Texas A&M University Press, 2009.

CHAPTER 13

Sansom, Andrew. *Water in Texas: An Introduction*. Austin: University of Texas Press, 2008.

Texas Water Development Board. *Water for Texas: 2017 State Water Plan*. Texas Water Development Board, 2017.

CHAPTER 14

Boswell, James. *The Life of Samuel Johnson, LL.D.*, Vol. 3. New York: Penguin Classics, 2008. Original publication 1791.

Briggle, Adam. *Field Philosopher's Guide to Fracking, How One Texas Town Stood Up to Big Oil and Gas*. New York: Liveright, 2015.

Nicot, Jean-Philippe, Robert C. Reedy, Ruth A. Costley, and Yun Huang. *Oil and Gas Water Uses in Texas: Update to the 2011 Mining Water Use Report*. Bureau of Economic Geology, University of Texas at Austin, 2012.

INDEX

Brown and Root (KBR), 23
Bunton, Lucius, 198–200, 202–203, 205
Burleston, 205
Burnett, Ronald S., 48, 50, 52
Burr, Carolyn, 158
Buttermilk Creek, 5

California, 30, 36, 72, 151, 170, 243
Canadian River Municipal Water
    Authority, 75
Carrizo-Wilcox Aquifer, 101, 158, 205,
    207
Caudle, Oren, 54–56, 131
Cedar Creek Reservoir, 42
Champion Lake, 212
Cheatwood, Gary Jr., 130, 133
Cheatwood, Gary Sr., 130, 133
Cipelo Creek, 163, 164–165
Cisneros, Henry, 200
Clark, Virgil, 155, 158–159, 163
Clawson, Terry, 108
Clayton, Billy, 201
climate change: causes of, 4; effect of, on
    extreme weather, 4, 16; effect of, on
    water sources, 63, 215
Coleman, Jason, 63, 64, 65
colonias: cultural differences in, 167;
    definition of, 159; lack of water sup-
    ply in, 163–166; state aid to, 166
Colorado, 30, 170, 173
Colorado River, 93; construction of
    dams on, 95–98; and water treaty
    with Mexico, 170–171, 174
Colorado River Municipal Water Dis-
    trict, 225
Comal Springs, 16–17, 187, 196–197
Comanche Springs, 66–69, 73, 79
commodification, of water: and afford-
    ability, 236, 240; challenges of, 189,
    240–241, 235–237; and development
    costs, 239–240; in San Antonio, 206–
    207; Williams' attempt at, 72, 74, 75
conjunctive use, 79–80, 111

Connally, John, 20, 202–203
conservation: cost as driver of, 241; in
    the DFW Metroplex, 43, 53–54; in
    farming, 64, 206; as important future
    strategy, 56, 123, 128, 241–242;
    negative consequences of, 64; in San
    Antonio, 32, 206; in Terlingua, 157
contamination. See groundwater; non-
    point source pollution; oil and gas;
    surface water
Corpus Christi, 210–211
Corralling the Colorado (Banks and Bab-
    cock), 92–93
correlative rights doctrine, 30
cotton, 72, 74
Crowder, William, 117

Dallas: and aquifer storage and recov-
    ery, 246; effect of drought on, 18, 42;
    growth of, 13. See also Dallas–Fort
    Worth Metroplex
Dallas–Fort Worth Metroplex, 114;
    conservation and reuse in, 53–54,
    118–119, 123, 128; effect of droughts
    on, 120–122; population and growth
    of, 44, 46, 122–123; potential new
    sources of water for, 53–54, 55,
    117–119, 123–124; water challenges
    and consumption in, 43, 46–47, 118,
    123, 124. See also Marvin Nichols
    Reservoir
dams: federal policy for, 40. See also
    individual dams
Daniel, Price, 19
Day/McDaniel case, 82–83, 207, 231,
    238
De La Rosa, Dymphna, 153, 155, 160
Denison, 36
desalination: of brackish groundwater,
    111, 131, 157, 227, 244, 246; cost of,
    151, 158–159; current and future
    use of, in Texas, 111, 151, 152, 155;
    and Dow Chemical, 105, 111, 150;

environmental concerns about, 46, 56, 151–152; history of, 148–149, 150; technological advancements in, 149–150. *See also* Gulf of Mexico; *and individual facilities*

de Vaca, Cabeza, 174–175

Donna, Texas, 212

Dow Chemical, 103–105, *104. See also TCEQ v. Texas Farm Bureau*

drought of record, 16–19, 42, 98, 106, 120–122

Drought Preparedness Council, 111

droughts, 5–6; effect of, on Texans, 9, 17, 93, 99–101, 230; effect of climate change on, 4, 16, 98; likelihood of future, 16, 229–230, 248; planning efforts for, 109–112; and storms, 16, 99; and surface water rights conflicts, 103–109; and water contamination, 215. *See also individual droughts*

Dust Bowl, 17–18

Dyrenforth, R. G., 135, 137–140

East, W. A., 36–37

East Bernard, 88–89

Eaton, David, 210–212, 214–215, 220

Edwards Aquifer: commodification of water in, 206–207; dependence on, 191; effect of droughts on, 187, 197, 200; endangered species of, 196–197; formation of, 4; and irrigated agriculture, 191–192; and protection of recharge zone, 218–219; regulation of, 192, 200–205; and rule of capture, 194–196, 208; uniqueness of, 185, 187; water levels of, 187, 192. See also *Sierra Club v. Babbitt*

Edwards Aquifer Authority (EAA): authority of, 203–205, 238; and Day/McDaniel case, 82–83, 208, 238; effects of, 205–207; establishment of, 195, 203–205, 238; as model for

centralized water authority, 206, 235, 237–238, 247

Edwards Aquifer Authority v. Burrell Day and Joel McDaniel. See Day/McDaniel case

Edwards Aquifer Recovery Implementation Program, 80, 204–205

Edwards-Trinity Aquifer, and the Williams family, 75–77

Edwards Underground Water District, 200

Electro Purification, 79

Elephant Butte Dam/Reservoir, 173, 181

Elms, Monroe, 163, 164–166

El Paso: attempts to sell water to, 81, 181; and desalination, 152, 157; drought plan of, 111; rainfall in, 14; and wastewater reuse, 244

El Paso Herald, 22

Emerging Contaminants Project, 220

eminent domain, 75, 101, 106, 126–127

Endangered Species Act, 238

Enoch, Craig, 81

environmentalists: and farm bureau case, 107; and fracking, 45–46; and Living Waters Artesian Springs Catfish Farm, 195, and Marvin Nichols Reservoir plan, 48–54, 118–119; and support of rice farmers, 102

Environmental Protection Agency (EPA), 124–125, 216, 217, 238

Environment Texas, 211

evaporation, 119, 245

E. V. Spence Reservoir, 226

Falcon Reservoir, 174, 181

firefighting, 5, 6

fires, 5–6

floods, 5–6; and Colorado River, 93–94; lack of statewide plans for, 89; and urban development danger, 219–220; and water contamination, 105

Sulphur River, 24, 118. *See also* Marvin Nichols Reservoir

surface water: contamination of, 210–212, 214–215; court battles over rights for, 103–109; effect of *derecho* concept on current policy for, 32–35; "first in time, first in right" policy for, 29, 34, 106, 181–182; increasing use of, 109, 111–112; and interbasin transfer policy, 238–239. *See also* conjunctive use; water policy

Sweet, J. R., 188

Tarrant Regional Water District, 39–40, 53

TCEQ v. Texas Farm Bureau, 103–109, 231, 246

Teff grass, 72

Terlingua, 4; characterization of, 156, 160–161, 167; community garden in, 161–162; conservation in, 157, 160–161; debate over municipal desalinated water versus rainwater in, 153–159, 162–163

Texarkana, 118, 126

Texas: agricultural economy in, 61, 88, 101; battle between rural and urban interests in, 101, 117, 200; construction of reservoirs in, 42, 111–112; fatalism in, 49; migration from rural to urban areas in, 13, 18; population rise in, 13, 24, 44; rainfall in, 14–16; river basins of, 224; unique challenges of, 6–7, 14, 110; urban development of, 87–90, 101. *See also* water policy; *and individual cities and regions*

Texas Commission on Environmental Quality (TCEQ), 182, 209, 210, 212, 246. See also *TCEQ v. Texas Farm Bureau*

Texas Conservation Alliance, 49–50

Texas Court of Appeals, 115, 146, 202

Texas Court of Civil Appeals, 69, 79

Texas Farm Bureau, 202. See also *TCEQ v. Texas Farm Bureau*

Texas legislature: and drought study, 229; and Edwards Aquifer, 197, 200, 203–204, 206; and 1968 Texas Water Plan, 22; and pollution control, 214; and regulation of water policy, 18–19, 30–31, 78, 80–81, 108, 231; and Senate Bills 1/2/3, 78, 80–81, 192–193, 204

Texas state water plans, 20; as collection of regional plans, 110, 229, 231–234, 247; current, 110–111, 127, 157, 228–229, 233–234, 241, 245; and Marvin Nichols Reservoir, 113; need for centralized, 132, 197, 228, 231–235, 237–238, 247. *See also* 1968 Texas Water Plan; water policy

Texas Water Commission (TWC), 199, 201–202

Texas Water Development Board (TWDB): formation of, 19, 42; and Marvin Nichols Reservoir plan, 56, 113, 115; and 1968 Texas Water Plan, *10–11*, 19, 22; responsibilities of, 20, 42. *See also* Texas state water plans

Thompson, Albert, 12

Thompson, Jim, 53, 117–118, 119–120

Thompson, Rick, 165–166

timber industry, 53, 129

Time It Never Rained, The (Kelton), 17

Toledo Bend Reservoir, 47, 53, 117–118

tornados, 15

Trinity Aquifer, 79

Trinity River: as alternative to Gulf Coast Aquifer, 108–109; contamination of, 209–210, 212; effect of drought on, 121; and interbasin transfer, 119

Tropical Storm Claudette, 14

Trump administration, 208, 238, 247
Turco, Mike, 108–109

United States Bureau of Reclamation,
	20–21, 125
United States Department of the Interior, 198–199
United States Fish and Wildlife Service,
	199, 204, 212
US Clean Water Act, 195–196, 210
US Oil Recovery, 215
Uvalde, 35

Villa, Pancho, 175–176
Vista Ridge Pipeline Project, 101, 205
Vonnegut, Bernard, 144–145
Votteler, Todd, 185, 191

Waco, 15
W. A. East v. Houston and Texas Central
	Railway Company, 37
wastewater reuse, 43, 131, 222, 242–244
watermasters, 108, 182
water policy: bureaucratic challenges to,
	124–125, 128; complexity of, 18, 29,
	78, 85, 100, 183; court battles over,
	37, 79–84, 180–184; federal intervention in, 20–21, 196, 197, 216; interconnectedness of individual regions',
	109, 228, 230–232; and potable
	water standards, 215–217; and
	property rights, 29–30, 36, 107–108,
	112; resistance to centralized, 110,
	231–232, 234; and separate treatment
	of groundwater and surface water,

29–31, 79–80, 218; and sources of
	"new" water, 111–112, 242–247; and
	"tragedy of the commons," 202, 208.
	See also conjunctive use; groundwater; surface water; Texas legislature;
	Texas state water plans; and individual court cases
weather modification: and cloud seeding, 143–145; and concussionism,
	137–142; effectiveness of, 146, 147;
	environmental concerns about, 146;
	military use of, 143, 145; and rule of
	capture, 146; state's position on, 147
White Rock Lake, 121
Wichita Falls, 230, 243–244
Williams, Clayton Jr. "Claytie," 71; bid
	for governor of, 73; oil and gas career
	of, 73–74
Williams, Clayton Sr., 67–69, 73
Williams, Jeff: characterization of, 73; on
	his family's settling in Texas, 67–69,
	72; proposal of, to export unused
	water, 75–77; rice crop of, 84–85;
	water use and commoditization
	philosophies of, 72, 74, 75
windmills, 59–60
wind turbines, 59
Wirtz, Alvin, 97
Wolfcamp Shale, 227
Wolff, Nelson, 195
Wright Patman Dam/Reservoir, 40, 47,
	53, 118

Yaquis, 2–3